T0274747

I Will Live
for Both of Us

CONTEMPORARY STUDIES ON THE NORTH

ISSN 1928-1722

CHRIS TROTT, SERIES EDITOR

I Will Live
for Both of Us

A History of Colonialism,
Uranium Mining, and
Inuit Resistance

Joan Scottie, Warren Bernauer, and Jack Hicks

UNIVERSITY OF MANITOBA PRESS

I Will Live for Both of Us: A History of Colonialism, Uranium Mining,
and Inuit Resistance
© Joan Scottie, Warren Bernauer, and Jack Hicks 2022

26   25   24   23   22   1   2   3   4   5

All rights reserved. No part of this publication may be reproduced
or transmitted in any form or by any means, or stored in a database
and retrieval system in Canada, without the prior written permission
of the publisher, or, in the case of photocopying or any other
reprographic copying, a licence from Access Copyright,
www.accesscopyright.ca, 1-800-893-5777.

University of Manitoba Press
Winnipeg, Manitoba, Canada
Treaty 1 Territory
uofmpress.ca

Cataloguing data available from Library and Archives Canada
Contemporary Studies on the North, ISSN 1928-1722 ; 9
ISBN 978-0-88755-265-6 (PAPER)
ISBN 978-0-88755-267-0 (PDF)
ISBN 978-0-88755-269-4 (EPUB)
ISBN 978-0-88755-271-7 (BOUND)

Cover design by Attigo Media
Interior design by Jess Koroscil
Cover photo by Russell Toolooktook

Printed in Canada

This book has been published with the help of a grant from the
Federation for the Humanities and Social Sciences, through the Awards
to Scholarly Publications Program, using funds provided by the
Social Sciences and Humanities Research Council of Canada.

The University of Manitoba Press acknowledges the financial support for
its publication program provided by the Government of Canada through
the Canada Book Fund, the Canada Council for the Arts, the Manitoba
Department of Sport, Culture, and Heritage, the Manitoba Arts Council,
and the Manitoba Book Publishing Tax Credit.

Funded by the Government of Canada   Canada

*This book is dedicated to the Paningaya'naaq
who was born before me.*

I have lived and will live for both of us.

Contents

Illustrations

I Will Live
for Both of Us

Introduction

My Christian name is Joan, but Paningaya'naaq is the name I was given when I was born. I am an Inuk, and I spent most of my childhood living on the land. I was born at a place called Urpilik on the shores of Qamanirjuaq Lake. When I was still young, we moved to a place on Ferguson Lake called Aglirnaqtuq. My family are Qairnirmiut, one of several groups of Inuit that lived inland year-round in the Kivalliq (formerly called "Keewatin") region of Nunavut. Like other inland Inuit, we depended mostly on caribou for our food and clothing.

Today, I live in the community of Qamani'tuaq (Baker Lake). Like other Inuit of my generation, I was forced to leave our life on the land to attend school. However, just because I spent much of my life living in Baker Lake and other permanent settlements doesn't mean I have left our life on the land behind me. Most of the healthy food I eat still comes from the land, and I hunt and camp with my family any chance I get. I have also spent a great deal of time fighting to protect our hunting way of life—from the uranium mining industry, in particular.

This book tells the story of my community's decades-long fight against the uranium industry, from my perspective. It provides readers with an introduction to the culture and history of Baker Lake Inuit more generally, as well as the history of recent conflicts over gold mining, caribou habitat protection, and the cleanup of abandoned mineral exploration projects. Readers will receive an overview and "on the ground" account of the Canadian government's colonization of Inuit after the Second World War. Some of the stories I share raise important issues related to the oppression of women in Inuit society. Other stories show the limitations of the regulatory processes used to make decisions about mining in Nunavut today. The underlying theme throughout is Inuit, especially Inuit women, resisting oppression and colonization.

Inuit, Colonization, and Nunavut

Inuit are an Arctic Indigenous people. Our homeland stretches from Siberia in the west, across Alaska and Arctic Canada, to Greenland in the east. Although there are several Inuit languages and many regional dialects, the languages we speak are closely related. We are all hunting people—most of our food, clothing, and tools traditionally came from the animals we hunted.

. Beginning in the nineteenth century *qablunaat* (non-Inuit, people of European descent) established a colonial relationship with Inuit in what is now Nunavut. New economic activities, like the commercial whale hunt and fur trade, created fortunes for *qablunaat* investors while my people were left with very little to show for our labour.[1] The Canadian government gradually established its authority over us. At first, this process was slow going, and most Inuit maintained their autonomy. We did not experience the full force of the Canadian state's power until after the Second World War, when government administrators began to apply a policy of assimilation to Inuit. Children like myself were taken from their parents and sent to residential schools. The government began promoting mining in the Arctic, expecting that Inuit would give up our life on the land and become miners instead. By 1970, almost all Inuit had stopped living on the land full-time and had moved into permanent communities like Baker Lake.[2]

But we did not simply accept *qablunaat* authority and the government's plans for our future. There are examples of Inuit resisting colonization every step of the way. For example, my father, Basil Scottie, was notorious for the way he refused to accept *qablunaat* authority and openly challenged government officials when they visited our camp. For many years he disobeyed their orders and refused to send me or my siblings away to school.

Perhaps the most well-known example of Inuit resistance in Nunavut is the negotiation of the Nunavut Land Claims Agreement (or Nunavut Agreement). Beginning in the 1970s, newly formed Inuit representative organizations like the Inuit Tapirisat of Canada lobbied the federal government to sign a land claim, a type of modern treaty. Their goal was to provide us with more control over our lives, land, and resources. Negotiations dragged on through the 1980s.[3] The Nunavut Agreement was finally signed in 1993. Our land claim provided us with many positive things, including monetary compensation, ownership of small sections of our traditional territory, and guaranteed hunting and fishing rights. The agreement also created a new co-management system so we could participate in decisions about land, water, wildlife, and mining. Famously, the Nunavut Agreement divided the Northwest Territories to create the new Nunavut Territory in 1999. In exchange for all of this, we had to agree to surrender or "extinguish" our Aboriginal title to our traditional territory.[4]

We expected that the land claim, and the new territory it created, would give us greater control over our future. I personally hoped that this landmark event would allow us to implement our traditional values and laws pertaining to wildlife and the environment. However, I now realize that my hopes were misplaced. In some ways, environmental protection has declined since the Nunavut Agreement was signed. Perhaps most disappointing is that the Inuit organizations that represent us, as well as the Government of Nunavut, have irresponsibly supported uranium mining without properly consulting my community.

Mining in Nunavut

The mining industry is an important part of the story of colonialism in Nunavut. Most of the benefits derived from mining in our territory go to non-Inuit living outside of the Arctic, while Inuit are left to deal with the mess that mining companies leave behind. Most of the key decisions about mining in Nunavut are made by people and institutions—such as the federal government and large corporations—that are based outside of our territory.

The mining industry arrived in my homeland after the Second World War. Mining companies began exploration work across the Arctic, including at Ferguson Lake where I grew up. Oil and gas companies also conducted seismic surveys and exploratory drilling, including in coastal and offshore areas.

The federal government provided financial incentives to support mining in the Arctic, hoping it would drive economic development in the region. However, the mining industry did not expand nearly as quickly as the government expected. The first mine in Nunavut was the Rankin Inlet nickel mine, which operated from 1957 to 1962.[5] The next mine in our territory—the Nanisivik lead-zinc mine near the community of Arctic Bay—did not open until 1974.[6] Several more mines came on line in the 1980s, including the Polaris lead-zinc mine in the

High Arctic in 1981, and the Lupin gold mine in the Kitikmeot region in 1982.[7] The Cullaton Lake gold mine began operations in the Kivalliq region in 1983, only to shut down two years later because of financial and logistical difficulties.

Proposed oil and natural gas development created a lot of controversy in our territory. Two proposals for natural gas extraction in the High Arctic islands were debated in the 1970s. The first was the Polar Gas Project. This would have involved building a pipeline across several ocean channels and caribou calving grounds, to connect with the pipeline network in southern Canada.[8] The Arctic Pilot Project, a proposal to export natural gas using icebreaking tankers, was the second. Both proposals were ultimately abandoned because of Inuit opposition, not to mention poor markets for natural gas.[9] In the 1980s, the small Bent Horn oilfield "demonstration project" began shipping token amounts of oil from the High Arctic islands each summer.[10]

These resources were taken from our land, but the economic benefits from these projects mostly went to non-Inuit. The profits were collected by the companies and their shareholders (none of whom were Inuit), while the royalties were collected by the federal government. With the exception of the Rankin Inlet nickel mine, none of these projects had a majority Inuit workforce. When Inuit were hired, it was usually for comparatively low-paying "unskilled" and temporary positions. Inuit also had very little say in decisions about mining during this period. In fact, many of these projects went ahead despite opposition from Inuit communities and organizations.[11]

Soon after the Nunavut Agreement was signed in 1993, the Inuit organizations that represent us—like Nunavut Tunngavik Incorporated (NTI) and the Kivalliq Inuit Association (KIA)—changed their positions and started to enthusiastically support mining in our territory. Like the federal government in the 1950s, our Inuit organizations and territorial government began to view mining as our best hope for economic development. However, our leaders' expectations for a booming mining economy remained elusive. The territory's mining industry utterly collapsed after the Nunavut Agreement was signed. This was because some mines reached the end of their lifespans and ran out of ore, while other projects became unprofitable because of changes in global markets and unforeseen technical challenges. The Bent Horn oil project was shut down in 1997, the Nanisivik and Polaris mines both closed in 2002, and the Lupin mine followed in 2005. By this point, Nunavut had no operating mines.

The mining industry slowly re-established itself over time. In the Kitikmeot region, the Jericho diamond mine was operated by Tahera Resources from 2006 to 2008. Shear Diamonds acquired the property and resumed activity in 2012, only to abandon the project several months later. TMAC Resources' Doris North gold mine, the only mine currently operating in the Kitikmeot region, began production in 2017.

In the Kivalliq region, Agnico Eagle operates several projects. The Meadowbank gold mine operated near Baker Lake from 2010 to 2019. Just before mining at Meadowbank ceased, Agnico began using the Meadowbank mill to process ore from the nearby Whale Tail mine (2018–present). The Meliadine gold mine near Rankin Inlet also began production in 2018.

Industry activity has been less extensive in the Qikiqtani (formerly Baffin) region. While numerous companies have conducted exploration activities, there is only one operating mine in the region as of 2021. The Mary River iron mine, owned and operated by Baffinland Iron Mines, began production in 2014.

Resource extraction remains controversial in Nunavut. While the Government of Nunavut and our representative Inuit organizations look to mineral and energy resources to drive economic development in the territory, many people are unhappy with their communities' experiences with mining. For example, as I will explain in Chapter 5, the Meadowbank gold mine near my community mostly benefitted non-Inuit and disrupted our hunting way of life. Moreover, most decisions about mining are still made by non-Inuit.

However, not all types of resource extraction are the same, as some bring more risks than others. For example, offshore oil and gas extraction is especially controversial because of potential oil spills and disturbance to marine mammals. Inuit in the Qikiqtani region recently used the courts to stop proposals for offshore seismic exploration in Lancaster Sound (2010) and Baffin Bay (2017).[12] These communities have also supported a federal moratorium on offshore oil and gas development in the Arctic—imposed in 2016 and set to expire in 2021—and have requested it be extended for at least a decade.[13]

Uranium mining is another especially controversial type of extraction in Nunavut. Because of the unique risks of radioactive contamination, along with moral and political concerns with nuclear weapons and waste, an anti–uranium mining movement developed in our territory in the 1980s. Documenting this movement from a grassroots perspective is one of the main purposes of this book.

Uranium in Nunavut

Nunavut has significant uranium resources. The largest proven deposits are in the Kivalliq region, near my home community of Baker Lake. While uranium has never been mined from our region, mining companies have conducted extensive exploration of these deposits since the 1970s. Uranium mining and exploration have caused many political conflicts in our territory since that time.

In the 1970s my community tried to stop mining companies from exploring for uranium in our hunting grounds. Such activities were negatively affecting the caribou herds we depend upon for food. With the help of the Inuit Tapirisat of Canada (our newly formed representative Inuit organization), we tried to force the federal government to stop issuing permits for uranium exploration on our land. Our efforts included petitions and a court challenge. While we failed to stop exploration, our activism resulted in new regulations to limit the negative effects of exploration on caribou.[14]

In the late 1980s a German company called Urangesellschaft proposed building a uranium mine, called Kiggavik, eighty kilometres west of Baker Lake. Our community and Inuit organizations soon came together and formed an alliance to stop the proposed mine. Several Inuit and regional organizations created the Northern Anti-Uranium Coalition to provide a unified and collaborative position opposing the mine. I helped found the Baker Lake Concerned Citizens Committee, a community group that helped inform local residents about the dangers of uranium mining and provided a voice for community opposition to the Kiggavik project. Our organizing work paid off. Baker Lake's municipal government held a public plebiscite in 1990 and slightly over 90 percent of residents voted "no" to the Kiggavik proposal. The company ended up withdrawing its proposal and the project was shelved.[15]

This united opposition to uranium mining fell apart shortly after the Nunavut Territory was created in 1999. In 2007, the Government of Nunavut and Nunavut's Inuit organizations issued policies supporting uranium mining.

In my opinion, these policy changes were made without public transparency or meaningfully consulting my community. Before long, a company called AREVA Resources submitted a revived proposal for the Kiggavik mine.[16]

In response, residents of Iqaluit created a new group called Nunavummiut Makitagunarningit, which I soon joined as vice-chair. Nunavummiut Makitagunarningit means "the people of Nunavut can rise up." People often called the group "Makita" for short. Makita campaigned for Nunavut's territorial government and representative Inuit organizations to reconsider their pro-uranium policies.

The Nunavut Impact Review Board—a co-management board created by the Nunavut Agreement—conducted an environmental assessment of AREVA's proposed uranium mine. During final hearings in 2015, several groups opposed the proposal, including Makita, the Baker Lake Hunters and Trappers Organization, the Kivalliq Wildlife Board, and Dene communities from northern Saskatchewan and the Northwest Territories. Unfortunately, Nunavut's territorial government and Inuit organizations continued to support the Kiggavik mine despite local opposition. When all was said and done, the review board recommended the proposed uranium mine not be approved and the federal government accepted this recommendation. Before long, AREVA put the Kiggavik project into "long-term care and maintenance"—in other words, AREVA cancelled its plans for the Kiggavik mine and stopped all exploration work, so the only activities at the Kiggavik site are occasional visits to care for and maintain some equipment and infrastructure. For a second time in my life, my community stood up against the nuclear industry and won.[17]

That being said, it was only a partial victory. As far as Inuit organizations and the Government of Nunavut are concerned, our territory is still "open for business" when it comes to uranium mining. What's more, they have supported mining and exploration work in very sensitive caribou habitat that community Hunters and Trappers Organizations have long sought to protect.

The Writing Process

This book is a collaborative project involving me, Jack Hicks, and Warren Bernauer. I first met Jack in 1988, when we worked closely together to stop

Urangesellschaft's proposal for the Kiggavik uranium mine. As executive director of the Keewatin Regional Council, he worked as the coordinator for the Northern Anti-Uranium Coalition. I met Warren almost twenty-five years later, when he visited Baker Lake as a graduate student in 2010 to conduct research about community perspectives on AREVA's renewed proposal for the Kiggavik uranium mine. As part of Warren's research, he volunteered with the Baker Lake Hunters and Trappers Organization to support our participation in the environmental review of AREVA's proposal. Jack, too, was involved in our second campaign against the Kiggavik project, especially as a member of Makita.

The book is written in the first person, from my perspective. My life story forms the backbone of the book and I am the senior author on this project. I had the final say on all editorial decisions and all the stories in the book were approved by me. A lot of the information in the book comes from my personal knowledge—things I've experienced myself, as well as things Elders and other knowledgeable people have told me. I have been a spokesperson and organizer for my community's resistance to uranium mining since the 1980s, and have worked with experts from the anti-nuclear movement to understand how our community could be affected by uranium mining. I have experience in local and territorial politics, having served on the Baker Lake municipal council, the Baker Lake Hunters and Trappers Organization, the Keewatin Inuit Association, the Nunavut Wildlife Management Board, the Beverly and Qamanirjuaq Caribou Management Board, and the Ukkusiksalik National Park Steering Committee. I've also been fortunate to be involved in many community research projects over the years, both as an interpreter and as a researcher. This work provided me with many opportunities to ask Elders about our traditional culture, history, and the effects of mining and mineral exploration on our environment and way of life. I have also collected a lot of documents over the years—speaking notes from meetings, letters published in newspapers and sent to politicians, and reports from research projects I've been involved with—all of which came in handy when writing this book.

A great deal of the information we consulted comes from research conducted by Warren and Jack. As a graduate student, Warren researched the politics of uranium mining in Nunavut. His master's thesis and doctoral dissertation contributed substantially to this book. As an organizer, Jack has amassed a substantial (some might say excessive!) collection of documents related to uranium mining in Nunavut and around the world. These documents also played an important role in our book. Most of the book was initially drafted by Warren and Jack; however, we each played a role in shaping its direction. As such, even though it is written from my perspective, it is truly a collaborative project.

The book took shape slowly, over several years. In the fall of 2014, Warren, Jack, my daughter Hilu Tagoona, and I spent a weekend at Jack's cabin in the Gatineau Hills, where we discussed the framework for the book and agreed upon a chapter outline. After our meeting, Warren drafted some initial chapters based on our conversations at Jack's cabin. He combined the stories and reflections I shared in interviews for his graduate research, with speeches, letters, articles, and other material I had written over the years. Warren and Jack's research— especially the documents related to our struggle against uranium mining— played an important role as well. Key documents for our book include regulatory documents (submissions to environmental assessments, transcripts of public meetings, and court files), statements from Inuit and community organizations (news releases, position statements, newsletters, and motions), and media coverage (especially coverage by *Nunatsiaq News*). All of these documents are clearly cited in the chapters and are available to the public through libraries, archives, and online sources.

Warren was inspired by George Manuel and Michael Posluns's 1974 book, *The Fourth World: An Indian Reality*. Their book has a lot in common with ours. Both are collaborative projects involving Indigenous activists and non-Indigenous academics who had worked closely together on political campaigns. Both combine the memories and reflections of Indigenous activists with research conducted by non-Indigenous academics. The life histories of the Indigenous activists give coherence and meaning to the history presented in both books. Moreover, both are written in the first person, from the perspective of the Indigenous activist.[18]

In the summer of 2017, we met at Jack's partner Lori's house in Saskatoon to discuss the book's first draft, make some necessary edits, and plan additional chapters. Hilu had recently found recordings of some interviews with my late mother; I worked with her to translate and transcribe them so we could include them in the book. After our Saskatoon meeting, Jack, Warren, and I worked on drafting additional chapters for the book. We sent these drafts back and forth, making edits and discussing the project whenever our paths crossed. In the fall of 2019, we met in Winnipeg to further edit the manuscript, which we submitted to the University of Manitoba Press the following year. Because the COVID pandemic made it impossible to meet in person for long stretches of time, revising the book for publication was a long and sometimes frustrating process. Fortunately, the staff at the University of Manitoba Press were very helpful and supportive. Based on helpful suggestions from peer reviewers, copy editors, and others we slowly revised and expanded some aspects of the book before submitting a final manuscript in early 2022.

Relationship to Other Books

There has been surprisingly little attention paid to the history this book examines. While many books discuss the colonization of Inuit after the Second World War,[19] most of this work pays very little attention to how Inuit resisted colonialism when they still lived on the land. There are some exceptions,[20] but for the most part history books imply that Inuit did not resist colonization until *after* we moved to towns.

The stories in Chapter 2 about my father resisting *qablunaat* authority in the 1950s and 1960s are an important yet underappreciated part of Inuit history. These resistance stories show that we were not simply hapless victims. They remind us that we have a long history of resistance, which is something I think Inuit need to celebrate and build upon today.

There is only one other book that examines Baker Lake's resistance to uranium mining in the 1970s and 1980s—Robert McPherson's *New Owners in Their Own Land*, which was published in 2003. While McPherson provides a useful overview of some of the events from this period, he writes from a perspective that is very different from mine. McPherson first came to Nunavut as a geologist working for a uranium exploration company. He eventually got a job with the Tunngavik Federation of Nunavut—the group that negotiated the Nunavut Land Claims Agreement—helping negotiators select the parcels of land where Inuit would own mineral rights. It is therefore not surprising that McPherson's book argues that mining is the key to economic development in Nunavut. Suffice to say, while my book covers many of the same issues and events as McPherson's, I tell this history in a much different way and I focus on aspects that he mostly neglects. We also draw *very* different lessons from this history.

A handful of academic articles and graduate theses examine resistance to uranium mining in Nunavut in the twenty-first century.[21] There are also several articles, theses, and reports dealing with my community's experiences with gold mining.[22] These academic papers contain important information that was helpful when writing this book. However, they mostly focus on either the impacts of mining on Inuit communities or on territorial level politics. My book focuses more on grassroots perspectives and helps contextualize these recent struggles in the longer history of the Baker Lake Inuit.

Chapter Overview

When I was young, I lived in a traditional Inuit hunting camp. Chapter 1 deals with this period of my life and describes different aspects of my family's life on the land, including our hunting practices, spirituality, and music. The end of the chapter discusses the oppression of women in historical Inuit society. This section deals with topics that some people might find painful to read about, including domestic violence and female infanticide.

Chapter 2 covers the colonization of Nunavut. Using my family's experiences as examples, I explain how *qablunaat* increasingly controlled our lives after the Second World War, as well as the different ways Inuit resisted their control. This chapter discusses several aspects of colonization, including residential schooling and the relocation of Inuit into permanent communities.

Chapters 3 and 4 deal with my community's resistance to uranium mining in the 1970s and 1980s. Baker Lake Inuit unsuccessfully tried to stop uranium exploration in the 1970s with petitions and legal challenges. Chapter 3 covers this history. Chapter 4 discusses Baker Lake's successful resistance to Urangesellschaft's proposed Kiggavik uranium mine in the late 1980s. It explains how Inuit from my region united to stop a threat to our way of life.

Chapter 5 introduces the 1993 Nunavut Land Claims Agreement and its provisions for mining. I use the example of my community's experiences with gold mining to explain some of the limitations of the Nunavut Agreement. Even though the agreement has provisions for community benefits, most of the economic benefits of mining still go to non-Inuit. Despite new ways to participate in decisions about mining, Inuit communities are still at a significant disadvantage in debates about mining in Nunavut.

Chapters 6 and 7 cover resistance to uranium mining after the Nunavut Agreement was signed. In Chapter 6, I explain how Nunavut's representative Inuit organizations overturned a moratorium on uranium mining without meaningfully consulting my community. Chapter 7 deals with the environmental review of AREVA's proposal for the Kiggavik uranium mine. It explains how my community successfully intervened in the review process and stopped the proposed mine for a second time.

Chapter 8 deals with other attempts my community has made to protect caribou habitat in the Kivalliq region after Nunavut was created in 1999. It focuses on our battles with mineral exploration activities in caribou calving grounds, as well as our attempts to have caribou calving grounds and water crossings designated as protected areas under a land use plan. This chapter also uses examples of abandoned mineral exploration projects to argue that environmental protection has not significantly improved since the Nunavut Land Claims Agreement was signed in 1993.

CHAPTER 1

Growing Up on the Land

My people are called the Qairnirmiut. Qairnirmiut means "people from the place with the smooth rock." The name refers to a big hill made of smooth bedrock where my people originated. Our land stretches from the Hudson Bay coast near Chesterfield Inlet, west through Baker Lake, to the Thelon River area. Today, most Qairnirmiut live in the communities of Baker Lake, Rankin Inlet, and Chesterfield Inlet.

Anthropologists once called us "Caribou Eskimo" or "Caribou Inuit." This is because caribou are everything to us. Most of our food, most of our clothing, even most of our tools all used to come from the caribou. To this day, caribou is the biggest source of healthy meat for Inuit in Baker Lake, and we still use the skins for clothing and the bones and antlers for artwork and handicrafts. However, a better name for us might be Nunamiut, "people of the land." Most other Inuit groups spent the majority of the year on the coast and out on the sea ice, fishing and hunting marine animals. But we lived inland year-round, hunting and eating caribou.

Along with the Qairnirmiut, there are several other inland Inuit groups from the Kivalliq region. The Ukkusiksalingmiut ("people from the place with stone cooking pots") are from the Back River area, north of Baker Lake. The Hanningayurmiut ("people from the place that is horizontal") lived in the Garry Lakes area, northwest of Baker Lake. The Akilinirmiut ("people from the Akiliniq hills") lived around Beverly Lake and the upper Thelon River. The Harvaqtuurmiut ("people from the river with the strong current") lived along the lower Kazan River, south of Baker Lake. The Pallirmiut ("people from the place with dried-up driftwood") lived farther to the south, on the Padlei River, Yathkyed Lake, and Nutarawit Lake, close to the treeline. The Ahiarmiut lived even farther south, in the Ennadai Lake area.

Today, people from these different homelands are spread across several communities in Nunavut. For example, the descendants of the Qairnirmiut

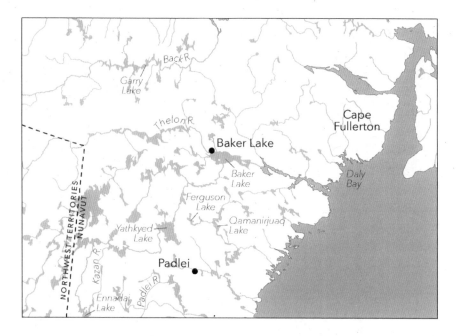

Figure 1. Map of the Kivalliq region, showing key locations from Joan's childhood. Map design by Julie Witmer.

now mostly live in Rankin Inlet, Chesterfield Inlet, and Baker Lake. Most Baker Lake residents are Ukkusiksalingmiut, Hanningayurmiut, Akilinirmiut, Harvaqtuurmiut, and Qairnirmiut.

This chapter is about what life was like for Qairnirmiut Inuit. It features stories from my family's experiences on the land before we were forced to move to the community of Baker Lake. It introduces the members of my family, describes our hunting way of life, and discusses the place of women in Inuit society.

My Family

My father's Inuktitut name was Tul'lulik, but in English he was called Scottie. However, Inuit had trouble saying the name Scottie, so they called my father "Hitkati"—and that's how I will refer to him throughout the book. Much later, when he was baptized, he took the name Basil.

My father was born in 1908 at Cape Fullerton. His father was Hugh Campbell McDiarmid, an officer in the North-West Mounted Police (later renamed the Royal Canadian Mounted Police, or RCMP). His mother was an Inuk woman named Jenny Tuluga'tuaq. When my father was one year old, McDiarmid left Cape Fullerton and returned to the south. My father stayed with his mother, Jenny, in the Cape Fullerton area. When he was in his early teens, Jenny passed away, leaving Hitkati and his newborn adopted sister Hilu all alone. Hitkati was taken in by the police inspector stationed at Cape Fullerton. I think the inspector must have felt responsible because Hitkati's father was a police officer. My father left the police outpost a few years later, taking his baby sister Hilu with him. I am not sure what happened, but I suspect the police inspector was strict or possibly even cruel.

When he was around the age of sixteen, Hitkati left Cape Fullerton altogether, moved inland, and took a much older Harvaqtuurmiutaq woman named Ikuutaq as a spouse to look after his baby sister Hilu. This relationship did not last long, however. Hitkati soon discovered she was being neglectful towards his baby sister. He had been purchasing powdered milk from the traders to feed Hilu. But one day he saw Ikuutaq forcing Hilu to feed from a female dog's teat, so she could drink the milk herself. He left her, and eventually moved to the Baker Lake area.

My father's next spouse was a Qairnirmiutaq woman named Mary Atangat. She was a widow, almost twenty years older than Hitkati, and was unable to bear children because of her age. However, she had children through another marriage, who were almost teenagers by this time. With Hitkati, Mary Atangat adopted my older brother, John Nukik, who was Mary Atangat's biological grandson.

Hitkati later took Mary Atangat's niece, Bessie Iquginnaq, as an additional spouse. Bessie Iquginnaq was a Pallirmiutaq woman from the Yathkyed Lake area. After becoming my father's spouse, she gave birth to my older brother Joseph Tuluga'tuaq Scottie.

My mother, Lucy Qaunnaq, was my father's next spouse. Lucy Qaunnaq was Mary Atangat's biological daughter from a previous spouse but was adopted at a young age. Lucy Qaunnaq had a daughter from a previous relationship, my older sister Marion Pattunguyak. Lucy Qaunnaq later had three children with Hitkati: me, my younger sister Susan Toolooktook, and my younger brother William Scottie.

My father's fourth spouse was Emily Nipiha'naaq. Emily Nipiha'naaq was Mary Atangat's youngest daughter and the biological sister of my mother, Lucy Qaunnaq.

Figure 2. Hitkati in caribou fur clothing. Photo courtesy of Joan Scottie.

Figure 3. (*left to right*) Mary Atangat, Hitkati, Emily Nipiha'naaq with Hugh
Ikoe in her *amauti*, Joseph Scottie, Bessie Iquginnaq, Lucy Qaunnaq with Susan
Toolooktook in her *amauti* and Joan Scottie at her feet, Marion Pattunguyak.
Photo courtesy of Joan Scottie.

Emily Nipiha'naaq was an older child when Mary Atangat became Hitkati's spouse.
When she was a young woman, Emily Nipiha'naaq also became Hitkati's spouse,
and gave birth to my younger brothers, Hugh Ikoe and Nicholas Nungnik. Later in
life, Emily Nipiha'naaq married a man named Michael Alerk and took his last name.

It was not uncommon for Inuit men to have more than one spouse. Hunting
was a dangerous job and many men died young in hunting-related accidents.
As a result, there were usually more women than men. Men who took multiple
spouses were usually very good hunters who could provide for a lot of people.
Sometimes men took additional spouses to rescue the women and their children
from famine or abuse. Their spouses were usually related to one another. This was
done to ensure that they would get along and promote harmony in the camp.

From Quurnguryuaq to Aglirnaqtuq

I was born in May 1948 at a place called Urpilik ("a place of willows"), on the northern shores of Qamanirjuaq Lake. My mother gave birth to me inside a small *iglu* (snow house) with a *qarmat* (skin roof). When I was born, I was given the name Paningaya'naaq, after Bessie Iquginnaq's mother.

Today, women from Baker Lake go to hospitals in Rankin Inlet, Yellowknife, or Winnipeg to give birth. When I was born, Inuit women would still give birth at their camps on the land, with the help of an *ikayuqti* (helper, or midwife). My mother gave birth to all her children on the land, with the help of the other women in the camp.

For the first two years of my life, our family's main camp was at a place called Quurnguryuaq, at the narrows of Qamanirjuaq Lake. I do not have many memories of our time at Quurnguryuaq because I was so young. While we were living there, the RCMP gave my father a very small cabin in exchange for a dog team. We used this cabin at our spring camp. For the rest of the year, we camped elsewhere around the Qamanirjuaq Lake area.

One summer in the late 1940s, we saw helicopters and planes flying overhead and travelling west towards Ferguson Lake. My father realized that there were *qablunaat* there, so he took Bessie Iquginnaq and my brother John Nukik and travelled up-river to see what they were doing. When they arrived, they found a small mineral exploration camp on the shore of Ferguson Lake. The *qablunaat* working there offered my father and brother occasional work, if they were willing to move to the area.

Hitkati decided to move us all to Ferguson Lake. Our main camp was on the shore of the lake, near the mineral exploration camp, at a place called Aglirnaqtuq. My father and brother worked for the *qablunaat* occasionally, although hunting and trapping were still how we made ends meet. I have very fond memories of a *qablunaaq* man named Les Arbuckle who worked at the exploration camp. Les was very kind. He gave me candy very often. One time I cut myself badly, and he performed first aid. On another occasion, I had a bad ear infection, and he helped us treat it. However, before long the mineral exploration project was abandoned. We stayed in the area and continued to live off the land, providing for ourselves from hunting and trapping alone.

Caribou Inuit

Like the other inland Inuit groups, our family relied on caribou (which we call *tuktu*) for almost everything. It was the mainstay of our diet. We would eat it as *uujuq* (boiled meat), *nipku* (dried meat), *piruyaq* (aged meat), and *quaq* (frozen raw meat). We collected the bones to boil for *imiraq* (broth) and used caribou to produce *punniqniq* (lard). Our favourite foods were the pieces of the caribou that were in limited supply—the tongues, the bone marrow, and the meat with fat attached to it.

We were also literally wrapped in caribou skin from the cradle to the grave. When babies were born, they would be placed in caribou calf skins because these

Figure 4. (left to right) Lucy Qaunnaq, Joan Scottie, Hugh Ikoe, Joseph Scottie, and Susan Toolooktook. Photo courtesy of Joan Scottie.

Figure 5. (left to right) Joseph Scottie, Bessie Scottie, Lucy Qaunnaq holding Susan Toolooktook, Les Arbuckle holding Joan Scottie, and unknown mineral exploration worker. Photo courtesy of Joan Scottie.

were the softest skins we had. Instead of diapers, we would use a *naliqqaraiqut* or *nangiq* (the front half of a caribou skin, which was placed as a pad under the baby when it was sleeping) to protect the bedding. An *akiumilitat* (skin from the caribou neck) was placed under the baby inside the *amauti* (carrying coat) and changed when soiled. Throughout our lives, we wore clothing and slept in bedding made of caribou skins. Historically, Inuit lived in caribou-skin *itsa* (tents) and hunted and travelled in caribou-skin *qayait* (kayaks). Some families still used skin *itsa* and *qayait* when I was a child, although my family did not. When people died, we would wrap their bodies in caribou skins.

For the most part, our camp followed traditional Inuit gender roles. Men were responsible for hunting, trapping, making tools, and trading with the *qablunaat*. Women were responsible for sewing clothing and tents, taking care of children, preparing food, and gathering willows for cooking fuel. These were typical roles for Inuit during this time. However, like all rules, this one had its exceptions—and I was definitely one of those exceptions. I was always more interested in travelling on the land and learning to hunt. I was not very interested in staying at camp and learning to sew. My father used to spoil me when I was a child, so he let me tag along when the men went hunting. As a result, I grew up to be a hunter. My grandmother Mary Atangat was not very impressed. She used to lecture me all the time when I was growing up, "You're a girl, not a boy." She would even get upset when I would play with a snow knife because it was a man's tool.

My sister Susan Toolooktook is the same. Susan enjoys sewing more than I do, but she is also an expert hunter. Even at times when the men in Baker Lake have no idea where to find caribou and come home empty-handed, I've seen Susan with a *qamutiik* (sled) full of caribou. She really puts the men to shame sometimes.

Our life at Ferguson Lake was affluent. Our camp included my father, his four spouses, their children, and grandchildren. We also had around forty dogs at our camp. My father had a very large dog team. My brothers John Nukik and Joseph Scottie, who were already young adults by then, also had their own dog teams. Those were a lot of mouths to feed.

We also owned several cabins. However, most were very simple and made with repurposed materials, not like the wooden cabins people use today. We used lumber that my father got from the nearby mineral exploration camp to build the walls. For the roof, we sewed together canvas bags that the exploration company used to collect rocks. The floor was made of the wooden trays the exploration company had used to store core samples. I remember taking the floor apart each summer, and washing the trays in the lake.

Usually, we had everything we needed to live happy and healthy lives. My father was a successful hunter and provided for our family very well. For example, during the winter of 1959–60, many families in the area experienced famine. They relied on "relief," in the form of food and supplies from the government. Some camps were relocated because they were at risk of starvation. However, in the patrol records from the RCMP, our camp at Ferguson Lake was described as the richest camp in the region. In a report from early January 1960, staff from the detachment wrote, "The only group of Eskimos not accounted for are those living at Ferguson Lake. E2-72 TOOLOOLE (Scotty), his two wives, his own family, one married son, and a widow with three children, make up the population. TOOLOOLE has yet to make a request for relief, and usually he is in a position to extend assistance to other less fortunate hunters."[1] Later that winter, when more families had been evacuated due to risk of starvation, the RCMP reported that "Ferguson Lake again appear[s] [to be] 'Keewatin's Haven' for energetic Scotty, E2-72 TOOLOOLE. This man not only supports his own two wives, four children, one married son, but also the widowed family of E2-108 KOWNAK and her three children. His two sons contribute to camp welfare as a result of TOOLOOLE's demanding approach to survival. . . . There is definitely not any need to express concern over the Eskimos camped at Ferguson Lake."[2] It was widely recognized that my father was a supremely competent and hard-working man.

Even though my family was affluent, we did experience shortages of food and other items from time to time. Sometimes we weren't able to catch enough caribou in the fall, and by the end of winter we would run out of meat. During these periods, we would mostly eat fish—I still think of fish as a sort of starvation food, as a last resort. My sister Susan Toolooktook was born during a winter when both food and fuel were scarce. That year, my family ran out of caribou meat. We only ate fish, when we were lucky enough to catch some. My mother was really worried that her unborn baby would not survive because she was eating so little. When she finally gave birth, we had run completely out of fuel. She had to give birth almost entirely in the dark. Her sister Emily Nipiha'naaq would light a match occasionally when she really needed to see. Otherwise, she had to do everything in total darkness. Susan was small when she was born, and at first my mother could not produce milk to feed her because she was malnourished. She was surprised Susan survived at all.[3]

The Seasons

During the winter, my entire family usually lived together at one main camp on the shore of Ferguson Lake. Early in the season, before there was much snow, my family would live in an *iglu* with a *qarmat*. Later, once more snow had accumulated, we would move into the snow *igluit* that Inuit are famous for.

Igluit were the warmest and most comfortable of all our housing options. They also had very good air circulation. We would live in *igluit* as long as possible. Even though we had several cabins at our main camp, they were not very warm and far too stuffy for us to live in during winter. Each of Hitkati's spouses had their own *iglu* where they lived with their children. Some *igluit* would be built for storage. We would also build a large *iglu* to use as a cookhouse, with an opening for smoke to escape. Here the women would use willow branches to make fires for cooking.

There were not very many caribou around our home during the winter months. Although some smaller groups of caribou remain on the tundra year-round, the major herds are migratory and return south to the treeline every fall. As a result, we mostly lived off the caribou meat we had cached the previous summer and fall.

The winter was trapping season. My father and my older brothers Joseph Scottie and John Nukik each had extensive trap lines. Together, they owned hundreds of leg-hold traps. They mostly focused on trapping fox but would also catch wolves and wolverines from time to time.

Winter was also the season to trade furs because it was easy to transport them over long distances using *qimmiit* (dogs) to pull *qamutiit* (sleds). My father would travel to different posts to trade: Baker Lake, Padlei, and Daly Bay were the posts he used to frequent the most. He would make several trips each winter.

In early November, when winter was just beginning, he would make his first trip of the season. By that point we were usually running low on supplies. He would make his second trip in March or April. In late May, immediately before the spring thaw, he would make his third trip—this is when he would stock up on supplies for the summer. Some years, if he was having a very successful trapping season, he would make an additional trip to trade at Christmas.

In May, once the snow began to melt, our *igluit* would be in danger of collapsing. When the roofs were about to cave in, we would remove each snow roof and replace it with a *qarmat*. Later, when the rest of the *iglu* melted, we would move into tents made of canvas. In the spring, we would leave our main camp at Ferguson Lake and our family would be divided between several hunting camps near caribou migration routes. Caribou would migrate through our area in great numbers during this season. Each camp would hunt what they could, and preserve as much as possible to be used the following winter.

My father had a set of *aul'laqutit* (flags) that he would use to influence the movement of small groups of caribou. He would place the flags in the ground in a line to divert caribou and make them easier to hunt. For example, if the caribou moved through a swamp, we would be unable to access them. In this case, my father might use the *aul'laqutit* to divert them around the swamp.

During May and June, we would dry caribou meat on *tuapak* (pebbles) or *qairtuq* (rock outcrops) to make *nipku*. Once it was ready, the *nipku* would be bundled in caribou skins and stored in caches under rocks so scavengers could not steal it. My family used very old stone cairns to cache the *nipku*. These cairns had been used by Inuit for generations. To us, they were ancient. Unfortunately, flies came out and began laying eggs in July. When that happened, we had to stop making *nipku* because the flies and maggots would spoil it. We would hunt caribou as we needed to in July and live off of fresh meat. Meat that was spoiled by flies was used for dog food.

During the open-water season, my father would travel between our hunting camps in a boat powered by an outboard motor. He had purchased the boat and motor with money he had earned trading furs. Throughout the summer and fall, whenever we had a break from hunting, we would gather willow branches, which we used to make cooking fires. My father had three canoes that he would fill with willows and tow behind his motorboat. I remember being worried that the canoes would capsize because he would fill them so full.

In August, we would hunt large numbers of caribou in preparation for winter. This was when huge herds of migrating caribou passed through our land, on their way south to the treeline where they would stay for the winter. It also started to cool off in August, so we could once again preserve meat in a cache made of heavy rocks without it getting spoiled by flies. My father kept a diary where he recorded the location of these caches, to ensure he would not forget about any meat he had stored for us. Caribou skins are perfect for making winter clothing during the fall migrations, so we also had to make sure we collected a lot of skins during this season. This was because fall is when caribou fur is the best quality.

Like many other inland Inuit, we did a lot of our fall hunting at caribou water crossings—the places caribou swim across lakes and river during their annual migrations. We would camp several miles away from the crossing, to ensure we didn't disturb the caribou. My father would watch the herds with a telescope, to see when they were getting ready to cross the water. When the caribou entered the water to swim across, my father would be waiting in his boat. When the caribou were about halfway across the lake, my father would begin to hunt them with a spear. Even though my father owned several rifles, ammunition was expensive, so when possible he used his spear to conserve bullets. This was a variation on the traditional Inuit method of hunting caribou at the water crossings, using a *qayaq* and harpoon.

The fall is also one of the busiest seasons for sewing. We were not able to reuse our winter clothing from one year to the next; the skins would become hairless, dried out, stiff, and eventually crack. Old clothing would sometimes suffice for people who remained around camp—children, Elders, and some women. However, those of us who needed to hunt, trap, and do other work away from camp required a new set of fur clothing every winter. As a result, the women in the camp would be very busy during the fall, making sure the hunters had a new set of clothing before winter set in.

In September, my entire family would return to our main camp at Ferguson Lake. We would continue to hunt caribou when we could, and live in our canvas tents. Once there was enough snow, we would move into an *iglu* with a *qarmat* and prepare for the winter trapping season.

Angatquit and Aglirniq

When I was a child, my family had already converted to Christianity. We had been given bibles by the Anglican Church. However, my childhood was a time when some Inuit still followed many of our traditional rules and beliefs. *Angatquit* (shamans) still performed services for Inuit, and certain people possessed special powers that some would call supernatural.

The traditional place-name for our camp at Ferguson Lake, Aglirnaqtuq, refers to *aglirniq*—the spiritual prohibitions Inuit traditionally followed (called "taboos" by *qablunaat* anthropologists). Aglirnaqtuq means "a place to observe taboos." It was a sacred place, where these rules had to be followed carefully. As a result, my family was very concerned about strictly following *aglirniq* when I was young.

There were many different types of *aglirniq*. For example, we were prohibited from eating certain parts of some animals. As another example, Inuit were not supposed to use the same pot to cook food from the land (like caribou) and food from the sea (like seal or whale meat).

Aglirniq were not necessarily universal rules that everyone had to follow, like modern laws and regulations. Instead, *angatquit* often instructed individuals to follow specific *aglirniq*. For example, after seeking the help of an *angatquq*, my father was instructed to never kill any dogs. If one of his dogs had to be put down, he would have to ask someone else to do it. My aunt Bessie Iquginnaq was instructed by the same *angatquq* to never eat meat attached to a bone—she could only eat meat that was separated from the bone before it was prepared.

In those days, *angatquit* were an important part of our lives. Inuit would seek their help with many issues, including illness, poor luck at hunting, or even bad weather. Bessie had to visit an *angatquq* several times during her life. When Bessie was a young woman, she required the help of an *angatquq* to heal from a gunshot wound. Years later, when Bessie had become my father's spouse, she was unable to have children because of the scarring from the gunshot wound. Hitkati went back to the same shaman to help Hitkati and Bessie conceive a child. The shaman arranged for them to have one son, my brother, Joseph Scottie.[4]

I have several childhood memories of meeting people who had special powers. When we lived at Ferguson Lake, we would often have Pallirmiut families visit us. After the trading post at Padlei closed down, these families had to come to Baker Lake to trade their fox skins, and they would visit us on their way. Some years, when caribou were scarce in the Yathkyed Lake area, my father would invite them to stay at our camp for the winter. During this time, the Pallirmiut were well known for having some of the most powerful shamans in the Kivalliq region.

One winter, an old Pallirmiut man named Pingitqaaryuk and his grandson stayed with us. The adults at our camp said that he had special powers, including the ability to foresee the future. One day Pingitqaaryuk told us all to pluck a hair from his head. He had a mixture of white hair and black hair. He said that everyone who picked a white hair would live a long life, while those who picked black hairs would die young. I did not take it very seriously, but I remember the adults in camp were very anxious and concerned about the outcome.

My brother Hugh Ikoe and I used to play with Pingitqaaryuk's grandson, who was close to our age. Together, we would get into a lot of mischief around camp. For example, we would play in my father's gun shed and canoe. Pingitqaaryuk did not feel comfortable with this sort of behaviour, so he would try to discipline us.

Eventually, Pingitqaaryuk demonstrated his powers to us. We were playing outside and getting into mischief as usual. Pingitqaaryuk came up and lectured us. He told us to stop causing so much trouble, and to obey what adults told us. He then said he was going for a walk, and told us to sit there and watch him. He insisted that we not take our eyes off him, just sit and watch. We sat down and watched him walk for a while. As he got farther and farther away, I started to get bored. I told Hugh and the other little boy, "Let's just play for a while, and then come back and watch him later." We started to play, and crawled into an *iglu*. We were shocked to discover that Pingitqaaryuk was sitting right there! It was as if he moved a kilometre in an instant. I think he wanted to demonstrate his powers to us, so we would start obeying him.

I have memories of another Pallirmiut man with powers. When we first arrived at Ferguson Lake, there was a Pallirmiut family living on the other side of the lake. At their camp, there was an old couple who had two sons and a daughter. One of the sons also had a spouse and his own children. We did not know the family very well, but we had heard that the old man had special powers. It was said that he could harm people he did not like.

At first, the Pallirmiut family got along well with my father. The old man would come to visit us in our camp during the summers, travelling in his traditional caribou-skin *qayaq*. After a while, however, and I am not sure why, my father became worried that the old man was upset with him.

One day, my father was out on the land, looking through binoculars. He saw the old man out on the land burying something and became concerned that he was preparing to use his powers to harm our family. My father came back to camp and held a meeting with everyone, even the children. He told us that we had to think of God and pray all the time, to protect us from this man's powers.

Music and Songs

The adults in my family made many types of music when we lived on the land. The *qilaut* (Inuit drum) was primarily played by men. *Pihiq* (vocal songs) were sometimes sung with a drum accompaniment, and sometimes without. Certain songs celebrated successful hunts; others mourned difficult times.

When there was a conflict between two people, sometimes they would argue and insult each other through song. For example, my grandmother Mary Atangat created insulting songs about a man she did not like. She made several songs about how ungenerous and stingy he was. Sharing—especially sharing food— is very important to our way of life, so generosity was highly valued. Calling someone selfish was a serious insult. In turn, the man also made insulting songs about her. I am not sure who started this exchange, but it went on for a long time.

My mother, Lucy Qaunnaq, made several songs during her life. A song she wrote for my brother William Scottie was recorded for a television program called *Takuyaksat*, produced by the Inuit Broadcasting Corporation.[5] This song was written from William's perspective when he was a baby. His aunt Bessie had just playfully thrown a clean *naliqqaraiqut* (caribou-skin bed pad for babies) at William. The song is supposed to be baby William's response to Bessie:[6]

Ayaaya pangmaiyaa ayaaya

Qanurlituu Uvanga pangmaiya ayaayaayaa

Ayaa Akitikhaqangi'namaa tuniythaqangi'nama

Tunimmiqtuqhima'mangaa Naliqqaqaiqqublunili

Pangmaiyaaya ayaaya

Ayaa Akitikhaqangi'namaa tuniyakhaqangi'nama

Ik&ingnaqtaqtuqanginmat Ik&igivangnigitpagit

Pituarivakapkilli

Akiumilitatkalu anaiyautitkalu Nangiralukulutkalu

Pangmaiyaaya ayaaya.

Ayaa ihumayunna ngi'namaa Piyangavakhinarama

Qitunaaq&amangaa Makitanaiq ayurama

Pangmaiaya ayaaya

Ihumayunnangi'nama piyangavakhinirama

Anguyungangitpakama qikturiyamigluniit

Pangmaiyaaya ayaayaa

Ayaa Ihumayunangi'namnuk piyangavakhinaramnuk

Anaanagalu imaa paiyimiangugamnuk

Pangmaiaya ayaaya ayaayaa.

Ayaaya pangmaiyaa ayaaya

How should I proceed? pangmaiyaa ayaaya

I have nothing to repay you, I have nothing to give

She gifted me the *naliqqaraiqut*

Pangmaiyaaya ayaaya

I have nothing to repay you, I have nothing to give.

I have nothing that is desirable.

Unless she wants the little I have

My *akiumilitat* [placing pad], *anaiyautit* [wipers], and
nangiq [placing mat]

Pangmaiyaaya ayaaya

I cannot form thoughts, because I am still helpless

You approached me while I am limp and unable to stay upright

Pangmaiyaaya ayaaya

I cannot form thoughts, because I am still helpless

I cannot hunt, not even for a mosquito

Pangmaiyaaya ayaaya

We cannot think, because we are helpless

My mother and I are left behind to be humble camp keepers.

Pangmaiyaaya ayaaya ayaaya

Today Inuit are probably most famous for *qiaqvaaq* (throat singing). This is a type of singing performed by women, as a duet. In earlier times, women would throat sing to entertain others, especially during celebrations. In the Kivalliq style, there was a series of words the women would have to sing in combination with wordless sounds. The words and sounds were very rhythmic, made by both inhaling and exhaling. This tradition was passed down from one generation to the next, for many years.

Both my mother and her sister Emily were very talented throat singers. Later in life, they became somewhat famous for their talents. They performed throat singing together at music festivals and similar events across Canada, in New York, and overseas. They also sang songs accompanied by drummers at celebrations throughout the country.

Women and Girls

The last aspect of my life on the land that I want to discuss deals with the way women were treated. I know that some people remember that women were treated well, and that there was a balance in power between men and women in traditional Inuit society. Unfortunately, this was not the experience of all women.

You should be aware that some of the stories I share in this section deal with infanticide and spousal assault. Some people will find them distressing. Please skip to the next chapter if you find these topics too painful to read about.

Some people might be upset that I am sharing these stories, or feel that I am presenting our culture and traditions in a negative light. In response to that, I want to be clear that I strongly support maintaining our distinct culture and have worked very hard to keep our hunting way of life alive. I think Inuit culture is great. But just because something is great does not mean it is perfect.

I am not the only one who feels this way. For example, Uqsuralik Ottokie, an Elder from the Qikiqtani (Baffin) region, said, "When I am telling you these stories about how life used to be, I am not saying that we were better than you are today. I am not saying our way of life was better than yours. In a lot of ways, it was not as good. But I certainly can say we were taught to lead a very good culturally strong life."[7] The way some women were treated in historic Inuit society was certainly not ideal. To help explain this, I want to return to the story of my mother, Lucy Qaunnaq.

My mother had a very difficult life. Her first spouse was a Pallirmiutaq. She had three daughters with him, but he and his parents were not interested in raising girls. They saw them as nothing more than mouths to feed. As a result, they took away two of her children, and left them to perish on the tundra when they were newborns. My mother was only permitted to keep one daughter, my older sister Marion Pattunguyak.

This practice was not uncommon, and was carried out under the advice of Elders. It was done for mostly economic reasons. The decision to not keep baby girls was often made during times of famine and hardship. Sometimes it had to do with whether or not the father was a good hunter and capable of providing for a new child. Also, daughters did not yield much of an advantage to the family because once they married they would usually move in with their spouse's family. Because sons usually stayed with their families, they were a longer-term investment. Many families would keep baby girls only if boys from other families were born around the same time—boys they could marry. If a girl was born without a potential spouse to arrange a marriage with, she would become an economic liability.

One winter, when my mother Lucy Qaunnaq was still married to her first spouse, my father Hitkati went to trade at Padlei post. When he arrived he saw Lucy Qaunnaq, and noticed that her face was covered with cuts and bruises. Her spouse had punched her in the face when she was wearing sunglasses. During that time, the Pallirmiut were experiencing food shortages. Hitkati invited Lucy Qaunnaq's family to live at his camp so they could be better provided for. Less than a year later, the family left Hitkati's camp. However, under pressure from Mary Atangat (Hitkati's spouse and Qaunnaq's biological mother), Lucy Qaunnaq remained at Hitkati's camp. Before long, Lucy Qaunnaq became Hitkati's third spouse. She did not have a choice in the matter.

After she became Hitkati's spouse, Lucy Qaunnaq gave birth to another daughter who was given the name Paningaya'naaq. This daughter died as an infant, although the cause of her death is not entirely clear to me. Before long Lucy Qaunnaq gave birth to another daughter, who she also named Paningaya'naaq. This second Paningaya'naaq was me.

When I was born, my mother expected that she would have to give me up, just like her daughters with her previous spouse. My mother and her sister Emily Nipiha'naaq cut the hood off an old *atigi* (woman's coat) and placed me inside it. My mother then breastfed me for a very long time. She would do this to all her daughters when she gave birth, so they could live for a few more hours on this Earth before passing away. However, my father and grandmother decided to keep me, and I was spared this fate. They also let my mother keep her next daughter, my sister Susan.

For many years, my mother did not talk to anyone about these experiences. She suffered quietly. Later, while recovering at a tuberculosis sanatorium, she opened up to another woman from the Baker Lake area named Julie. She described the impacts these experiences had on her emotionally. She told Julie that every year, while collecting willows, she would look for her babies' remains. Each winter, when ponds froze, she would look through the ice to see if she could find her babies' bones beneath the water. Her experience of having so many children taken from her was clearly very painful.

In the 1980s my mother discussed some of these experiences on a television program produced by the Inuit Broadcasting Corporation. She told a story of having to give up one of her daughters when she was still married to her original spouse, during a time of illness and famine:

> If we had known about weeks, it was about that long that my spouse's eldest brother was sick. He was not sick very long, and then he died. I was so frightened.
>
> It was during late summer. We were getting ready [to move camp] and we were storing the possessions that we will leave behind. It was our seasonal camp-moving, when it was time to *piruyi* [cache caribou meat]. Our *piruyat* [cached meat] would be our main food for the winter. Soon we would be relocating our camp and we were getting our belongings ready.
>
> Then he died unexpectedly. Our *utuqaak* [Elders] could not agree [on what to do next]. They were devastated and crying a lot. We would just watch them, not knowing, with our immature minds, what else to do.
>
> It was just our family, my spouse and his brothers. We finally tried to travel to our new camp, then my spouse and his other brother became sick. His brother was so sick that he was unconscious for a while. I was so terrified.
>
> We would put him on the *qamutiik* and pull him with our dogs. It was late summer. Our Elder, he had poor eyesight. His two sons were very sick. We were also lacking caribou. The Elder would always be scouting with a telescope. He was always looking through the telescope. It was his main duty.
>
> He saw some caribou through the telescope and wanted me to come with him to be his seeing-helper. We walked toward the caribou, but scared them. I did not know anything about approaching or hunting caribou and this was my first time accompanying a hunter. We did

not catch them. He burst into tears. I felt so bad for him, frightened and loved him. He was feeling very emotional.

By then lakes were freezing and my spouse and his brothers were still sick. Our Elder was, as always, looking through the telescope [and] saw a tent. They were offered food to eat. The Elder just ended up [in] tears.

We moved to the camp, and my baby daughter, the younger sister of Pattunguyaq, was very underfed and skinny. We had no food to eat for a very long time. She had been born the past spring.

My mother-in-law started to talk about my aunt. At that time my spouse and his brother were both still sick. She started telling me that my aunt loved her spouse and that she had choked her daughter . . . she kept repeatedly telling me, hinting that it was an option for me, for this poor baby daughter of mine. I was a daughter-producer, from the time I had children . . . there would have been four that had died.

I *ilirahuk* [felt intimidated and afraid] as she kept repeating it to me. She would say that my aunt, when her spouse was ill, that she had choked and killed her daughter. *Iliranatuapalaurmat* [It was a state of being constantly afraid and intimidated]. *Iliranatuapalaurmat*, when I was young, young as I was.

Then one evening, my spouse started repeatedly asking me, "Is she still alive?" I would respond, "Yes." Then he started criticizing me, claiming that I valued her more than him, that I would grieve more about her than him.

My spouse kept asking about my baby daughter. She was born that spring and by then [late summer] the weather had gotten cold. I had put her on the back of my bedding. *Iliranatuapalauman-ilaa* [I was constantly afraid and intimidated and felt like I had no choice]. I had placed her on the back, on a *nangiq* [skin mat for babies]. That's all, nothing else. *Iliranaʼtuarmat* [I was feeling so daunted/frightened].

As soon as we woke up, my mother-in-law would *uqapiluk* [nag me in a cruel and mean-spirited way]. Iquginnaq was the name of my little

girl. She was named after my paternal step-grandmother, she was the
mother of my adopted father. As always, *iliranatuapangman-ilaa*
[I was afraid and intimidated and felt like I had no choice]. It was part
of life when were young. My mother-in-law, would be admonishing/
telling-off at me again.

We used to use cut-off necks of caribou skin for *nangiq*. I had one.
I placed my daughter on it, nothing else. We did not have much of
anything. The only items we had were things given by our Elders.

That's all! Just a *nangiq*, nothing else. It was the only cover I had.
I had placed her on my bedding at the back of the tent. She
made a crying sound. I paid no mind. *Iliranatuapalauma-ilaa.*
My sister-in-law, she and I were both *ilirahuk*, together we both
faced intimidation.

You might need some context to appreciate just how scared my mother was
at this time in her life. She was still quite young and had recently moved to live
with her spouse's family. She would have felt isolated and disconnected from
her own relatives. The eldest brother and most capable hunter died first, leaving
the group without a leader. Afterwards, her spouse and his other brother—both
young and previously healthy men—became so sick they could not walk. No one
at the camp was able to hunt caribou during the late summer, when they should
have been caching caribou meat for the winter. It's not at all surprising that the
combination of illness, famine, and isolation would leave my mother terrified.

After telling her story, my mother performed a very sad song she had written
to express the grief and manipulation she felt when one of her daughters was
killed. When introducing it she said, "Now, I'm going to sing my pitiful song,
which I avoided sharing in the past. It is to share my experience how we lived
among our Elders when we were young. Nowadays, we [Elders] just cooperate
with our youth, hoping they will lead a good life." She continued,

This song I made is about my baby daughter, she was a younger sister
of Pattunguyaq. Now, I am being recorded, my voice is not the best,

and I may make mistakes as I go along. I have started to forget as my memory is not as it used to be.

Aaiya aiyayiyiyaa iyayaiyayiyaa

Aaiya iyayaiayaa aiyaayii

Aaiyaa aiyiyiyaa

Why me?

Aiyaa iyayaiyaa aiyaayii yaa

Aiyayiyiyaa

Why me? feeling depressed at this frozen lake in early winter

Aiyaayiyiyaa iyayaaiyayiyaiyaa aiya ayii

Aiyaa aiyayayaa

But so loved, but so loved, this child was placed at the
back of bedding

Aaiyaayiyiyaa iyayaiyaiyaaiyaa aiya ayii

Aiyaa aiyayiyiyaa

But loved, but loved, child at the back of bedding, sounds of whimper

Aiyayiyiyaa aiyayaiyayiyaa aiyaiyayaiyaa aiya aiyii

Told good for nothing, not being a boy

Told good for nothing like a bitch

Aiyaa yiyiyaa aiyayaiyaiyaa aiyaa iyayaiyaa aiya ayii

Aiyaa aiyapipiyaa

Then all of our daughters are like bitches . . . all of them

Aiyayiyaa iyayaiyayiyaa aiyaa iyayaiyaa aiya ayii

Aiiyaa aiyayiyiyaa

Cannot help but love them, cannot help but love those
poor eyes pleading

Aiyayiyiyaa iyayaiyayiyaa aa aiyaaayii aiyaa aiyayayi

I can only remember us feeling afraid and intimidated

Aiyayiyiyaa iyayaiyayiyaa yaa aiya ayii

In this song, my mother is using a metaphor of "bitches" (female sled dogs) to explain how baby girls were not valued. Female dogs are not very good for pulling sleds, so most female puppies would be killed. We would only keep a few for breeding purposes. From my mother's perspective, her daughters were treated similarly.

When Inuit gave birth, the mothers and midwives used to do certain things to help shape the baby's future personality and abilities. During an interview for a midwifery research project in the early 1990s, my mother described what she did when I was born:

> When a baby was first born, the baby was given directions to influence who they would be as a person. I myself have witnessed this come to be. This one, Joan Paningaya'naaq, do you know her?

> You must understand that in my youth, I could not speak up to anyone. Well, I blurted out to my daughter at her birth, and gave her a small lecture. We were cautioned about this, that doing so could truly determine [a child's] future. Well, I could never defend myself, no matter how badly I had been treated or lied about, as I was afraid. I thought about myself when I told my daughter, who I had just given birth to, that if she wants to talk back about what she felt or thought, no matter who the person was, she WOULD NOT stay silent.

> It even came back to me, as she will answer back to me as well. It came to be.[8]

This story shows how oppressed my mother felt at the time of my birth. She wanted me to have a better life, and not be afraid to defend myself and stand up for myself.

My mother also internalized the oppression she experienced. When I was growing up, she constantly reminded me, "*aqnakuluugavit*" ("you are cursed") for having been born a girl. The only way I would be able to live a happy and fulfilling life, she insisted, was if I could find a good husband. Looking back on my life, I can say with confidence that my mother was wrong. Even though I never married, my life has been filled with blessings. I was more than capable of making a happy life for myself and did not need a man to do it for me.

My mother's experiences provide just one example of how some Inuit women were mistreated and oppressed. Another example can be found in the experiences of my aunt Bessie Iquginnaq Scottie. In the 1980s, Bessie Iquginnaq told her life story to my friend David Pelly, who recently published a paraphrased version.[9] Pelly explains how Bessie Iquginnaq's father had been cruel and abusive towards Bessie, her mother, and her sisters:

> Their [Bessie Iquginnaq and her sisters'] father was a mean man and their mother plotted to leave him. She was the fourth of his four wives and, therefore, required to live with her three little daughters in the porch of the *iglu* with the dogs. There was no light or heat whatsoever.
>
> Slowly, she collected some small pieces of wood and frozen caribou skins, hoping to build a *qamutiit* for her two younger daughters, who were too small to walk. A man who happened by understood what was going on and gave her two small toy *qamutiit*, which he'd built for his own children. Unfortunately, the mean father found them and put them on the fire, ruining the plan.
>
> But word of the mistreatment spread to other camps, and two other men came to take the mother and three children away. They moved to the area of Aberdeen Lake, on the Thelon River, where Iquginnaq grew up.[10]

Even though she and her children were being abused, Bessie Iquginnaq's mother was not simply a passive victim. She did everything she could to escape the horrible situation and eventually succeeded. Also, other people clearly recognized that Bessie Iquginnaq's father's treatment of his spouse and daughters was wrong, and helped them leave this abusive man.

Earlier I explained why families were hesitant to keep baby girls, and how this often resulted in the infants' deaths. But just because there were reasons for this practice doesn't mean that it was easy for the mothers who had to give up their children. As my mother's experience shows, it could be very painful for women to give up their baby daughters. It was unfair to subject them to this pain.

Having said that, the fact that our historical culture had aspects that I think were unfair *in no way whatsoever* justifies the way *qablunaat* took control over our lives. Inuit were not "savage" or "primitive" because of these practices. We certainly were not inferior to *qablunaat*. These historical practices simply mean that we were not perfect—just like everybody else.

I Will Live for Both of Us

In the early 1990s I was working closely with Darren Keith, a *qablunaaq* researcher working for Parks Canada. Darren liked to go on long trips out on the land. In 1992 Darren travelled from Gjoa Haven to Baker Lake by snowmobile. He continued on to Arvait, and I accompanied him halfway there, along with a man from Baker Lake named Percy Tutannuak.

The following year, Darren was returning to Baker Lake from Arvait, and again I met him halfway. I brought my aunt Emily Nipiha'naaq along because we would be travelling near Qamanirjuaq Lake. I wanted to ask her questions about Urpilik, the place of my birth, Quurnguryuaq, my father's main camp at Qamanarjuaq Lake, and other places where my family had lived and hunted in the area.

On April 19, the anniversary of my father's death, we stopped at Quurnguryuaq. Darren had broken a lot of the crossbars on his *qamutiik*, so we went looking for wood at my father's old camp to fix them. While we searched for wood, Emily showed me some graves. One of them was for Paningaya'naaq, the little girl who was born before me.

I went back to help Darren fix his *qamutiik* and let Emily visit some of the graves by herself. But before long she came back and told us it was too difficult to do on her own. I went back out with her, to Paningaya'naaq's small grave. I looked at Emily, but at first I did not know what to say. Eventually, I looked at the grave and said, "I will live for both of us." That moment was when I decided I wanted to write a book about the experiences of the women in my family.

CHAPTER 2

Qablunaat, Moving to Town, and Going to School

My youth was a time of great change for Inuit. After the Second World War, the Government of Canada began to exert more control over us. *Qablunaat* (non-Inuit, people of European descent) dictated how we lived our lives. We experienced many colonial interventions, including coerced relocations and residential schooling. Because of the government's actions, Inuit moved off the land where we had lived for generations and into the towns we live in today.

This chapter is about the Kivalliq Inuit experience with colonization. It recounts my family's experiences with *qablunaat* authority figures, schooling, and moving from the land into the town of Baker Lake. It is based on my memories, supplemented with some secondary sources.

Qablunaat and Colonialism

Beginning in the late nineteenth century, Kivalliq Inuit were drawn into a colonial relationship with Canada. An unequal power relationship slowly developed between Inuit and *qablunaat*. In the late nineteenth and early twentieth centuries commercial whalers and fur traders created a new dependency among Inuit on European and Canadian manufactured goods.[1] The federal police helped assert Canadian sovereignty over Inuit lands and Canadian laws over Inuit society.[2] Christian missionaries helped extend *qablunaat* authority over Inuit by displacing Inuit spiritual leaders.[3]

At first, most Inuit families maintained their independence and autonomy. There were very few *qablunaat* living in the Arctic then, and most Inuit only saw them occasionally—when Royal Canadian Mounted Police (RCMP) officers or missionaries visited their camps, or when Inuit went to trading posts to trade furs. As a result, *qablunaat* authority over Inuit was limited, and traditional leaders continued to make important decisions. Also, the federal government decided not to apply its assimilationist policies—like residential schools and the Indian Act—to Inuit, at least for the time being.[4]

This began to change during the Second World War. Canadian and American military bases were built across the Inuit homeland, resulting in a massive influx of *qablunaat*.[5] At the same time, the price of furs plummeted, leaving many families destitute and dependent on relief from the government.[6] After the war, the federal government began to intervene in Inuit society. Its policy of assimilation, which First Nations in southern Canada had been subjected to since the nineteenth century, was extended to Inuit.[7] Children were separated from their families and sent to residential and boarding schools, where they were taught a curriculum that was irrelevant to life on the land.[8] Gradually, Inuit were drawn into the permanent communities that dot the map of the Arctic today.[9]

By 1970, almost all Kivalliq Inuit had stopped living in camps full-time and had moved to communities like Baker Lake. Different families left the land for different reasons. Most of the children left the land because they were taken away for schooling; some adults left the land to be closer to their children. Others were taken to town for medical treatment. Some families migrated to town to seek employment, while others moved to escape famine. Others were relocated by the government.

Once Inuit moved to town, the *qablunaat* gained an unprecedented amount of control over them. At camp, we still maintained some independence. Traditional leaders still made most decisions, even if they were sometimes constrained by *qablunaat* rules. However, in the towns, *qablunaat* held all the positions of authority.[10] Government administrators, police officers, teachers, and nurses were all *qablunaat*. As a result, Inuit understood that moving to town would mean abiding by their rules.

Colonialism and *Ilirahungniq*

Most Inuit did not clearly protest when *qablunaat* told them to send their children to boarding schools or move to the town of Baker Lake. At the time, most Inuit felt it was impossible to talk back to *qablunaat*. The concept of *ilirahungniq* helps us understand why this was the case.

Ilirahungniq is an Inuit emotional concept with no direct equivalent in English. It refers to a type of fear and intimidation. People who feel *ilirahungniq* usually avoid conflict and confrontation with any person who makes them feel this way. As a result, *ilirahungniq* can sometimes make people say yes to things they want to say no to.

Inuit often use words related to *ilirahungniq* when discussing oppression and inequality. For example, in the previous chapter, I wrote about my mother's experiences with female infanticide. When my mother discussed these experiences later in life, she often used words like *ilirahuk* (intimidated), *iliranatuapalaurmat* (a state of being constantly intimidated/afraid), and *ilirana'tuarmat* (daunted/ frightened) to explain how she was pressured and manipulated into giving up her daughters.

Sometimes, when *qablunaat* academics and bureaucrats write about this concept, they just use the root of the word ("*ilira-*").[11] However, this doesn't make sense in Inuktitut and sounds very awkward. You'll also see some Inuit write the word as "*ilirasungniq*" instead of "*ilirahungiq*." This is simply a difference between Inuktitut dialects.

Inuit politicians and public intellectuals use the concept of *ilirahungniq* to explain Arctic colonialism to the Canadian public. Sheila Watt-Cloutier, former chair of the Inuit Circumpolar Council, uses the concept of *ilirahungniq* to explain why Inuit "followed directions that were clearly contrary to their culture, their wisdom, and their own self-interest" in the 1950s and 1960s. She states, "In those days in interaction with *qablunaat* men—church missionaries, Hudson's Bay [Company] officials, and government representatives—our people often felt intimidated. The *qablunaat* had tools and technology that were foreign to us. And they clearly had power and a willingness to exercise it. What's more, their behavior was often at odds with our quiet, restrained way of approaching others."[12] In a series of blog posts, Inuit singer/songwriter Susan Aglukark uses the idea of *ilirahungniq* to explain the contemporary effects of colonization on the Inuit emotional well-being, especially the sense of inferiority many Inuit have internalized. In one blog post, she writes, "some of us (second generation New Inuit) still carry that kind of *ilira* around with us. I certainly felt that way when I first moved to Ottawa."[13] In another, she admits, "I have pursued my career almost always feeling *ilirasuk*."[14]

Inuit political organizations have used the notion of *ilirahungniq* to explain colonial history to commissions of inquiry. For example, in 1993 Rosemarie Kuptana, then president of the Inuit Tapirisat of Canada, used the concept of *ilirahungniq* in testimony to the Royal Commission on Aboriginal Peoples. Kuptana argued that the concept of *ilirahungniq* helped explain why Inuit did not seem to protest when *qablunaat* officials told them to move from northern Québec to the High Arctic. She explained that "this relationship [of dependence], and the feeling of *ilira* to which it gave rise, meant that whatever the *qablunaat* suggested or wanted was likely to be done. *Qablunaat* could make the difference between success and disaster, sustenance or hunger, and Inuit responded to their desires and requests as if they were commands. In this cultural setting, a challenge to the authority of the *qablunaat* or a defiance of their requests was almost unthinkable."[15] The Qikiqtani Truth Commission—a commission of inquiry that was initiated and funded by the Qikiqtani Inuit Association—used the concept of *ilirahungniq* to explain why Inuit could not say no to "requests" from the police in the 1950s and 1960s: "In customary contexts, *ilira* was a positive method of social control, but in relationships between RCMP and Inuit the feeling of *ilira* stopped Inuit from speaking out against injustices. The police were the most intimidating of all *qablunaat* with which they came into contact. If Inuit failed to listen to RCMP, or didn't adequately understand the police, they could be taken away and imprisoned."[16]

Several non-Inuit scholars have also used the concept of *ilirahungniq* to explain colonial power dynamics, most famously anthropologist Hugh Brody. In *The Other Side of Eden*, Brody wrote, "The word *ilira* goes to the heart of colonial relationships, and it helps to explain the many times that Inuit, and so many other peoples, say yes when they want to say no, or say yes and then reveal, later, that they never meant it at all. *Ilira* is a word that speaks to the subtle but pervasive results of inequality. Through the inequality it reveals, the word shapes the whole tenor of interpersonal behaviour, creating many misunderstandings, mistrust and bad faith. It is the fear that colonialism instils and evokes, which then distorts meanings, social life and politics."[17] Many other non-Inuit scholars have drawn from Brody's insights and applied the concept of *ilirahungniq* to colonial dynamics in the postwar period.[18]

It is important to understand that many *qablunaat* encouraged these feelings among Inuit. The church played a particularly important role in fostering feelings of *ilirahungniq*. Missionaries told us that we shouldn't question instructions we were given by the clergy and other *qablunaat* like police officers because *qablunaat* knew what was best for us.

Talking Back to *Qablunaat*

While most Inuit would not talk back to *qablunaat* in the 1950s and 1960s, there were some important exceptions. My father, Hitkati, was well known in the Baker Lake area for the way he repeatedly refused orders from *qablunaat* and publicly challenged their authority.

My father refused to obey many of the rules the police and clergy were trying to impose on our way of life. For example, in the 1950s, wildlife biologists were worried that caribou herds were declining, so they made it illegal for us to feed caribou to our dog teams. They did this without even consulting us. Some Inuit were convicted of criminal offenses as a result.[19]

Hitkati did not obey this law. He really loved his dogs—they were precious to him. A strong and healthy dog team contributed to his success as a hunter, so he treated his dogs very well. My mother and the other women in camp would sometimes complain that the dogs ate better than we did! There was no way my father was going to stop feeding caribou meat to his dogs. When I was young, my dad would always coach us before the *qablunaat* came to visit our camp. He would tell us what to say if they asked us questions. He always reminded us, "If they ask what we feed the dogs, tell them fish, only fish."

Another example of Hitkati's defiance is the way he refused to obey the church's rules for most of his life. While my father had accepted Christ into his life, he refused to give up three of his four wives, even though our tradition of having multiple wives was not permitted by the church. And, as I mentioned earlier, my father still sometimes went to an *angatquq* (shaman) for help with some issues when I was young, even though the missionaries discouraged us from doing so.

Another example of the way my father used to talk back to *qablunaat* is the story of my brother John Nukik's wedding. John Nukik told the story to a researcher a few years ago. It began with Hitkati using the radio at the mining exploration camp to contact Anglican Church representatives in Baker Lake:

Hitkati wanted to talk to Tapatai (Thomas) in Baker Lake on the radio. The radio was on and Hitkati requested that they fetch Tapatai to listen to the radio. The radio operator told Hitkati that Tapatai was now listening. Hitkati then told Tapatai, who was Anglican catechist, "I want my adopted son to get married. I do not want to spend three weeks in Baker Lake. (It was the Anglican Church's customary law to announce an impending marriage three times before the wedding could go ahead.) I want the wedding to take place the very next day after our arrival. I want to head home right away because it is spring." Hitkati was giving orders through the radio and asking Tapatai to tell Reverend Canon James.

We then travelled to Baker Lake and met my in-laws-to-be en route. My wife-to-be was told to get on my sled, since she soon will be my wife. The Elders said, "Since she will be your wife, she has to ride on your sled." We were travelling by dog team, and how successful I felt with my wife-to-be on my sled!

We arrived at Baker Lake and that same evening Canon James wanted me and my wife-to-be to come. He said he will teach us what we will need to do. We were wearing caribou skins, since we certainly did not have fancy clothes to get married in. How hot the house was! We found the house too hot. He offered us coffee and then he taught us what we will need to do and say. I finished my coffee and Canon James ordered, "Now kiss each other." My, here we were embarrassed and this minister telling us to kiss. I thought, "He just wants to see us kissing." Much later I learned it was part of the wedding custom and we were simply going through the routine procedures. Here we were, sweating from a hot house and, with the minister looking on, I had to kiss my future wife!

As I had said, Hitkati radioed Tapatai and he got the message back that Canon James agreed to his request. We spent only two nights in the community for the wedding ceremony and I was happy about that since I had never spent time with a crowd of strange people and I was terribly embarrassed.

This is one of my favourite stories from my brother John Nukik. I always laugh when I think him as a young man, wearing caribou-skin clothing indoors, sweating buckets, being told by a priest that he must kiss his bride-to-be, worried that the priest just wants to watch them be intimate. The story also speaks to my father's willingness to talk back to *qablunaat*. Most other Inuit could not believe that he would go on the radio and start issuing orders to the clergy.

My father also blatantly refused to send his children away to school or move into the community of Baker Lake. Every August, government officials visited our camp and told my father that he had to send his children to school in Baker Lake. But my father always stood his ground and said no. As a result, unlike most other Inuit my age, I did not go to school when I was young. Still, my mother tried to prepare me for school, just in case my father lost his fight against the government. She explained that if I went to school, I would have to wash my face every day. I used to practise, should I ever need to go to school eventually.

By the 1960s, the federal government began to encourage everyone, young and old alike, to move to Baker Lake permanently. Once people moved to Baker Lake, they were almost entirely under *qablunaat* authority. My father did not want to have anything to do with these plans and he simply refused their orders. He was one of the last Inuit living on the land full-time.

However, my father did more than simply refuse to follow orders from *qablunaat*. He also went out of his way to publicly challenge their authority. For example, Hitkati was usually very unwelcoming to the *qablunaat* police officers and government administrators who came to visit our camp at Ferguson Lake. He didn't like *qablunaat* showing up and telling us how to live our lives, so he tried to discourage them from visiting us whenever possible. He never offered them tea, or any of the other standard hospitality Inuit typically show to guests. The *qablunaat* would always bring him a gift of snuff as a sort of peace offering. One year, the police showed up and handed him a big carton of chewing gum. He took one look at it, threw it on the ground, and said to the officer (in Inuktitut), "Where's my snuff?" The other people at camp were *so* scared. His wives felt *tunniaq*—a feeling you get when someone close to you, like a family member, is being too aggressive (even if they are right). At the time, this was very extreme behaviour for an Inuk. Most Inuit couldn't imagine responding to a police officer in that way; my father was acting without *ilirahungniq* for *qablunaat*.

Very few Inuit challenged *qablunaat* authority in the same way as my father. I am not entirely sure why he was an exception. I think he may have been bullied or mistreated by some of the *qablunaat* police officers he encountered as a child, and this abuse gave him a life-long dislike of *qablunaat* authority figures.

Unfortunately, the way Hitkati would talk back to the *qablunaat* frightened my mother and the other women in our camp. They were terrified that his aggressive behaviour would have negative repercussions. However, I am glad my father had such a strong personality. He set a very good example for me. He taught me that Inuit could be proud people, and that we did not have to blindly accept everything *qablunaat* officials told us. If he had not set such a good example, I might not have grown up to be so outspoken about Inuit rights later in my life.

Moving to Town and Going to School

After a while the pressure from *qablunaat* became too much, even for a powerful person like my father. Gradually, members of our family began to move to Baker Lake. The government program that caused most of us to move to town was health care.

My first trip to Baker Lake was in the summer of 1957, when I was nine years old. A small government float plane landed near our camp at Ferguson Lake. I had a swollen neck, likely from the mumps, so they wanted to take me to the nursing station in Baker Lake. My father agreed because he felt that health care was a legitimate reason to go to town. After I arrived in Baker Lake I developed a cold or a flu, so I had to stay several weeks longer than expected. This was a very common experience. Whenever we encountered people from Baker Lake—for example, when people from our camp went there to trade—we would usually become infected with a cold or flu.

My next trip to Baker Lake took place during the winter of 1958–59. Titus Seeteenak, an Inuk working for the RCMP as a special constable, came to our camp late that winter and told us that we had to visit Baker Lake to be screened for tuberculosis. My whole family (except my mother, my sister Susan, my brother William, and my aunt Bessie) travelled to Baker Lake by dogsled to have chest X-rays taken. Luckily, we were all healthy and none of us had to be sent to sanatoriums in the south. We returned to Ferguson Lake that spring. The snow was melting very quickly by then, and I remember our sleds getting stuck in the soft snow over and over.

I took my third trip to Baker Lake in 1961, when I was twelve years old. That winter, a government plane landed on the lake ice in front of our camp. An RCMP officer, a federal administrator, and a nurse were on board. My mother had injured her back earlier that fall and was still having difficulty moving around. The *qablunaat* told my father to send her to Baker Lake for treatment. He agreed. My mother was taken to town, accompanied by my sister Susan, my brother William, and me. Although I did not know it at the time, I would never move back to the land full-time again.

In those days, the town of Baker Lake was still very small. It was home to a Hudson's Bay Company trading post, Anglican and Catholic churches, a nursing station, and an RCMP detachment. There was also a school and some small hostels where the Inuit students stayed. The *qablunaat* teachers, nurses, police officers, and clergy all lived in houses. A few Inuit families who had been living in town and working for *qablunaat* for some time also lived in houses. However, most of the Inuit families in Baker Lake lived in *igluit*, tents, and shacks made of scrap materials. When we arrived in Baker Lake, someone built an *iglu* for us.

Not long after we arrived, the *qablunaat* administrators told my mother that her children had to attend school. Unlike my father, my mother was too weak to talk back to *qablunaat*. As a result, my brother, my sister, and I began attending classes at the Baker Lake federal day school. It was not always easy, going to school while living in an *iglu*. We were also very poor because we had no one to hunt for us. We had to rely on whatever other people were willing to share. We did not have very much caribou because people mostly just shared fish with us.

Around the same time, church representatives insisted that we be baptized. We were all required to choose Christian names as part of joining the church. Canon James—the Anglican cleric in Baker Lake at the time—gave us a book with different English names listed in it. I chose the name Janet, as I thought it was the most beautiful-sounding name. I turned to him and pointed to "Janet" in the little book. However, he must not have been paying attention very closely because he wrote "Joan" on my paperwork.

We got sick often during our first few months in Baker Lake. This was almost always the case when people first moved to town. My mother eventually contracted tuberculosis. Like all the other Inuit who caught that terrible disease, she was sent to a tuberculosis sanatorium in southern Canada for treatment. With no guardian, I was sent to live at the school hostel, along with my brother and sister. This was the start of a very dark period in my life. I cried often. I missed my parents so much and wanted so badly to go back to the land. But school officials would not even let me visit. Even though other students were able to visit their families, during that first year I was not allowed to go. I remember going to the administrator's office, and begging him, "Please, let me go back to my father, I want to go back to Ferguson Lake." But he would not budge. I think they were worried my father would keep us and not allow us to return to school.

I really hated living at the hostel. My strongest memory of living there was being hungry all the time. It seemed like every meal was porridge, which was not enough for me after growing up on the land with a healthy diet of caribou meat. My stomach always felt empty when I lived in that hostel. In fact, this was my first real memory of hunger. As I discussed in Chapter 1, when I was very young, my family endured a winter when food was not as plentiful as usual. However, I do not remember that time clearly, and only know about it from the stories my mother and aunts told me when I was older. The first time I clearly remember experiencing real hunger was after I had moved to town.

But the worst part of my experience at school was not being able to protect my younger siblings. I felt responsible for them because I was the oldest. However, sometimes there was nothing I could do to protect them when they were in trouble. I was as powerless as they were. An example of this occurred when my brother was mistreated by a teacher. After a year at school, I had dropped out of classes to work for the school making food. It was my job to make students hot cocoa every morning and hot lunches three times a week. For this, they paid me seventy-five dollars a month. One evening, as I was cleaning up after the other students went home, I could hear a child screaming and crying very loudly from another room. I snuck over and quietly looked in. It was my brother. A teacher was beating him with a yardstick. I was *so* mad, but there was nothing I could do to stop it. I hid somewhere and waited for them to leave the building. After they left, I went into the room, took the yardstick that was used to hit my brother, and broke it over my knee. Then, I went through the entire school, into all four classrooms, and broke every yardstick I could find. I left the broken yardsticks in a pile on that teacher's desk, as a message.

From Baker Lake to Churchill

A few years later, I grew tired of living in Baker Lake and decided to move to Churchill in northern Manitoba. I was sixteen years old at the time, and wanted to look for a better job. I knew of a government charter plane that went back and forth between Baker Lake and Churchill. One day, without a ticket or even asking anyone, I just got on the plane.

When I arrived in Churchill, I soon found a job working as a live-in babysitter for a young *qablunaaq* couple. I worked for them for a while, but the couple eventually insisted that I should go further with my schooling. As a result, after a few months I enrolled as a student in the new Churchill Vocational Centre, a residential school that had been for Inuit students from what is now Nunavut and Nunavik. It focused on providing vocational training to mature students. The young men learned skills related to trades—for example, building construction, electrical, plumbing, and heating installation. Young women were taught cooking, how to budget, and other skills to prepare them for family life. Some of the young women also did on-the-job training to be hospital ward aides and food service workers.[20]

I had a much more pleasant time at the Churchill Vocational Centre than I did at the school in Baker Lake. I was a little older, a little wiser, and more comfortable living on my own. The teachers were mostly kind and encouraging, and I found the atmosphere much more pleasant than at the Baker Lake federal day school. I am not the only one who had positive experiences there. For example, Sheila Watt-Cloutier wrote in her memoir that her years in Churchill "were the best of [her] teenage life."[21]

However, despite these positive experiences, school in Churchill was not always easy for me. It involved a very strict lifestyle, and some of the instructors and other staff could be quite controlling. Also, because I received so little schooling in Baker Lake, I was behind many of the other students my age. It took a lot of hard work to catch up with my classmates. The school also brought people together from different regions, with different dialects and traditions. That was really interesting for me, but also difficult as sometimes we didn't all get along.

Project Surname

When I was living in Churchill in the late 1960s, the federal government launched an initiative called Project Surname. It was a program designed to give Inuit surnames, following *qablunaat* naming conventions. Many families chose to use the father's Inuktitut birthname as their surname. However, it was complicated for us. My mother no longer lived with my father. Also, the Church was pressuring us to only use our father's name if our parents had a Christian marriage.

My mother Lucy ended up choosing her birthname (Qaunnaq) as her surname. My sister Susan (Toolooktook) and brothers John (Nukik), Hugh (Ikoe), and Nicholas (Nungnik) did the same. To honour my father, I chose "Scottie" as my last name, as did my brothers William and Joseph.

Back to Baker Lake

In 1967, I decided to return to Baker Lake for the summer break from school. While I was in town, women regularly came to visit my mother in hopes of arranging a marriage between me and one of their sons. I absolutely refused to be subjected to any sort of arranged marriage. It was very disturbing to have other people negotiate my future love life for me. I was determined to put a stop to this, so I found the men whose mothers had tried to arrange marriages with me and embarrassed them. I yelled at them, said that there was no way I would ever marry them, and mockingly asked why they had to send their mothers to find them wives instead of doing so themselves. Finally, I warned that I would continue to embarrass them if their mothers persisted with trying to arrange a marriage with me. That fall, I went back to school in Churchill.

In 1968 I returned to Baker Lake again, this time to stay. The town had changed quite a bit since I had first moved away to Churchill. The most obvious change was that fewer Inuit were living in tents, *igluit*, and so-called matchbox houses (shacks). This was largely because, in 1967 and 1968, the government built sixty-seven new three-bedroom social housing units in Baker Lake.

I soon found a job working as a cashier at the HBC store. After I'd saved a little money, I bought a small motorized scooter from a *qablunaaq* administrator. I felt really proud of myself driving around town on it because in those days it was rare for woman to drive motorized vehicles. However, my scooter didn't last long. I got confused when I was fuelling it up and put fuel oil into the gasoline tank. The engine was ruined.

Before long I left my cashier job to work in the settlement office as an interpreter. Along with interpreting and translating for the government workers stationed there, it was also my job to distribute social assistance payments to members of the community. One of the tasks I remember well was working as an interpreter for the area administrator's wife. It was her job to teach Inuit how to live in, and how to maintain, the new three-bedroom houses. Before anyone could move into this new style of housing, they were required to take the course she offered.

Together, we taught a series of lessons on topics including washing dishes, waxing floors, using a gas stove, and operating a furnace and thermostat. There was also a lesson on children's nutrition. These may seem like very mundane topics, but they were all new (and sometimes strange) concepts for people moving off the land. While we were all more than capable of living on the land, these simple everyday tasks are very different in Western-style housing. In particular, I remember that a lot of Inuit were quite scared of furnaces and automatic thermostats.

At the end of the course, there were oral and practical exams. Everyone had to demonstrate that they could perform the tasks we taught them (for example, lighting a stove) and answer questions about what they had learned. Some people had a lot of difficulty with these tests and had to repeat them several times before they were allowed to move into the new housing. My sister Marion Pattunguyak was one of them. I recall one oral exam, where the administrator's wife placed a lot of different food items on the counter, and asked her, "What would you feed your children for breakfast?" She pointed to the ice cream. I was *so* embarrassed for her. The instructors were clearly not thrilled, and asked my sister rather sternly, "Why would you feed your children ice cream in the morning?" My sister said, "Because I want them to wake up quickly, by eating something cold." I thought that was a pretty good answer.

Hitkati Moves to Town

By the time I moved back to Baker Lake, most members of my family had already left Ferguson Lake and moved to Baker Lake as well. Three of Hitkati's spouses—Mary Atangat, Emily Nipiha'naaq, and my mother, Lucy Qaunnaq— had all moved to town for medical reasons. My brother, John Nukik, had moved to town with his wife Martha because he'd been hired as a construction worker.

Hitkati remained on the land with only one spouse—Bessie Iquginnaq—and two adopted granddaughters. In those days, my father was becoming quite paranoid. He was worried that the *qablunaat* authorities would punish him because he had broken so many of their laws. Other Inuit had been arrested and sent to prison for things that my father considered to be minor, such as hunting muskox. He was constantly scared that someone would testify to the authorities about his past transgressions. For example, a widower with a son came to our camp at Ferguson Lake, to request marriage to my sister Marion Pattunguyak. The widower lived with us for a year, then moved away with my sister. One summer, he died by suicide. My father became very concerned that the man had taken his own life out of guilt, presumably because the man had testified against him and told the authorities that my father was not following Canadian laws. My father was always worried that someone was plotting against him. After my mother and her sister Emily moved to town, he worried that they had sided with the government and would someday testify against him as well.

My father remained on the land until 1973. By this time his health had begun to deteriorate. We learned that he had passed out several times while on the land—we suspect it was from heart problems. That winter he was supposed to come to town after freeze-up but did not arrive on time. I asked the government administrator to send a plane to his camp to make sure everything was all right. A plane was sent, but my father refused to travel back to Baker Lake by air with the *qablunaat*. He said he would come by dog team with Bessie and his granddaughters in due time. Worried for his safety, I ended up travelling to his camp by snowmobile with two men, using government-provided snowmobiles and sleds. We met my father on his way to Baker Lake. When he arrived in town, my father and Bessie Iquginnaq moved into a housing unit where he lived for the rest of his life.

The transition to living in Western-style housing was very difficult for Bessie Iquginnaq. She and my father moved to town years after the introductory course was offered, so they were confused by many aspects of living in their new house. For example, they tried to continue sleeping on caribou-skin bedding, which is totally impractical in a warm house. They also had a lot of trouble adjusting to an automatic thermostat. They fiddled with it endlessly. Whenever Hitkati wanted to heat up the house, he'd turn the thermostat up all the way. Then Bessie Iquginnaq would get scared that the house would catch fire and turn it back down all the way. Eventually, I successfully explained to Bessie Iquginnaq that they were supposed to leave it at a comfortable temperature somewhere in the middle, instead of turning it on and off constantly. However, I was unable to explain this concept to my father, so they kept moving the thermostat back and forth all the time.

The biggest source of stress for Bessie Iquginnaq was housekeeping. When they moved in, they were required to sign a contract that included a promise to keep the house clean. Bessie was always scared that they would get kicked out of their house for not fulfilling their end of the agreement. She was especially anxious because my father treated the house as if it were a tent or an *iglu*. For example, every time my father had something to eat, he would use the curtains as a napkin—they were always dirty and bloody from my father wiping his hands and face on them. Also, my father used to chew tobacco, and would often make a mess on the floor from his spit can.

Even after moving to town, my father remained firmly connected to our hunting lifestyle. He continued to travel and hunt on our land until his dying day in 1978. He also maintained a very strong will and continued to talk back to *qablunaat*. He did this even though he could no longer hear and did not know how to speak English. Whenever he met a new *qablunaaq*, he would gesture to them as if to say, "You, get on a plane, and go back to the south."

CHAPTER 3

Uranium Exploration, Petitions, and a Court Case

Mineral exploration and mining companies began work in the Kivalliq region soon after the Second World War. In the late 1940s, a small mineral exploration camp briefly operated near my family's camp at Ferguson Lake. Exploration activity increased significantly in the late 1960s after uranium was discovered near Baker Lake.

By 1969, the Baker Lake area was overrun by uranium exploration companies. That year, the federal government issued prospecting permits for one-third of our hunting grounds.[1] As time went on, the amount of exploration activity near Baker Lake kept increasing. Hunters began finding more and more drill rigs out on the land; operations that made a lot of noise and left behind plenty of garbage. Helicopters flew above our hunting grounds constantly, moving people and supplies to and from base camps, drill sites, and the town of Baker Lake.[2] These companies were doing their exploration work without any regard for Inuit or the caribou we hunt. Their low-flying helicopters and noisy drilling disturbed migration routes. They set up equipment and camps in sensitive caribou habitat, next to major caribou water crossings, and right in the middle of the caribou calving grounds. We grew up with strict rules about how to treat these areas, so it was very upsetting to see *qablunaat* come and treat them with such disrespect. As a result of all of this activity, the caribou herds started to change their migration routes. Soon, our hunters had difficulty catching enough caribou to feed their families.[3]

Our community decided to fight back. We used our new municipal government and representative Inuit organizations to express our opposition to uranium exploration. We used petitions, letter-writing campaigns, and even went to court to try to stop mineral exploration in our hunting grounds. In the end, we failed to stop it. However, because of our efforts, the government introduced new and much stricter regulations that minimized the disturbance of exploration activities on caribou.

In this chapter, I discuss the creation of new community and Inuit representative organizations in Nunavut and explain how we used them to fight uranium exploration. I describe the development of these organizations and our legal and political battles against the uranium industry from my point of view. My perspective on this history comes from my personal experience as a Settlement Council member, interpreter, community researcher, and federal land use inspector.

Municipal Government, Inuit Organizations, and Land Claims

In 1969, a Settlement Council was created in Baker Lake. This council was the first real municipal government in Baker Lake that Inuit could participate in. Government administrators had created an "Eskimo Council" in Baker Lake in the late 1950s. However, this council was advisory only, and had no legal jurisdiction.[4] I was elected as a council member for the first three years of its operation—in 1969, 1970, and 1971. I was in my early twenties and had just returned to the area after attending school in Churchill. Sitting on the council was an important learning experience for me. It taught me about working with representative politics to fight for Inuit rights. However, because I was young, I did not participate in most of the discussions and debates.

In 1973, I moved to Arviat to start a new job as a social worker. This required spending some time in Brandon, Manitoba, studying social work at the college. I returned to Arviat to work in the field, but I really hated the job. I especially hated the apprehension of children from their families. Eventually I quit and moved back to Baker Lake.

When I returned to Baker Lake, I took a temporary job as an interpreter for the Inuit Land Use and Occupancy Project. This was a massive research project driven by Inuit Tapirisat of Canada (ITC), the national Inuit organization. ITC (later renamed Inuit Tapiriit Kanatami, or ITK) was created in 1971 to represent all Inuit in Canada. ITC's first major action was to lobby the federal government to negotiate a land claim agreement with Inuit, to protect our rights to the land, wildlife, and other resources. According to the government's policy, we were required to document our land and resource use before our claim would be considered. The Land Use and Occupancy Project was created to gather this evidence in support of Inuit land claims. The final report, released in 1976, ended up playing a very important role in future negotiations for the Nunavut and Inuvialuit land claims.[5]

Together with Dr. Milton Freeman (an anthropologist and director of the project) and Tony Welland (the researcher for the Kivalliq region), I helped interview hunters and Elders in Baker Lake, Chesterfield Inlet, Whale Cove, and Coral Harbour. We asked them to tell us all of the places they hunted, fished, trapped, travelled, and camped. Some of the people we interviewed seemed very hesitant to answer our questions—they were likely worried that the government might use this information to impose new restrictions on hunting or fishing. I think some of them might have left out a lot of information, worried it would be used against them.

The Canadian Uranium Industry Moves North

The Canadian uranium mining industry was established during the Second World War to support the United States' nuclear weapons program. The first uranium mines in Canada were in Dene territory—northern Saskatchewan and the Northwest Territories. These mines provided the raw materials used to develop the atomic bombs that were dropped on Nagasaki and Hiroshima in 1945, killing hundreds of thousands of people.[6]

In the 1950s, the nuclear arms race between the United States and Soviet Union resulted in continued demand for Canadian uranium from the American military. Canadian uranium production quickly expanded, with most activity taking place in northern Saskatchewan and Northern Ontario. However, this "boom" of uranium mining collapsed in the late 1950s, after the United States developed domestic supplies of uranium for its weapons program. The price of uranium dropped and, as a result, most of the uranium mines in Canada closed.[7]

The development of nuclear power plants in the late 1960s caused the market for uranium to partially recover. Uranium companies resumed their frenzied search for uranium in northern Canada.[8] This is what originally led uranium mining companies to the Baker Lake area. However, just before this new uranium boom could really take off, the global uranium market collapsed again. Protectionist economic policies in the United States, introduced in 1971, forbade the use of imported uranium in American nuclear power plants. The global price of uranium soon hit an all-time low, threatening the viability of several Canadian mining companies.[9]

In response, a secretive and illegal cartel was established in 1972, involving governments and uranium companies from Canada, France, Germany, Australia, and South Africa. The cartel's purpose was to inflate the price of uranium by controlling the global supply. Despite only operating for two years, the cartel achieved its goal—by 1976, two years after the cartel had ceased operations, the price of uranium had increased over 700 percent.[10] This spike in the price of uranium caused a rapid expansion of uranium exploration activity near Baker Lake in the 1970s.

The cartel was publicly exposed in 1976. Evidence of its existence was stolen from an Australian uranium company and leaked to the media. Canada later faced significant public criticism for its role in the cartel, not only because of its illegal nature but also its legitimation of apartheid South Africa's extraction of uranium from occupied Namibia.[11]

I think it's important for us to think about this history when we deal with uranium companies in Nunavut. Spokespeople for the nuclear industry always claim they mine uranium to create jobs and produce alternative sources of energy. However, the truth of the matter is, the Canadian uranium industry has its origins in the nuclear arms race, shadowy cartels, and illegal dealings that helped apartheid South Africa—one of the most brutal, oppressive, and racist regimes of the twentieth century—develop nuclear weapons.

Petitions and a Land Freeze

Before long, the Baker Lake Settlement Council spoke out about the negative effects of uranium exploration on our land and the caribou we depend upon.

In 1974 it submitted a petition to the federal government, protesting planned uranium exploration near major caribou water crossings on Baker Lake, the Kazan River, and the Thelon River. It stated,

> We, the undersigned people of Baker Lake, do not accept the position
> of the federal and territorial governments, to allow exploration to
> continue to take place on Inuit land. We, the residents of Baker Lake,
> do not want exploration to take place on Inuit land until:
> 1) The Inuit land claims have been settled to the satisfaction of the
> Inuit peoples;
> 2) Formal approval has been received from the residents of Baker
> Lake to allow exploration to go ahead.[12]

The petition explained that low-flying aircraft, blasting, and drilling were disturbing the caribou we hunt, and that this was a threat to our community's economy and the survival of the caribou herds.[13] The government basically ignored this first petition.

In 1975 the Settlement Council worked with our newly formed Hunters and Trappers Association (HTA) to prepare a proposal for a "land freeze." HTAs (later renamed Hunters and Trappers Organizations, or HTOs) are community organizations that provide Inuit hunters with a voice to represent their interests in the management of wildlife and wildlife habitat. The Settlement Council and HTA carefully mapped out the areas we wanted to protect, and asked the government to put a halt to exploration in those places. The community put a lot of work into the proposal, which documented the cultural and economic significance of the areas they wanted protected.[14] Once again, the government ignored us.

Inuit Tapirisat of Canada helped us lobby the government for a land freeze. In 1977 the president of ITC was Michael Amarook, a hunter from Baker Lake who grew up on the land. Amarook wrote to Warren Allmand, minister of Indian Affairs and Northern Development, calling for a land freeze in the Keewatin region. The letter explained that mineral exploration was negatively affecting caribou hunting. "We have seen the disturbance and damage they [exploration companies] have caused to our animals and our hunting areas," he wrote.

Amarook concluded by stating that Inuit would "not stand by any longer and see our hunting lands invaded while our legitimate concerns are ignored."[15]

Finally, the government responded. Minister Allmand granted us a partial land freeze. The government stopped issuing new exploration permits for one year, from 1977 to 1978. This did not stop companies from continuing work on existing permits, but it did prevent the level of activity from increasing, for the time being at least.[16]

The Baker Lake Study

During the one-year freeze on new permits, the federal government contracted a Winnipeg-based consulting firm called Interdisciplinary Systems Limited to study the impacts of uranium exploration on wildlife and Inuit hunting. The firm reviewed scientific literature, interviewed fifty men from Baker Lake, and worked with an advisory committee of local hunters.[17]

I was offered a job as a community researcher for the Baker Lake study, which I accepted. At the time, I was a single mother with a baby, so I was happy to find some part-time employment. It was my job to visit people's homes to interview Elders and hunters about their knowledge of the land, animals, and our hunting lifestyle. I travelled between Baker Lake and the company's Winnipeg office many times during my work on this project. I met with the other researchers to discuss our findings, and then went back to the hunters and Elders for clarification on some issues. Unfortunately, the transcripts from my interviews have been lost. However, I still remember how passionate the hunters were about protecting the land, especially caribou migration routes and water crossings.

I really enjoyed this job. It was interesting, getting to hear from so many different Elders. But the job wasn't always easy. There were some Elders who intimidated me that I did *not* want to interview. One was my father, the other was Thomas Tapatai. I respected them both a lot, and I was worried it would be disrespectful or annoying for me to ask too many nosey questions. I decided to interview them together—that way they could just talk to each other and I could take notes, keeping my questions to a minimum.

My experience as a researcher on this project had a big impact on me, and it's one of the reasons I've fought so hard to protect the land from the mining industry. Those interviews taught me just how important migration routes, water crossings, and calving grounds are for both caribou and Inuit. I also learned how easily mineral exploration and mining can disturb these special places.

Caribou usually follow predictable migration routes from year to year. If the caribou change their migration route, it can negatively affect our ability to hunt. Our ancestors were not just wandering aimlessly around the tundra searching for food. They knew where the caribou would be at different times of year.

Inuit have several rules, called *pitqussiit*, that we follow to ensure that caribou keep the same migratory paths year after year. The word *pitqussiit* refers to the Inuit way of doing things, our "rules, values, customs, and norms that have been passed down through generations."[18] Unlike the *aglirniq* (taboos) I discussed in Chapter 1, many of us still strictly follow *pitqussiit* when we hunt, fish, and travel on the land and water.

One example of a *pitqussiit* related to caribou is that Elders teach us not to hunt the first caribou in a herd. The caribou at the front of the herd are leaders, and the rest follow where they go. If you hunt the first caribou, the herd may scatter and change its migration.[19] We are also taught not to disturb the caribou's migratory paths. When I was growing up, my family would not camp directly on the migration routes. Instead, we would camp a short distance away so we would not disturb that land. We would also make sure to keep the major migration routes clean, and remove carcasses and any other remains from our hunting activities. We weren't even allowed to defecate near the migratory routes. Changes in migration still harm our communities today. If a herd avoids our hunting grounds, even just for a season or two, it will affect our ability to feed our families.

Water crossings have always been one of the most important hunting places for inland Inuit. Traditionally, we would hunt caribou in *qayait* (kayaks) at the crossings, spearing them when they were in the water.[20] To this day, we still hunt near crossings on the Kazan River, Thelon River, and parts of Baker Lake.[21] The importance of water crossings is embedded in our culture—there are traditional songs about hunting at water crossings,[22] and many traditional place names refer to caribou water crossings.[23]

Caribou are very sensitive to disturbance at and near water crossings. Even the smallest disturbance can cause them to scatter or change their migration route. When I was a child, there were a lot of *pitqussiit* we had to follow when we hunted and camped near water crossings. The shore of the river where caribou enter the water was not used for camping, hunting, skinning animals, or caching meat—basically, we avoided that side of the river as much as possible. We usually built our camps on the opposite shore, some distance away from the crossings, so caribou would not see, hear, or smell us when they cross. We took great care to clean up any evidence of our presence near the crossings, and we would not leave carcasses and other remains in the area. We would even clean up the guts and blood from the land when we skinned caribou near water crossings and migration routes by burying it under the tundra.[24]

Caribou are also very sensitive to disturbance where they give birth and where they nurse their newborn calves. Biologists call these areas "calving grounds" and "post-calving grounds." Since the 1970s, biologists have recommended protecting caribou from disturbance in these areas.[25] To this day, most of the biologists I have met have recommend we protect these areas. They say that caribou cows tend to abandon their calves if disturbed during this time. Also, caribou need to graze more than usual during this season, so they can produce enough milk to feed their young. If they become disturbed, they won't be able to eat enough for their calves to survive.[26]

Mining and exploration activity can negatively impact the caribou. The low-flying helicopters, the noise from drilling, and the noise and dust from roads can cause herds to scatter, change their migrations, or even cause their populations to decline. They can be especially sensitive to disturbance from humans—if you are out on the land, caribou will often hear and smell you before they are close enough for you to see them. Many hunters have stories of their hunting being affected by low-flying helicopters and other disturbances. This is why we work so hard to protect the migration routes, water crossings, and calving grounds from mining and exploration. Hunters from Baker Lake are still fighting to have these areas protected to this day.

The Baker Lake study's final report recommended that the federal government develop measures to protect the area's water crossings, calving grounds, and post-calving grounds. It recommended a mixture of protected areas and seasonal restrictions. However, the decision to act on these recommendations was ultimately up to the government.

The Government Responds

The federal government responded to the report in the spring of 1978. It announced that it was, in fact, developing measures to protect caribou from disturbance, and that these measures would provide seasonal restrictions in calving grounds, post-calving grounds, and at water crossings. In these sensitive areas, activity would be prohibited during the calving, post-calving, and migration seasons. Unfortunately, the government also announced that the land freeze would be lifted, and more exploration permits would be issued near Baker Lake.[27]

Delegates from Baker Lake raised this issue at ITC's annual general meeting in March 1978. They complained that the one-year freeze on issuing permits had not been enough, and expressed disappointment that the government planned to issue further permits. Our delegates presented a petition, addressed to the prime minister, calling for a halt to all mineral exploration in the area. The ITC assembly passed a resolution declaring its support for our struggle.[28]

On April 7 Hugh Faulkner—then minister of Indian Affairs and Northern Development—came to Baker Lake and met with the Hamlet Council, the Hunters and Trappers Association, and the Land Claims Committee. Representatives from ITC were also in attendance. The minister told us that the land freeze would be lifted on April 14—a mere one week later. This was before the new protection measures had even been finalized, let alone implemented.[29]

We did our best to explain our position to the minister. William Noah, chair of the Baker Lake Hamlet Council, had hosted a radio call-in show a few days earlier. He told Faulkner that the overwhelming majority of callers wanted the land freeze extended. Noah also explained that the Hamlet was prepared to go to court over the issue. Edwin Evo, vice-president of the Hunters and Trappers Association, argued that further research was needed to identify caribou calving grounds before the new protection measures could be finalized. Emile Oklaga, chair of the Land Claims Committee, told the minister that Baker Lake residents wanted the land freeze to continue until land claims were settled.[30]

Unfortunately, Faulkner wouldn't budge. I attended the meeting as a Hamlet councillor. I asked the minister if he would at least consider waiting to lift the land freeze until the new protection measures were finalized and implemented. He refused.[31]

The Baker Lake Court Case

William Noah immediately began to organize a legal challenge. I remember listening to him speak on community radio, asking us to visit the Hamlet office and sign our names onto the court action. I signed my name, as did many of my family members, including my mother Lucy Qaunnaq, my aunt Bessie Scottie, my sister Marion Pattunguyak, and my brothers William Scottie and John Nukik.[32]

In April 1978, the Hamlet of Baker Lake, the Baker Lake Hunters and Trappers Association, the Inuit Tapirisat of Canada, and 111 residents of Baker Lake sought a court order to halt all mineral exploration in our hunting grounds. Our application argued that uranium exploration was infringing upon our Aboriginal land rights. We also applied for an "interlocutory injunction." In other words, we asked the judge to order a halt to the exploration planned for the summer, so there would be time for the case to be heard in court.[33]

Our application for an interlocutory injunction was heard in a Toronto courtroom at the end of the month. William Noah brought some Baker Lake community members to the hearing, so they could explain the importance of the land and animals to the judge. My mother, Lucy Qaunnaq, was part of that delegation. I remember these events very clearly, because it was the same week my father died.

The judge issued an initial ruling in our favour. He concluded that "the balance clearly weighs in favour of an injunction: the minerals, if there, would remain; the caribou, presently there, may not." However, he did not order the full halt to exploration that we had wanted. Instead, he simply ordered the government to implement especially strict regulations on exploration for that summer. Practically speaking, the "injunction" only provided a deeper legal requirement for the government's seasonal restrictions on activity in calving grounds, post-calving grounds, and water crossings.[34]

The case went to court in the summer of 1979. Inuit testimony was heard in Baker Lake; legal arguments, technical evidence, and expert witnesses were heard in Toronto. Baker Lake Inuit, our legal counsel, and our expert advisors argued that caribou numbers in the Baker Lake area had declined because of harassment from uranium exploration, negatively impacting our Aboriginal rights to harvest wildlife. The defendants argued that this decline was related to a broader decline in caribou populations, allegedly because of overhunting. They also argued that we had no Aboriginal rights to harvest wildlife.

At the Baker Lake hearings, some of our hunters appeared as witnesses. They explained how uranium exploration was seriously disrupting caribou hunting. Barnabas Piryuaq told the court about his upbringing on the land, how he had lived entirely from caribou hunting, fishing, and fox trapping. He said that in the late 1960s caribou migrations had shifted—they no longer passed through traditional water crossings where Inuit hunt. He claimed that low-flying aircraft were responsible for this change in the animals' patterns.[35] William Noah told the court that in the 1950s hunters could catch up to two hundred caribou each year. By the 1970s, according to Noah, this was no longer possible, and as a result many families "[did not] have enough food at home." He said that noise from mineral exploration had scared caribou away: "More and more these caribou are moving away. It doesn't have anything to do with people in the community, but [rather] activities from mining groups."[36] Hugh Ungungai told the court that he had not seen caribou at the Kazan River crossings in a decade. "I believe the cause of all that . . . has been a lot of mining exploration and aircraft flying around."[37] Michael Amarook told the court he had directly witnessed helicopters chasing away a group of caribou he was attempting to hunt near a water crossing. He reiterated that noise from mineral exploration had scared caribou away, and that migrations would return to normal if the disturbance was removed.[38] John Avaala told the court that caribou had also failed to cross the Thelon River in large numbers in recent years, and that low-flying aircraft were at fault.[39]

At the hearing in Toronto, lawyers Aubrey Golden and David Estrin argued our case. Professional geographers, anthropologists, archaeologists, biologists, and archivists presented evidence in support of our claims. Together, they argued that Inuit had a ten-thousand-year history of land use and occupancy in the area, and that mineral exploration was disturbing caribou.[40] Lawyers representing the federal government and uranium companies claimed that Inuit had no Aboriginal rights to land. Government biologists claimed that Inuit overhunting had caused a general decline in caribou populations. They argued that this population decline, not uranium exploration, explained the poor caribou harvests in recent years.[41]

A decision was released in the fall of 1979. For Baker Lake Inuit, the trial's outcome was both a victory and a loss. On the one hand, the judge ruled that we had not provided enough evidence that mineral exploration was the cause of a decline in caribou. The injunction issued in 1978 was lifted, which meant exploration for uranium could not only continue, but increase. On the other hand, he found that we did indeed possess Aboriginal rights to our traditional lands.[42] This recognition of our Aboriginal title ended up playing a big role in the Nunavut Land Claims Agreement and the creation of Nunavut, many years later.

Caribou Protection Measures and 1½ Helicopter Crashes

The seasonal restrictions the government placed on exploration activity eventually became known as Caribou Protection Measures. To support these measures, the government created Caribou Protection Areas around the calving grounds and post-calving grounds. All activity was banned in these areas from the middle of May until late July, to ensure caribou were not disturbed when they gave birth and nursed their young. Exploration activity was also banned near water crossings during the spring, summer, and fall. The government hired caribou monitors to survey the animals from airplanes each spring. If they spotted large numbers of caribou approaching an exploration camp between May and July, even if the camp was outside of the Caribou Protection Areas, the camp would be shut down. The protection measures also required aircraft to maintain minimum altitudes to decrease disturbance to caribou.[43]

These new regulations did help decrease disturbance to caribou. The caribou populations started to climb again, and by the 1990s we were getting *lots* of caribou near Baker Lake. But the new regulations were not perfect. Stopping all activity for a few months during calving season seems like very strong protection in some ways, but it leaves a lot of issues unresolved. The protection measures were only designed for *exploration*, and only during certain seasons. However, if a company happened to find a mineral deposit, they were going to want to mine it. I do not think seasonal restrictions or other special measures could acceptably manage the impacts of a full-blown mine in the calving grounds. Moreover, these measures do nothing to protect the lands that are culturally important to

Elders. These lands are like a part of our spirit, and the thought of seeing them destroyed tears some of us up inside.

I have first-hand experience with these regulations. In 1978, I was hired by the federal government as a land use inspector to enforce various land use regulations. I worked out of the Department of Indian Affairs and Northern Development's district sub-office in Baker Lake. From May 15 to August 15, I would travel by helicopter to visit all the exploration camps in the area. It was my job to inspect the camps and ensure that companies were following regulations and meeting all conditions for their land use permits. For example, I had to make sure that fuel was properly stored and that no garbage was being left on the tundra. I also helped enforce the Caribou Protection Measures. If the caribou monitors saw that caribou were migrating towards an active exploration project during the calving season, they would call me and I would tell the company they had to stop operations. I would also be called to investigate if hunters reported seeing low-flying aircraft harassing the caribou.

One memorable day in 1981, I was on my way to do an inspection at Yathkyed Lake, which is inland and very far away from any communities. I had two summer students with me that day. The weather was bad, so our helicopter was flying low below the clouds. Suddenly, an alarm went off—the helicopter's engine had failed. My first instinct was to take my seatbelt off, so I would not get trapped. But I smartened up quickly and put it back on. The next thing I remember is waking up with a loud ringing in my ears. We had crashed. I was worried the helicopter might explode, so I tried to get out as fast as possible, but my door would not open. Eventually I kicked the door open, crawled out, and looked for the pilot. He made his way out of the helicopter, followed by the two students. After a long wait, another helicopter arrived to bring us back to Baker Lake.

I was very shaken up by this event, but kept working as a land use inspector. Incredibly, we had another incident the following year. That day, the helicopter pilot had just dropped the district geologist off to do some exploration work west of Baker Lake. When we were back in the air, the pilot asked me if I smelled something burning. At first, I thought maybe the geologist had left a lit cigarette on board. But then I saw heavy smoke coming out of the top of the helicopter. That's when I started to get nervous. We were carrying a lot of extra fuel that day, and I was worried it might catch fire and explode. I told the pilot to land. As soon as we were on the ground, I jumped out and ran away from the helicopter. Something was burning close to the base of the blades, so the pilot tried to radio back to Baker Lake for help. No one answered his calls. The pilot decided he would fly back to the nearest camp, which was a twenty-minute flight. We got back into the helicopter and started the engine, but it started to smoke again. I got right back out and insisted that I was not going anywhere in that helicopter. The pilot told me he would send another helicopter for me and then flew off.

I was alone. I had nothing useful with me, not even a lighter. All I had was my notebook for land use inspections. I walked to the nearest hill to wait for the promised helicopter. After three hours of waiting, I started getting really nervous. I was worried that the pilot had crashed and died. No one knew where I was, out on the land. I thought people would just assume that I died in the crash with the pilot, and would not bother coming to look for me. I did not even know which way to walk to get back to Baker Lake. Finally, I heard a helicopter off in the distance. As it turned out, the pilot had forgotten to record where he left me—they had spent the last three hours flying back and forth looking for me.

After these experiences, I decided to take some time off from my job as a land use inspector. I took educational leave in 1983 and moved to Fort Smith. I returned to my land use inspector job in Baker Lake the following year, but I was still uncomfortable with flying in helicopters. As a result, I resigned from my job in 1985. I still hate flying in helicopters and avoid it as much as I can to this day.

CHAPTER 4

Kiggavik Round 1: The Urangesellschaft Proposal

By the late 1980s, a German company called Urangesellschaft had discovered a large uranium deposit west of Baker Lake. In March 1988 the company submitted a proposal for the "Kiggavik" uranium mine to the federal government. The proposal called for an open pit uranium mine and milling operation to be built eighty kilometres west of Baker Lake, as well as a winter road connecting the new mine to the town of Baker Lake.

As a community organizer, I worked hard to inform local residents about the dangers of uranium mining and coordinate local opposition to Urangesellschaft's proposal. I did much of this work as founder of the Baker Lake Concerned Citizens Committee. Our goal was to ensure that people's concerns were heard, so Inuit would be able to influence the final decision about the proposed mine. I worked closely with Jack Hicks, who was the coordinator for the Northern Anti-Uranium Coalition. This was a regional umbrella group created to coordinate Inuit organizations and other groups from the Kivalliq region that opposed the Kiggavik project.

The Kiggavik proposal was reviewed by the Federal Environmental Assessment and Review Office. However, the review was never completed because Urangesellschaft withdrew its proposal midway through the process—because of technical concerns raised by communities, government, and Inuit representative organizations, and because our community expressed overwhelming political opposition to the project.

In this chapter, I tell the story of how Baker Lake Inuit worked with allies from around the world to stop Urangesellschaft's proposed uranium mine. Our experiences show that a small group of Indigenous people can stand up to the global nuclear industry and win.

Returning to Ferguson Lake

In the fall of 1987, I moved to Rankin Inlet to work for the Government of the Northwest Territories on a casual basis. From October of that year until May 1988, I did clerical work for different government departments, including health, finance, communications, and human resources. However, I couldn't stand staying in Rankin Inlet over the summer. Being cooped up in an office felt horrible when I just wanted to be out on the land.

Luckily, I found seasonal work at a fishing lodge on Ferguson Lake. The lodge was owned by a *qablunaaq* businessman named Keith Sharp, who lived in Rankin Inlet. He was married to an Inuk woman and was very much a part of the community. I worked at the lodge as a guide, taking tourists out fishing in the Ferguson Lake area. This allowed me to return to the land of my childhood and revisit the places where my parents had raised me. The owner of the lodge even let me bring my pet German shepherd and my daughter Hilu. It felt just like being at home.

Spending time at Ferguson Lake stirred up a lot of feelings. It made me realize just how much I had lost by moving to Baker Lake when I was a child. It made me confront the fact that, in many ways, my connection to the land had been severed. At the same time, it provided me with an opportunity to renew my relationship with my homeland. It also reminded me of the strong spiritual bond I have with my childhood home.

For the most part, I enjoyed my job. I took guests out fishing every day, made them a shore lunch, and helped fillet their catch when the day was done. I was outdoors most of the time, which was really nice. Most of the clients were very wealthy people. I remember guiding for doctors, magazine editors, and famous photographers among others. Some of them were pleasant but a lot of them could be really obnoxious. They drank beer in my boat even when I told them not to. Some guests could be very bossy. Some of them were obviously sexist and treated me like I didn't know anything because I was a woman. Some of them also acted like huge creeps to the female staff. As camp employees, we weren't supposed to talk back to guests. Sometimes it was very difficult for me to not tell them off.

Keith Sharp did a good job of hiring mostly Inuit guides. I got along well with most of my coworkers. However, one summer he hired a *qablunaaq* couple as camp cooks, and I didn't get along with them at all. I remember they were extremely stingy with food. The wife started hiding the tea bags from us, because she didn't want Inuit staff drinking tea unless it was mealtime. Once, she even scolded me for serving tea to an Elder outside of mealtime! Being stingy with food goes against the values I learned as a child. When I was a little girl, we always shared everything, even during times of famine. It's almost unthinkable to have an Elder visit you and not offer them tea and food.

Two days later I got into an argument with the husband. We had been using a nearby island to dump food scraps from camp. I agreed to this plan, so long as it was only biodegradable food waste. That day, when I stopped at the island to prepare shore lunch for some guests, I discovered that the cook had been dumping other garbage on the island as well. When we got back to camp that afternoon, I gave him a piece of my mind. The next day the husband suddenly fell seriously ill and had to be airlifted out of camp to receive medical care. His wife went with him, so we were stuck without a cook. The whole situation felt very strange. The day before he seemed perfectly healthy, then all of a sudden he was so sick he couldn't even stand up.

Ever since that day I've always wondered if his illness had something to do with the strong spiritual power at Ferguson Lake. As I mentioned earlier, the place where my family lived when I was young was a sacred place where *aglirniq* (traditional spiritual rules or "taboos") had to be closely observed. The adults in our camp were always very careful to follow our traditional rules and customs because of the spiritual power of the area. I still wonder if that man fell ill because he and his wife were so disrespectful to me, my culture, and my land.

The Baker Lake Concerned Citizens Committee

While staying in Rankin Inlet in the fall of 1987 and the winter of 1987–88, I started hearing that a company called Urangesellschaft was planning to build a uranium mine west of Baker Lake at a site they called Kiggavik. I wasn't too pleased with the idea of a mine in our hunting grounds, so in the spring of 1988 I returned to Baker Lake.

My father had taught me to care for our land and wildlife, and it was very upsetting to know that caribou migrations would be disturbed if this mine went ahead. I had also heard a little bit about the nuclear industry, and I realized that this was not an ordinary mining proposal. If we allowed Urangesellschaft to build the uranium mine, we would be putting our land, water, wildlife, and health at great risk. I was inspired to do something about it.

At that time, local radio stations played a big role in northern communities. We were informed of everything of importance through local radio. If a community meeting or some other event was coming up, an announcement would be read out over the local radio. It also served as a way for people to send messages to everyone in town. From birthday greetings to wedding announcements, everything was communicated over the airwaves. It was my generation's social media, similar to the way people use Facebook today.

I wrote a message expressing my concerns about the Urangesellschaft mine proposal. I submitted what I'd written to Baker Lake community radio, and it was read on the air. A lot of people called in to the station, voicing their support for my position. As young people today say, it went viral. I wasn't on the Hamlet Council or any other community body, but because I had spoken out, many people trusted me to express the community's concerns. Because of the overwhelming response to my message, I became resolved to stop Urangesellschaft's proposed uranium mine.

My first tactic was to start a petition. I began collecting signatures as a way to demonstrate that area residents opposed the mine. It was slow to begin with, but when all was said and done my petition had hundreds of signatures. People in other Kivalliq communities soon caught on, and started their own petitions opposing the mine.

I soon realized that people in Baker Lake needed assistance accessing basic information about uranium mining. Many of us, myself included, had many unanswered questions. For example, we knew very little about the history of uranium mining in other regions, or the possible health implications of uranium mining, or even what uranium was used for. I also realized that we needed funding if we wanted to communicate our position in an effective way. There was a lot of work to be done. We had to write letters, make long-distance phone calls, and hold public meetings. All of these things cost money, and I had none. In order to legitimately speak for the community, we needed to organize a formal committee. This would help us qualify for grants and other funding opportunities, as well.

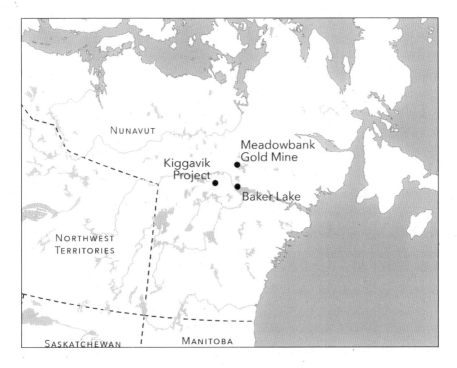

Figure 6. Map showing location of the Kiggavĭk project and Meadowbank gold mine. Map design by Julie Witmer.

For this reason, I helped form a community-based non-government organization (NGO) called the Baker Lake Concerned Citizens Committee (BLCCC). Several Baker Lake residents played important roles in the BLCCC, including Samson Jorah, Fred Ford, Barnabas Piryuaq, and Martin Kreelak. As one of the group's founders, I became chair of the board. However, we soon realized that we needed a staff-person who was well networked, familiar with the issues, and skilled in office administration. Since I fit the bill, I stepped down from the board and became the volunteer secretary for the BLCCC. I wrote many letters and corresponded with other concerned organizations and individuals who had experience with uranium mining.

We received a small amount of funding from the Northern Anti-Uranium Coalition, an organization I will tell you more about later. We rented a small house that we used as a drop-in centre, a place where people could ask questions and pick up handouts we had prepared. We did a lot with the limited funding we had available to us. Meanwhile, Urangesellschaft had a nice office in Baker Lake with all kinds of full-colour pamphlets—and there was no lack of coffee and baked goods for visitors. In contrast, we were grateful for the private donation of an electric typewriter, a card table, and some well-used chairs.

One of the BLCCC's most important activities was our participation in radio call-in shows. We collected the questions that people asked when they phoned in, and then asked experts in nuclear issues who Jack had identified to provide us with answers. After months of hearing from community members and discussions with experts, we identified many serious concerns with the proposed mine. Among them were three major topics:

1. Contamination—especially in the case of an accident. Both the "yellowcake" (uranium concentrate) that is produced from mining and the tailings that are left behind are radioactive. If released into the environment, these substances could contaminate land, water, vegetation, wildlife, and people. Companies always claim that, even though some accidents and mishaps have happened in the past, "modern" uranium mining is safe because of new technology and regulations. However, technology and regulations do not really address our concerns. We are not worried about what will happen if everything goes according to the company's plans; we are worried about what will happen if those plans fail. If an accident causes yellowcake or tailings to be released into our environment, the results could be catastrophic. The Baker Lake area is notoriously difficult to fly in and out of through most of the year, due to blizzards, fog, and high winds. It could potentially take weeks for a cleanup crew to respond to an accident if the weather was not cooperative.

2. Opening the region to further uranium mining. If we allowed the Kiggavik uranium mine to open, other uranium mines would surely follow. Uranium exploration was taking place all around Baker Lake, even in sensitive caribou habitat like calving

grounds and water crossings. If the Kiggavik mine were built, other potential projects might become more profitable because they could use Urangesellschaft's infrastructure to save on capital costs. Also, it would be politically impossible for us to say no to uranium mining in the future if one mine had already been approved. People became very concerned that Kiggavik was only the beginning: other uranium mines would likely follow, and this would lead to substantial disturbance of caribou and their habitat.

3. Moral issues with nuclear weapons and waste. Many Baker Lake residents found it morally unacceptable to allow our lands to be used by an industry connected to the creation of atomic weapons, nuclear waste, and nuclear accidents. The government insists that international agreements prevent Canadian uranium from being used in nuclear weapons. However, we know for a fact that Canadian uranium has been used in the development of nuclear weapons despite these agreements. The high-level nuclear waste created by nuclear reactors is an irresponsible burden we are leaving to future generations. Nuclear reactor accidents (meltdowns) bring significant human and environmental costs. For example, the fallout from the Chernobyl accident contaminated reindeer in Scandinavia, and large amounts of reindeer meat was destroyed due to radioactive contamination.[1]

To this day, these three issues remain serious concerns for many Kivalliq Inuit, and continue to drive local opposition to uranium mining.

During our discussions with community members, a major challenge the BLCCC faced was translation, as there were no terms in Inuktitut for many technical English words. Take radiation, for example. How do you explain to an Elder something that you can't see, taste, or smell? Even the word uranium has no Inuktitut translation. We ended up using the term *nungusuittuq* (it never goes away), as this seemed the best way to describe the properties of uranium.

During my work with the BLCCC, we learned that uranium remains radioactive for a very long time. Uranium-238—the most abundant uranium isotope on Earth—has a half-life of almost 4.5 billion years. Uranium-235—the uranium isotope used in nuclear reactors and weapons—has a half-life of over 700 million years. Many of the chemicals left behind in uranium tailings also remain dangerously radioactive for a very long time. Thorium-230 has a half-life of over seventy-five thousand years. As my friend and colleague Gordon Edwards likes to say, in human terms, uranium tailings remain radioactive forever.[2] The term *nungusuittuq* was chosen to translate "uranium" into Inuktitut because it describes how long it remains radioactive.

Inuit also use the word *nungusuittuq* in other contexts. For example, I have heard it used to describe a millionaire: He was so rich, his money would never run out. So, you see, *nungusuittuq* is a very good description of uranium in a double sense. For Inuit hunters, it is a danger that will last forever. For the mining industry, it is a way to make endless amounts of money.

Another tactic the BLCCC used was to approach organizations and request that they support our position against uranium mining. One of the first organizations I approached was the Beverly and Qamanirjuaq Caribou Management Board (BQCMB). They happened to have a board meeting in Baker Lake in the spring of 1988, and I decided to attend. I was a little bit intimidated because I was worried that an organization like this would be too busy to listen to my concerns. I did not want to go to the meeting alone. As it turned out, a friend of mine had a crush on one of the board members, so I asked her to accompany me. I told her, "I need your help, to be by my side while I request their support. Maybe your big crush will help us if you speak up too."

At the time, I didn't know much about the BQCMB, its mandate, or its jurisdiction. Because it had "caribou" in its name, I thought it was worth showing up and asking if they would support us in opposing the Kiggavik mine. I later learned that the BQCMB is a co-management board that provides advice to various levels of government regarding the management of the Beverly and Qamanirjuaq caribou herds and their habitat. It had been created in the early 1980s, shortly after the Baker Lake court case was decided. At the time, caribou management was in crisis. Hunters did not trust wildlife biologists, wildlife biologists did not take Indigenous knowledge seriously, and Indigenous communities were clashing with the mining industry.[3] The BQCMB was created to try to resolve some of these conflicts over the Beverly and Qamanirjuaq caribou herds, which have ranges that include what is now Nunavut, the Northwest Territories, Manitoba, and Saskatchewan. The board was made up of representatives from Indigenous communities that use the herds, as well as representatives from federal, provincial, and territorial governments.[4]

I didn't have much difficulty convincing the BQCMB to support our cause. After a brief discussion, the board members agreed to pass a motion officially opposing the mine. However, that was just the beginning of the BQCMB assisting us in our fight against Kiggavik. The board was a very useful organizing space because it brought together caribou hunting communities from across the North. It helped spread awareness of the Baker Lake struggle to First Nations and Métis communities in Manitoba, Saskatchewan, and the Northwest Territories, many of which also supported us in our fight against uranium mining.

National and International Inuit
Organizations Oppose Uranium Mining

Before long, our representative Inuit organizations declared their opposition to the Kiggavik mine. This was partially because—at the national and international levels—these organizations already held anti-uranium and anti-nuclear positions. Kiggavik was not the first proposed uranium mine that Inuit had opposed, and it was not the first time we risked being negatively impacted by the nuclear industry.

Inuit Tapirisat of Canada (ITC) opposed uranium mining. This position was developed because of a proposed uranium mine near the Inuit community of Makkovik in Nunatsiavut on the coast of northern Labrador. Labrador Inuit, with the support of ITC, successfully opposed the proposed Kitts Michelin mine in 1979.[5] The following year, ITC lobbied the federal government for a moratorium on uranium mining on all Inuit territory in Canada.[6]

The Inuit Circumpolar Conference (ICC)—which brings together Inuit living in Greenland, Canada, the U.S., and Russia—also adopted an anti-nuclear position in the 1980s. This position was developed because of ITC's concerns with uranium mining, as well as broader concerns with the nuclear industry, especially nuclear weapons. Because the issue of nuclear weapons in the Arctic is complicated, I am going to take a moment to give you some context.

During the cold war between the United States and Soviet Union (1947–1991), the Arctic took on great strategic significance. The shortest route between Moscow and Washington goes over the North Pole and the Inuit homeland. As a result, the Americans built military bases and deployed nuclear weapons to the Canadian Arctic, disrupting our way of life and leaving a legacy of environmental contamination.[7] In Greenland, Inuit were forcibly relocated to make way for an American military base.[8]

Fallout from nuclear weapons testing contaminated our food. The United States, the Soviet Union, and the United Kingdom conducted more than five hundred above-ground nuclear weapons tests between 1946 and 1963, when a limited test ban treaty was signed. The tests sent radioactive material into the stratosphere, where it remained for several years and gradually dispersed globally. Some of this fallout eventually settled to earth in the Kivalliq region.

It may surprise you to learn that higher concentrations of radioactivity have been found in caribou (and, in the Sámi regions of Scandinavia, in reindeer) than in any other large terrestrial mammal on the planet. This is because lichen—the primary source of food for caribou—easily absorbs radioactive fallout from the atmosphere.[9] Cesium-137 bioaccumulates (becomes concentrated) in caribou meat. Inuit hunt and eat caribou, lots of it, and the radioactivity then accumulates in their bodies. One couldn't design a more effective way to transfer radioactivity from the atmosphere into the human body than the atmosphere => lichen => caribou => human pathway.

Once this pathway was discovered, scientists began monitoring cesium levels in Arctic Indigenous peoples.[10] In 1967, 190 Inuit from Baker Lake were tested for cesium-137 levels. This study found that they had very high body concentrations of cesium-137—much higher than in most other communities in the Northwest Territories where testing took place, and far higher than in southern Canada.[11] Radiation levels in the northern environment declined slowly over time, but these experiences show how big a threat nuclear weapons are to the Inuit way of life.

There were other encounters between Inuit and nuclear military technology during the cold war. One especially bizarre example is Project Chariot, a proposal in the late 1950s to blast a deep-sea harbour in Alaska using nuclear weapons. Luckily, nearby Inupiat communities managed to stop this horribly stupid idea before it was carried out.[12]

Another example was much closer to home for me. In 1978, a malfunctioning Soviet nuclear-power reconnaissance satellite called Cosmos 954 disintegrated upon re-entering the Earth's atmosphere. It scattered radioactive debris over a six hundred–kilometre swath of northern Canada.[13] An extensive joint Canada/ US cleanup operation called Operation Morning Light took place. Baker Lake was the easternmost point of the search area.[14]

When all was said and done, it turned out the debris from Cosmos 954 fell to the west of Baker Lake, mostly in Dene territory. However, the experience frightened a lot of Baker Lake residents. A man from Baker Lake named David Simailak worked as an interpreter for the government officials who tried to explain the situation to our community. He later reflected: "How the hell do you interpret such terms as nuclear reactors, uranium—they don't understand those terms, they never had any need to. . . . People are wondering exactly what is going on."[15]

With this context in mind, it is not difficult to understand why the ICC became concerned with nuclear and military issues. From the time it was formed in 1977, the ICC took a stand against the use of our homeland for military purposes.[16] At its 1983 circumpolar conference, it passed a motion calling for the Arctic to be declared a "nuclear free zone." The motion resolved:

1. That the Arctic and Subarctic be used for purposes that are peaceful and environmentally safe;

2. That there shall be no nuclear testing or nuclear devices in the Arctic;

3. That there should be no nuclear dump sites in the Arctic and Subarctic;

4. That exploration and exploitation of uranium, thorium, lithium, or other materials related to the nuclear industry in our homeland be prohibited.

The resolution concluded that the ICC would "lobby the United Nations and various international organizations to encourage members of the United Nations to adopt a policy for a nuclear free zone in the Arctic."[17] Throughout the 1980s, ICC representatives like Aqqaluk Lynge[18] and Mary Simon[19] continued to call for the demilitarization of the Arctic.

The Northern Anti-Uranium Coalition

With clear Inuit opposition to uranium mining at the national and international levels, it was not surprising that the Inuit organizations representing the Kivalliq region quickly and forcefully made their opposition to the Kiggavik proposal known. The Keewatin Wildlife Federation (KWF)—an umbrella group representing the community Hunters and Trappers Associations (HTAs) of the region—publicly opposed Kiggavik in 1988, shortly after Urangesellschaft had submitted its proposal. In November of that year, Tagak Curley (then president of the KWF) wrote to a letter to Dennis Patterson, leader of the Government of the Northwest Territories, declaring his opposition to uranium mining and the Kiggavik proposal. Curley wrote,

> I shudder to think what could happen to Keewatin Inuit, and the wildlife we depend on for our livelihood and cultural subsistence.
>
> The end uses of uranium must also be kept in mind. There are only two major commercial uses for uranium: nuclear weapons and nuclear reactors. So the final products of the uranium industry are bombs and radioactive wastes.
>
> I have personally come to the conclusion that this proposed uranium mine must be stopped. Forever. I have three reasons for this. First, no uranium mine can be guaranteed environmentally safe, especially in an area where the environment is so fragile. Second, no one can guarantee that uranium produced in the NWT will only be used for peaceful purposes. And third, if we allow a uranium mine to proceed, after years of public and political consensus against uranium mining, the international reputation of Inuit as a peaceful people who are careful custodians of our environment will be destroyed. Forever.[20]

This was the first of many letters and motions from the KWF opposing the Kiggavik project.

The Keewatin Regional Council (KRC)—a coalition of the region's seven mayors—was also quick to adopt a position opposing the mine. In 1988, Jack Hicks had moved to Rankin Inlet from Resolute Bay in the High Arctic to start a new position as executive director of the KRC. Urangesellschaft announced its Kiggavik proposal the same week Jack began his new job. At the first KRC meeting about the mine proposal, Chair Louis Pilakapsi, a very strong and principled leader, said that the mine would go ahead "over [his] dead body." It was therefore Jack's job to work to stop the proposed mine, something he was more than happy to do.

The Keewatin Inuit Association (KIA)—the organization representing all Inuit in the Kivalliq (at that time called "Keewatin") region—soon followed suit. At its 1989 annual general meeting, KIA passed the following motion opposing the mine:

Whereas this mine will result in the widespread exposure of radioactive contaminants; and

Whereas these contaminants pose an unacceptable hazard to the health of the Inuit of the Keewatin and to the environment and its wildlife;

Now therefore be it resolved that the Annual General Meeting of the KIA, in recognition of the hazards posed by the radioactive contaminants which would result from the operation of this mine, vehemently opposes the establishment of this uranium mine.[21]

Resolutions reiterating the KIA's position were passed at subsequent annual general meetings.

The Tunngavik Federation of Nunavut (TFN)—the organization that was negotiating the Nunavut Land Claims Agreement—also passed a motion opposing the mine. The motion read:

WHEREAS The Tunngavik Federation of Nunavut opposes development of minerals, oil, and gas in the North prior to land claim settlement;

NOW THEREFORE BE IT RESOLVED THAT TFN supports the Keewatin region in their opposition of the proposed Kiggavik uranium mine.

It is important to note one key aspect of TFN's position. They moved that development should not proceed until the negotiation of the Nunavut land claim was complete, not because of the arguments the other groups made about uranium mining.

These organizations all came together to form a coalition opposing the proposed mine. The name Northern Anti-Uranium Coalition was chosen because the acronym, NAUC, is phonetically similar to *naung*—the word for "no" in the Kivalliq dialect of Inuktitut. If anyone asked us what we thought about uranium mining, we would say, "NAUC!"

NAUC's membership included representatives from the Keewatin Inuit Association, the Keewatin Regional Council, the Keewatin Wildlife Federation, and the Tunngavik Federation of Nunavut. The Baker Lake Concerned Citizens Committee also became a member of NAUC, and I sat on NAUC's board as the committee's representative. Tagak Curley, president of the Keewatin Wildlife Federation, was the primary spokesperson for NAUC. Jack Hicks served as the group's organizer and coordinator.

We continued to ask other groups for their support. Sometimes, powerful politicians tried to stop us. For example, Jack and I once made a presentation at a meeting of the Keewatin Regional Health Board (KRHB), hoping to get them to join NAUC. We gave our presentation, and to our delight Jean Simailak—the representative from Baker Lake—made a motion that the KRHB should become a member of NAUC. The other Inuit delegates in attendance all agreed, and the motion was carried unanimously. We were surprised and delighted.

This clearly upset the *qablunaaq* chair of the KRHB. He came from a mining-industry family, and later became executive director of the NWT and Nunavut Chamber of Mines. In any case, this guy had a problem—to which he found a solution. One member of the KRHB, a *qablunaaq* woman, had been delayed while travelling to Rankin Inlet for the meeting. She arrived just after Jack and I had left. We learned later that she had asked the board to revisit the question of the KRHB joining NAUC, and had seconded a new motion stating that, while the KRHB would join NAUC, it would not take a position for or against Kiggavik. In other words, KHRB had decided to join a coalition opposed to a proposed mine, while stating they were not opposed to the proposed mine!

When Jack and I saw the minutes of the meeting, we noticed that the first motion—the one we had watched with our own eyes be approved unanimously—was missing from the transcript. It was as if it had never happened. This was a striking example of how *qablunaat* can sometimes manipulate the system to get their way.

Baker Lake Hamlet and Government of the NWT Remain Neutral

Just because the Inuit representative organizations all opposed the proposed mine didn't mean that everyone in the region opposed it. In Baker Lake itself, and elsewhere in the region, many small-business owners—mostly *qablunaat*, but some Inuit as well—stood to profit considerably from the construction and operation of a nearby mine. These business owners held a lot of power in our communities. People were often hesitant to publicly oppose what these owners wanted, out of fear that they (or their relatives) would be denied employment in the future.

Some of these business owners used their positions of power to pressure the Baker Lake Hamlet Council to remain "neutral" on the question of the Kiggavik mine. Officially, the council stated it would wait until the proposal's environmental review had been completed before it adopted a position on the matter. However, because several council members also owned businesses, we were very concerned that the Hamlet was going to support Kiggavik in the end.

The Government of the Northwest Territories (GNWT) took the same approach, and decided it would remain neutral until the environmental assessment was complete. In part, this was because the GNWT did not have a clear stance on uranium mining. Like our Inuit organizations, the GNWT had also debated uranium mining and other nuclear matters in the early 1980s. However, unlike our Inuit organizations, it did not adopt a clear position on the issue.

In 1981 and 1982 expert witnesses—including Gordon Edwards—testified before the Legislative Assembly of the Northwest Territories on the dangers of uranium mining. These debates took place due to the insistence of backbench Members of the Legislative Assembly (MLAs), especially Dennis Patterson, who was the *qablunaaq* representative for Frobisher Bay at the time. Unfortunately, the assembly was dissolved before members were able to debate the issue and adopt a clear policy on uranium mining.[22]

In 1986, Dene MLA Sam Gargan tabled a motion titled "Declaration of a Nuclear Free Zone." The motion declared "the Northwest Territories, land, coastal waters, and airspace a nuclear weapons free zone." It also stated opposition to the "exploration and exploitation of materials related to the nuclear weapons industry." Dennis Patterson and several Inuit MLAs gave passionate speeches supporting the motion and opposing uranium mining. Patterson said, "The critical ingredient [in nuclear weapons] is uranium and I would like to say here that I am opposed to the exploration and mining of uranium in the Northwest Territories.... There is no satisfactory way of dealing with the tailings and the waste that result from the mining of uranium. There is no proven, long-term method of dealing with uranium tailings.... The truth is that Canadian uranium goes into nuclear weapons." However, because of pressure from the mining industry, some members pushed through an amendment and removed the resolution's references to uranium mining. The motion's title was changed to "Declaration of a Nuclear Weapons Free Zone." It passed with fifteen in favour, none opposed, and one abstention.[23]

Dennis Patterson became government leader of the Northwest Territories in 1987. Urangesellschaft submitted the Kiggavik mine proposal in March 1988. Given Patterson's history of opposing uranium mining, many of us thought it was strange that the government's official position on Kiggavik was neutrality. Many of us also felt betrayed because, as soon as he became government leader, Patterson stopped speaking out on these important issues. In an open letter, Keewatin Wildlife Federation President Tagak Curley asked him, "How can you personally stay silent on an issue for which you once had such passion? ... As a political leader who clearly understands the facts about uranium mining, you have a responsibility to everyone in this region to show leadership on this issue."[24] Dennis Patterson never did so. He later joined the Conservative Party and was appointed to the Senate on the advice of Prime Minister Stephen Harper.

Federal Environmental Review

Prior to the settlement of our land claims, if a mine or other "development" was proposed in our territory, the proposal was sometimes reviewed by the Federal Environmental Assessment and Review Office (known by the rather strange acronym FEARO). As part of their process, FEARO appointed a panel to study Urangesellschaft's proposal. This panel would ultimately recommend whether or not the project should proceed. Panel members included Thomas Kudloo, a highly respected Inuk man from Baker Lake, and Bob MacQuarrie, a *qablunaaq* former high school principal from Baker Lake who had since moved to Yellowknife (where he was elected MLA).

The Northern Anti-Uranium Coalition and the Baker Lake Concerned Citizens Committee had a two-track strategy. On the one hand, we felt that both organizations had to participate in the review process. We knew it would have a major impact on the final decision about the mine. We also knew that debates during the review process would have a substantial influence on public opinion in Baker Lake. On the other hand, we didn't limit ourselves to the review process because we had to educate and mobilize Inuit in our communities. All the expert submissions we sent to the review panel would be meaningless if we didn't have the people on our side, and public opinion (even big protests) would have a limited effect if we didn't also submit technical information to the review panel.

The review panel had a limited amount of funding available for intervenors— organizations with official standing in the review process. Because NAUC had representatives from the Inuit and regional organizations, it received most of this money. NAUC then provided the BLCCC with the funds required to support our community-based work.

Environmental reviews in Canada usually focus on a document called an Environmental Impact Statement (EIS), which is prepared by the company. The company is supposed to study the potential impacts of its proposal and explain how it will minimize negative effects and maximize benefits for the region. Review panels generally provide a set of EIS Guidelines to the company. These guidelines outline what issues the company has to look at when preparing its EIS. Once the company submits an EIS, the document is circulated to government agencies and other intervenor groups. These agencies and groups then have the opportunity to provide comments in writing and (usually) orally at a public hearing. After a public hearing, the review panel considers all of the information and arguments that were presented and writes its final report. In this report, the panel makes recommendations as to whether or not the project should proceed and, if so, under what conditions. In Nunavut, the final decision is usually made by federal government ministers.

The FEARO review of Urangesellschaft's Kiggavik proposal broke new ground for environmental review processes in Canada. This review was different because the panel consulted intervenor groups when creating the EIS Guidelines. The panel circulated draft EIS Guidelines to intervenor groups, and invited comments on how the guidelines could be improved. Members of NAUC decided that this was a major opportunity for us. If we spent a lot of our time and energy trying to toughen up the EIS Guidelines, it would make Urangesellschaft's job more difficult. We prepared a thick document called "Who Takes the Risks? Who Gets the Benefits?" and were delighted to see that large sections of our work appeared in the final set of EIS Guidelines. This really raised the bar in terms of what was expected of Urangesellschaft.

Throughout the review process, individuals who held a lot of power and influence claimed that representatives of the BLCCC and NAUC were uninformed and implied that we were misleading the public. After all, Urangesellschaft claimed that their experts had determined that uranium mining was safe. Some of the business owners in Baker Lake started to suggest that we were exaggerating the potential negative impacts of uranium mining. Jack Anawak, then the Liberal member of Parliament for the riding of Nunatsiaq (covering what today is Nunavut), claimed that we were reacting with emotion, and were not objectively considering the issue of uranium mining. Gordon Wray, the MLA for Baker Lake at the time, went so far as to claim that we'd been telling community residents that, if the mine went ahead, they could have "deformed babies"![25]

Another prominent Liberal in the Kivalliq region, wily Rankin Inlet–based businessman John Todd, suggested that we were kidding ourselves if we thought that community-level resistance to the proposed mine would have any impact on the decision-making process. Todd told a CBC television interviewer, "All I'm saying is, you have to be practical as well as being emotional. You have to try and separate the two. You have to put pressure on the government to start to cut a deal if it becomes a reality. Don't cut the deal after the fact." The decision whether or not the mine should be built, he continued, "will not be made by northerners, for or against."[26]

The Federal Government's Information Workshop

In response to our political agitation, the federal government decided to hold an information workshop on uranium mining. This event took place in Baker Lake on March 1 and 2, 1989. NAUC had arranged for acclaimed investigative reporter Paul McKay to attend the workshop. According to McKay,

> [It] was a two-day cheerleading session on uranium mining, good corporate citizenship and the unimpeachable credibility of Canada's nuclear industry regulators. The Inuit were not even given their own place on the agenda. . . . It was a disaster. There was not even a hint of impartiality. The meeting was chaired by a bumbling, incoherent [federal government] geologist whose performance embarrassed even his own government colleagues. His first task was to explain to the 150 Inuit meeting in the Baker Lake hockey arena why the agenda for the meeting and all the print and audio-visual materials were in English only, and why the Inuit organizations had no place on the agenda. It went downhill from there.[27]

McKay's description of the meeting was accurate. It showed very clearly that the federal government was more interested in promoting uranium mining than listening to what we had to say.

To support us at this workshop, NAUC had also invited an expert from the anti-nuclear movement in the south, Dr. Jim Harding. Jim was a professor of social justice at the University of Regina who had spent decades opposing uranium development in his home province of Saskatchewan. He brought important insights about public inquiries and reviews, industry-public relations campaigns, and pro-nuclear propaganda being introduced in schools.

As the room was being set up for the workshop, Jim noticed an official from the Atomic Energy Control Board (AECB; the federal regulator of nuclear power and materials in Canada) placing documents on a table. These documents were handouts from Atomic Energy of Canada Limited (AECL; a federal Crown corporation that develops, designs, and markets nuclear reactors) and the Canadian Nuclear Association (CNA; the representative organization of the nuclear industry in Canada). This material was being placed beside other freebie publications that community residents could take away. The fact that someone from a government regulatory body (AECB) would see fit to openly help out his friends in the industry (AECL and CNA) by carrying their literature to Baker Lake and making it available to the public spoke volumes. It was a prime example of the close government–proponent relationship that characterizes the nuclear industry.

We were struck by the fact that neither the government nor Urangesellschaft realized how this close government–industry relationship looked to Inuit. Speakers at the workshop alternated between government officials and company officials, and they both looked and sounded alike. The transcript of the workshop records the chair referring to "buildings or equipment [that] will be used at the mine." It was one thing for Urangesellschaft to always say "will" (rather than "would") when referring to the proposed mine, but government officials also said "will"—as if the proposal had already been accepted. This gave the community the impression that the outcome was fixed—it seemed that regardless of the review process, approval of the Kiggavik proposal was a foregone conclusion.

Both Urangesellschaft and the government officials spoke to residents of Baker Lake as if we were stupid. They were so convinced of their cause that they couldn't conceive that any thinking person could disagree with them. When I asked an Urangesellschaft official whether a similar ore body located eighty kilometres upwind and upstream of the city of Toronto would pass environmental review, he assured me that it would. I didn't believe him, and I doubt that anyone else did either.

It would have been smarter for the government to have told us that uranium mining had been banned in parts of Canada and the United States, and to have explained why they thought those decisions had been unjustified. Instead, we learned from our own research that the provincial governments in British Columbia and Nova Scotia had banned uranium mining in their jurisdictions, and that state governments in New Jersey and Vermont had done the same. So, when the government and the company told us that there was absolutely nothing for us to worry about, we knew that they were taking us for fools.

The low point of the workshop came when an Urangesellschaft official showed a hand-drawn sketch of what the tailings storage plan would be. It looked like something the company had prepared on the back of an envelope during lunch hour. Urangesellschaft had spent time and money preparing detailed computer-designed blueprints for the mine and the mill, but when it came to the aspect of the proposal of greatest concern to Inuit—how to safely store the radioactive tailings for thousands of years—they saw nothing wrong with showing us an amateurish sketch. Even some of the government officials seemed shocked when they saw it.

I should also mention that the government workshop was where the funniest moment in the whole process took place. We were perhaps the very first intervenors in an environmental review process in Canada to raise the question of climate change. The topic came up because Urangesellschaft's plan was to simply leave fifty million tonnes of radioactive waste on the surface of the tundra and let it freeze. That was it—their entire tailings "storage" plan. But we had spoken to scientists who'd told us that they wouldn't build an outhouse on the tundra and expect to find it standing upright in fifty years' time. Already in the late 1980s they were predicting that permafrost would eventually melt and cause damage to buildings and other infrastructure.

Jim Harding therefore asked if the greenhouse effect might pose problems for Urangesellschaft's plans for tailings management. (What we today call climate change was then called the "greenhouse effect.") A government official scoffed at Jim's question about the greenhouse effect, calling it a "red herring"—something that is, or is intended to be, misleading or distracting. A very skilled Inuk woman named Mikle Langenham was in the interpreter's booth at the time. She jumped up, took off her headset, and shouted at the government guy, "Isn't the effect of a green house a red fish?! Would you please speak proper English?!"

The NAUC/BLCCC Public Meetings

In response to the federal government's one-sided workshop, NAUC and the BLCCC organized our own public meetings in both Baker Lake and Rankin Inlet the following month, April 1989. We brought in five guest speakers with experience fighting the nuclear industry:

- Dr. Gordon Edwards, president of the Canadian Coalition for Nuclear Responsibility. Gordon has an encyclopedic knowledge of the nuclear industry, from uranium mining to nuclear power to nuclear weapons to the storage of nuclear waste.

- Robert Del Tredici, photographer and educator. His 1987 book *At Work in the Fields of the Bomb*, which portrayed the nuclear industry in the United States from uranium mining to nuclear weapons and the high-level waste from nuclear power plants, had received the 1988 Olive Branch Award for the most outstanding book on the subject of world peace.

- Dr. Rosalie Bertell, Catholic nun, epidemiologist, environmental activist, president of International Institute of Concern for Public Health, and author of the book *No Immediate Danger: Prognosis for a Radioactive Earth*. Rosalie had conducted pioneering research on the effects of ionizing radiation and had worked with Indigenous peoples around the world.

- Dr. Nettie Wiebe, a former president of the National Farmers Union and a professor of church and society at the University of Saskatchewan. Nettie had played a leading role in stopping a proposed uranium refinery near her hometown.

- Mike Simons, a journalist from England who specialized in coverage of the nuclear industry worldwide. He had covered the 1986 Chernobyl disaster and the health impacts of the nuclear industry in Britain.

Figure 7. (*left to right*) Nettie Wiebe, Gordon Edwards, Rosalie Bertell, Mike Simons, and Robert Del Tredici. Photo by Jack Hicks.

We had held radio call-in shows ahead of time, asking callers to share any questions they had about uranium mining. We wrote down everyone's questions and gave them to our guest speakers to help them prepare their presentations. At the public meetings, each of our speakers communicated clearly using language that was easily understood, and answered all the questions that were asked of them. They also gave Inuit a very clear message: If you're worried about the nuclear industry setting up shop in your homeland, you have good reason to be worried. More than that, the speakers stressed that the nuclear industry had been stopped before, and it could be stopped again. Nettie Wiebe told participants in our workshop that stopping the proposed uranium refinery near her home community "was a real lesson in how as an individual, as a lone voice, you both feel and often are powerless—but as a collective, when you work with each other and together for something, you can be politically very effective, *surprisingly effective.*"

Figure 8. Baker Lake Concerned Citizens Committee spokesperson Samson Jorah speaking to Rosalie Bertell. Photo by Jack Hicks.

Figure 9. Joan Scottie attending a public meeting about Urangesellschaft's proposed Kiggavik uranium mine. Photo by Jack Hicks.

Later, Gordon Edwards and Rosalie Bertell helped us even further. They reviewed all of the information we'd prepared for public distribution and submission to the review panel in the months that followed, to ensure that it didn't contain any errors. Back in the days before email, this process involved sending them hundreds of pages of faxes, and receiving many faxed pages from them in return. Even though Urangesellschaft, politicians, and business owners accused us of misleading people or of being overly "emotional," neither the company nor the government ever found any factual errors in our submissions. We knew that every sentence we wrote would be studied by people seeking to discredit us, so we took great care to make sure we got things right.

In Rankin Inlet, schoolteacher Alan Everard hosted regular meetings of our supporters at his house. He, Gary Weber, Janet Onalik, Sue Shirley, Nick Burns, and others were our "eyes and ears" in the regional centre, where many meetings

Figure 10. (*left to right*) Lucy Qaunnaq, Joan Scottie, and Suzanne Paalak Mautari'naaq attending a public meeting about Urangesellschaft's proposed Kiggavik uranium mine. Photo by Jack Hicks.

were held, and they put up posters challenging Urangesellschaft's propaganda. We in Baker Lake very much appreciated their solidarity with us.

Mounting Opposition

In early 1990 the public perception of the proposed Kiggavik mine only got worse. As I said before, people in the community were worried that Kiggavik was only the beginning. They were afraid its approval would lead to further uranium mining near Baker Lake, possibly in sensitive caribou habitat. By this time, Baker Lake residents discovered that Urangesellschaft had another exploration property north of Kiggavik, in the Beverly caribou herd's calving grounds. When the public found out about this, they became very concerned.

Figure 11. Baker Lake Concerned Citizens Committee member Barnabas Piryuaq speaking to Urangesellschaft spokesperson Mick Stuart. Photo by Jack Hicks.

Our hunters and Elders became worried that if Kiggavik was approved, Urangesellschaft would eventually want to start mining in the calving grounds.

At the same time, Urangesellschaft was doing a poor job at community relations. Mick Stuart, the company's project manager, came across as very patronizing. For example, an Elder once tried to explain caribou migrations to Stuart at a public meeting. Stuart turned around and said, "No, that's not right, the caribou do not migrate that way." This sort of behaviour, talking back to an Elder and belittling their knowledge, is entirely unacceptable in Inuit society. Stuart was also a very awkward man, and had trouble connecting with anyone.

The federal government also unwittingly did a lot to galvanize opposition. In early 1990, we received a leaked internal document in which the Department of Indian Affairs and Northern Development's regional director general for the Northwest Territories stated his "considered prediction"—arrived at after

Figure 12. Louis Pilakapsi (president of the Keewatin Inuit Association) attending a public meeting about Urangesellschaft's proposed Kiggavik uranium mine. Photo by Jack Hicks.

"candid conversations that [he] had with deputy ministers in the Territorial Government"—that the Kiggavik proposal would be approved. This angered a lot of people. All along, the Government of the Northwest Territories had said it would wait until the environmental assessment was complete before it took a position on the Kiggavik project. In private, senior GNWT officials were signalling the federal government that the project was a sure thing.

Government of the Northwest Territories Debates Kiggavik

Even though the Inuit representative organizations and municipalities from the Kivalliq region had declared where they stood on the Kiggavik proposal by 1990, the Government of the Northwest Territories still refused to budge from its position of neutrality. Government Leader Dennis Patterson continued to insist that the "responsible" course of action was to wait until the environmental assessment was complete before adopting a position. Even more frustrating to us was the fact that the MLA for Baker Lake also refused to take a stand on the issue. While he expressed concerns with the project when questioned by the media, he did not take a clear position one way or another.

We had much more support from the MLA representing Rankin Inlet, Piita Irniq (then Peter Ernerk), who ended up being our voice in the Legislative Assembly of the Northwest Territories. He openly declared his opposition to the proposed Kiggavik mine and attempted to get the legislative assembly to support our position. On February 27, 1990, Irniq introduced a motion titled "Opposition to Exploration and Mining of Uranium in the NWT." The preamble to the motion began by acknowledging the widespread grassroots opposition to the Kiggavik proposal:

> WHEREAS the great majority of Inuit and other residents of the
> Keewatin region strongly oppose uranium mining in the Arctic
> and have adopted informed, considered, and determined positions
> against the Kiggavik proposal, both as individuals and through their
> representative organizations;

WHEREAS this opposition has been demonstrated by approximately 1,700 signatures on petitions circulated in 5 Keewatin communities, including approximately 600 signatures on the petition circulated in Baker Lake;

The preamble also referred to the many organizations that already had passed motions opposing the Kiggavik proposal:

WHEREAS the Kiggavik proposal is opposed by the Keewatin Inuit Association; the Keewatin Regional Council; the Keewatin Wildlife Federation; the Beverly-Qaminirjuaq Caribou Management Board; the Inuit Tapirisat of Canada; the Tunngavik Federation of Nunavut; the Concerned Citizens' Committees which have been formed in Baker Lake and Rankin Inlet; the Northwest Territories Federation of Labour; Ecology North; and Nuclear Free North;

WHEREAS the 5th General Assembly of the Inuit Circumpolar Conference, held in Sisimiut, Greenland in July 1989, passed a motion stating that the ICC will "support Inuit of the Keewatin region in opposing the proposed Kiggavik uranium mine";

WHEREAS the Kiggavik proposal is strongly opposed by the Chipeweyan and Cree of northern Saskatchewan, who have lived in the vicinity of uranium mines for more than a decade and have witnessed the effects of uranium mining on their communities and their wildlife;

WHEREAS a Dene Nation Leadership Meeting, held in Fort Franklin in June 1984, passed a motion which stated that "the Dene oppose any uranium development in Denendeh or anywhere else in Canada";

Irniq's motion went on to declare that uranium mining and the nuclear industry ran contrary to the values of northern Indigenous peoples:

WHEREAS economic activity which makes a contribution to the production of nuclear weapons and also generates dangerous waste which threatens the health of people and wildlife for thousands of years CANNOT be considered a form of sustainable development which is acceptable to Inuit and Dene values.

It resolved that the assembly "declares its unequivocal opposition to the proposed Kiggavik uranium mine" as well as its "unequivocal opposition to the exploration and mining of uranium anywhere in the Northwest Territories."[28]

However, before Irniq was able to complete his opening comments on the motion, Mike Ballantyne, the minister of Justice who was close to the mining industry (and, like Dennis Patterson, a prominent member of the Conservative Party), moved that the motion be referred to committee for discussion. As the Committee of the Whole was significantly backlogged at the time, many saw this as a move to prevent the issue from being discussed in the assembly. Reflecting on the situation, Irniq later told the press, "It's very frightening that the government isn't letting the people of the Northwest Territories know where it stands. Referring the motion to the committee for debate means that [the motion] could be delayed until next fall's session."[29]

While industry-friendly politicians derailed Irniq's motion in the legislative assembly, GNWT staff were completing their review of Urangesellschaft's Environmental Impact Statement. They did a very thorough job. The GNWT's submission to the FEARO panel was surprisingly critical of the company's plans. Nellie Cournoyea, the pro-development minister of Energy, Mines and Petroleum Resources, issued a Minister's Statement to the effect that there was so much missing information and uncertainty in Urangesellschaft's EIS that the GNWT was not prepared to support the Kiggavik proposal. In other words, even though the GNWT did not oppose the Kiggavik mine *in principle*, it opposed the proposal Urangesellschaft had developed.

Hamlet Plebiscite

Meanwhile, in response to growing public anger, the Baker Lake Hamlet Council had announced that it would abandon its position of neutrality on the Kiggavik issue. In a media release on February 15, 1990, Baker Lake Mayor Garry Smith announced that the Hamlet would hold a plebiscite. It stated:

At a meeting held February 14 the Baker Lake Hamlet Council considered the question of Kiggavik, the proposed uranium mine west of Baker Lake.

It was decided that for council to have maximum influence representing Baker Lake on this issue it is important that Council make a public statement before the FEARO process ends. It is also important that this public statement is in tune with the view of the majority of the adults of Baker Lake.

With this in mind the Hamlet Council of Baker Lake has decided to hold a plebiscite on the Kiggavik question as soon as legally and administratively possible.[30]

We viewed this plebiscite as a major opportunity—if we could show a unified position through a fair and democratic vote on a secret ballot, it would be very hard for Urangesellschaft or the government to justify proceeding with Kiggavik.

The Baker Lake Hamlet Council held its plebiscite in late March. I remember that day as if it were yesterday. First thing in the morning, Tunngavik Federation of Nunavut President Paul Quassa phoned in to the community radio station. He made the case that Inuit should oppose all non-renewable resource development until the land claim was settled. He explained that Inuit would not receive financial benefits from mining without a land claim in place. While most people in Baker Lake had already made up their minds to oppose Kiggavik, Paul's speech probably helped convince those who were undecided.

I was so anxious, waiting for the plebiscite results; the day really took a toll on me. People were phoning me constantly. Some were asking me for rides to the polling station, which was located in the old curling rink. Others were asking if they could assist me in any way and offering to be scrutineers. It was one of the longest days of my life, and I just wanted it to end.

Finally, they announced the results. Jack, who was a scrutineer, came out and told me the good news. Slightly over 90 percent of the community's residents had voted NO to Kiggavik! This was the greatest news I could hope for. I knew there was a community bingo being held just down the hall from the polling station.

I ran over, burst into the room, and yelled, "We won!" It had been a very long and exhausting few years, and I was so happy that all of our hard work had paid off.

On April 3, 1990, Mayor Garry Smith wrote an open letter to Urangesellschaft, asking the company to withdraw the Kiggavik proposal:

> Dear Mr. Stuart:
>
> I am writing to you on behalf of the Hamlet Council and the people of Baker Lake.
>
> We are asking you to abandon the Kiggavik project.
>
> On different occasions you have publicly stated that if the people of Baker Lake did not want this proposed uranium mine to go ahead then your company would not proceed.
>
> At a recent meeting of the Hamlet Council the Council unanimously voted to oppose Kiggavik. Of course the plebiscite, with results of 397 "NO," 43 "YES," confirms this is the wishes of the people of Baker Lake.
>
> With the foregoing in mind we ask you to keep your word and abandon this project.
>
> By a copy of this letter we are asking your partners to reconsider their involvement.
>
> We await a reply at your convenience.
>
> Sincerely,
> Mayor Garry Smith[31]

Project Abandonment

In a press release on July 5, 1990, Urangesellschaft requested that the environmental review panel "delay indefinitely its planned environmental assessment hearing of the Kiggavik uranium mine project."[32] The company claimed that a substantial delay was necessary for it to properly respond to the review panel's request for additional information. In the end, Urangesellschaft never did respond to the review panel's request for information, nor did it ever acknowledge the results of the plebiscite in Baker Lake. The company essentially abandoned its plans for the Kiggavik mine, and the proposal remained shelved through the 1990s.

The fight to stop the Kiggavik mine had been a huge experience for everyone involved. It was truly very empowering. Only a few decades earlier most Inuit were too intimidated to talk back to government officials. With Kiggavik, Inuit from across our region stood together to say NO to a proposed mine that threatened our physical health and our hunting way of life. More importantly, we won!

My life became a lot quieter after Urangesellschaft walked away from their Kiggavik proposal. After being so focused on that issue for so long, it was a bit odd not to have to worry anymore—though most of us knew that another company would likely attempt to open Kiggavik in the future. Looking back over this period in my life, I realize that it ended on an extremely positive note.

A few years later, I was invited to speak at the World Uranium Hearing in Salzburg, Austria. In September 1992, Jack Hicks and I made the trip, with a stop in London on the way. It was very strange sitting on the top of a double-decker bus going the "wrong" way down the city's crowded streets. Thankfully, Salzburg was a far less hectic place. But I was pretty nervous when it was my turn to speak before such a large hall full of people. I read carefully from the text I had prepared. When I got to the part about the 90 percent no vote in the plebiscite in Baker Lake, I was startled by the noise that the audience made. Everyone in the hall was on their feet, clapping and whooping! It went on and on. As I gazed in amazement at the crowd, I realized that tears of joy were running down my cheeks.

CHAPTER 5

The Nunavut Agreement and Gold Mining near Baker Lake

In 1993, Inuit in what is now Nunavut signed the Nunavut Land Claims Agreement (often referred to as the Nunavut Agreement) with the federal and territorial governments. The Nunavut Agreement "extinguished" our Aboriginal title—the legal right to exclusively use, occupy, control, and benefit from the lands and resources in our traditional territory. Even though the federal government and mining industry had not honoured our title (especially our right to control our lands and resources), many Inuit felt very uneasy about giving up our inherent rights to our homeland.

In exchange, we received money, title to small portions of our original lands, and clearly defined rights. The agreement is probably best known for the creation of the Nunavut Territory, a political jurisdiction where the great majority (85 percent) of residents are Inuit. Through the new Government of Nunavut, which was created in 1999, we hoped to gain further self-determination. The agreement created other new political and regulatory organizations, some with authority over mining in Nunavut. Negotiators of the agreement claimed it would allow Inuit to participate in decisions about mining in Nunavut, and to benefit from it as well.

I supported the Nunavut Agreement because I thought it would give Inuit more power and allow us to uphold our traditional laws and values. I thought it would give hunters more control over how our lands were used. I expected that everything would now be done on our terms. I assumed that the Government of Nunavut would find a way to take our Inuit *pitqussiit* (Inuit rules, customs, and social norms) and turn them into modern regulations. However, more than two decades after the new territory and new government were created, our government and Inuit organizations have yet to implement traditional rules around wildlife—especially when it comes to the mining industry.

In general, I'm very disappointed with the outcome of the Nunavut Agreement, particularly its influence on mineral exploration and mining. Despite provisions for environmental protection, we still experience significant negative effects to our environment and our hunting way of life. Most of the benefits from mining in our territory still go to non-Inuit, even when mining companies sign impact and benefit agreements with our representative Inuit organizations. Our ability to participate in decisions about mining also remains limited because mining companies are in a position of power that allows them to manipulate our community leadership and co-management processes.

This chapter introduces the Nunavut Agreement and its provisions for mining. I use the Meadowbank and Whale Tail gold mines as examples, to explain how communities experience mining in Nunavut today. These mining experiences show that, even after our land claim agreement was signed, not much has changed: most benefits still go to non-Inuit, Inuit (especially Inuit women) still suffer negative effects, and most decisions about mining in Nunavut are still made by non-Inuit. Our experiences with gold mining also validated one of our biggest concerns with the Kiggavik proposal: if we approved one uranium mine near Baker Lake, more would inevitably follow, and our community would be powerless to stop them.

The Nunavut Land Claims Agreement

After we defeated Urangesellschaft's Kiggavik proposal in 1990, the issue of uranium mining faded into the background as our political leaders became preoccupied with the negotiation and implementation of a land claim agreement. The Nunavut Land Claims Agreement was signed in 1993 after more than fifteen years of negotiations. It is one of the most famous modern treaties because of the way it changed the map of Canada: the Northwest Territories was divided in two, creating the new Nunavut Territory as an Inuit homeland.

The Nunavut Agreement extinguished our Aboriginal title to our traditional homelands. In return, we received:

- $1.14 billion in compensation;

- ownership of roughly 20 percent of our homeland
  (Inuit Owned Lands);

- mineral rights to roughly 2 percent of our homeland;

- specific rights for Inuit, including the right to hunt, fish, and trap
  throughout our traditional homeland; and

- the division of the Northwest Territories, the creation
  of the Nunavut Territory, and the creation of the new
  Government of Nunavut.[1]

The Nunavut Agreement also created a new system of governance in the territory. This resulted in new representative political organizations and co-management boards that are now key players in decisions about our territory's
lands and resources.

New Political Organizations

Several new political organizations were created by the Nunavut Agreement.
The Government of Nunavut (GN) is the public government for our territory.[2]
By "public government" I mean that all residents, regardless of their ethnicity,
can run for a seat in the Legislative Assembly of Nunavut and vote in elections.
This is not a form of Inuit self-government. The structure and powers of the GN
are similar to those of other provincial and territorial governments in Canada.
It has jurisdiction over many important issues, including health, education,
and terrestrial wildlife resources. Because Nunavut is a territory rather than a
province, it does not have jurisdiction over Crown lands and resources. The GN
is currently negotiating a devolution agreement with the federal government
that would give it some authority over Crown lands and resources. However,
until an agreement is reached, the federal government will continue to make
most decisions about mining in our territory.

New organizations were created to represent our interests as Inuit. Nunavut
Tunngavik Incorporated (NTI) superseded the Tunngavik Federation of Nunavut
as the primary representative organization for Nunavut Inuit. NTI manages the

land and money Inuit received under the terms of the Nunavut Agreement. It shares these responsibilities with three Regional Inuit Associations. The Kivalliq Inuit Association (KIA) is the regional association for Baker Lake and the six other communities in the Kivalliq region. Prior to 1999, KIA was known as the Keewatin Inuit Association.

Several organizations represent the interests of Inuit hunters. Each community in Nunavut has a Hunters and Trappers Organization (HTO). HTOs are responsible for managing local hunting and representing hunters' rights at the community level. Each HTO has a board of directors that is elected by its membership, and an executive (chair, vice-chair, and secretary treasurer) are selected by the board. Before the creation of Nunavut, HTOs were called Hunters and Trappers Associations.

Each region of Nunavut also has a regional wildlife board. The Kivalliq Wildlife Board (KWB) superseded the Keewatin Wildlife Federation as the organization for my region. These boards are responsible for wildlife management and Inuit hunting rights at a regional level. Regional wildlife boards consist of HTO chairs from each region.

Unfortunately, the way these organizations were established has put Inuit hunters at a serious disadvantage. Nunavut Tunngavik Incorporated and the Regional Inuit Associations are large institutions with significant resources. NTI has an executive with a full-time president and over one hundred staff divided over thirteen departments. The Kivalliq Inuit Association similarly has a full-time president and thirty-nine people on staff. HTOs, by comparison, have no full-time political representatives and only one or two full-time staff. The Kivalliq Wildlife Board also has no full-time political leadership and only two people on staff. To make matters worse, NTI and the Regional Inuit Associations—the institutions with most of the power and resources—face a conflict of interest when it comes to mining and Inuit rights.

The Nunavut Agreement, Mining, and Economic Benefits

The Nunavut Agreement provided our Inuit organizations and territorial government with an opportunity to economically benefit from mining in our territory. These economic benefits vary, depending on the category of land being mined.

Crown lands (roughly 80 percent of Nunavut) are owned and administered by the federal government. When mineral and energy resources are extracted from Crown lands, the federal government collects royalties. A relatively small portion of these royalties is shared with Nunavut Tunngavik Incorporated—50 percent of the first $2 million, and 5 percent of any further royalties, each year—per Article 25 of the agreement. This means NTI will receive a significant share of royalties if mining activity is slow, but it will only receive a small proportion if there is a mining boom.

The Government of Nunavut also collects some revenue from mining in the territory, in the form of corporate and income taxes. But, as I mentioned earlier, the GN is in the process of negotiating a devolution agreement with the federal government. If such an agreement is reached, the GN may be eligible to receive royalties from resource extraction on Crown lands, as well. This dream of devolution and royalties provides a lot of incentive for the GN to support the expansion of mining in our territory.

Inuit Owned Lands (IOL), in comparison, are administered by Nunavut Tunngavik Incorporated and the Regional Inuit Associations. The Nunavut Agreement created two categories of Inuit Owned Lands: Surface IOL and Subsurface IOL.

Surface IOL (roughly 18 percent of the land in Nunavut) are managed by the Regional Inuit Associations. The Nunavut Agreement requires mining companies to negotiate Inuit Impact and Benefit Agreements (IIBAs) before any "major development project" proceeds on Surface IOL. Like impact and benefit agreements in other jurisdictions, IIBAs usually provide consent to extraction in exchange for various benefits, including financial compensation, preferential hiring of Inuit, and preferential contracting to Inuit businesses.

When the Nunavut Agreement was signed, each community in Nunavut was provided with the opportunity to select Surface IOL. These lands were usually selected for their cultural and heritage value, and most Surface IOL parcels correspond to important hunting grounds and traditional homelands. Some Surface IOL parcels were also chosen because they corresponded to areas with potential for mining. However, it isn't always clear if communities selected areas with mining potential because they intended to support (and benefit from) development, or if these areas were chosen because communities wanted to prevent the development of these ore bodies.[3]

Subsurface IOL (roughly 2 percent of the land in Nunavut) are managed by Nunavut Tunngavik Incorporated. Mining companies must negotiate exploration and production agreements with NTI to access Subsurface IOL, which can provide royalties and other financial benefits. Subsurface IOL parcels were selected by TFN, with the assistance of geologists. Their primary goal was to select lands with high mineral and energy resource potential. Cultural, environmental, and political questions were generally not taken into consideration during the selection process. As a result, TFN succeeded in gaining partial ownership over some of the most promising ore bodies in Nunavut, including some associated with the Kiggavik uranium project near Baker Lake.[4]

This system of land ownership has placed Nunavut Tunngavik Incorporated and the Regional Inuit Associations in a conflicted position. It has given these organizations financial incentives to promote mining in some of the most important wildlife habitat and heritage sites in our territory. The system of land ownership created by the Nunavut Agreement also gives these organizations an economic interest in risky types of extraction, like uranium mining.

Because of the very poor royalty sharing provisions for mining on Crown lands, there is a strong financial incentive for these organizations to promote mineral extraction on Inuit Owned Lands. Because Surface IOL primarily consist of historical camping and hunting areas, Regional Inuit Associations now have a strong interest in extraction specifically in some of the most important areas for Inuit hunting and cultural heritage. There are many IOL parcels—both surface and subsurface—corresponding to promising uranium ore bodies. A large number of IOL also overlap with sensitive caribou habitat like calving grounds.

For someone dedicated to our hunting way of life and traditional values about the land, this conflict of interest within our Inuit representative organizations is a very big problem. It breaks my heart to see our Inuit organizations selling off our homeland to the highest bidder. As I will discuss in the next few chapters, this has led to conflicts between these organizations and Inuit hunters like me.[5]

Co-Management and Decisions about Mining

The Nunavut Agreement also created four co-management boards that allow Inuit to participate in decisions about land and resource use in Nunavut. These boards have members that are appointed by the federal government. However, some of these appointments must be based on nominations from NTI and the Regional Inuit Associations. These boards are also mostly advisory—that means final decisions still mostly lie in the hands of government, especially where mining is concerned.[6]

The Nunavut Wildlife Management Board (NWMB) has a mandate to make decisions and recommendations about wildlife harvesting in Nunavut. For example, it determines the total allowable harvest of different wildlife species in our territory. The NWMB also provides advice to the federal government and GN about the impacts of mining on wildlife.

The Nunavut Planning Commission (NPC) drafts and implements land use plans for the territory. These plans can help protect the land and animals by placing restrictions on the mining industry, among others. For example, a land use plan can restrict mining in sensitive wildlife habitat, such as caribou calving grounds. If a company wants to explore for minerals or open a mine in Nunavut, its proposal is first sent to the NPC to see if it conforms to existing land use plans. If the NPC rejects a proposal, the company can ask the federal government for an exemption.

If the proposal passes the NPC's conformity check (or receives an exemption from the federal government), it next goes to the Nunavut Impact Review Board (NIRB). NIRB is responsible for screening and reviewing proposals for mineral exploration and mining. Environmental reviews by NIRB are similar to those conducted by the Federal Environmental Assessment and Review Office in the 1970s and 1980s. The mining company is required to write an Environmental Impact Statement, based on guidelines issued by NIRB. Government agencies, Indigenous organizations, and members of the public are invited to comment on the proposal in writing. NIRB then holds final hearings, where the mining company, intervenor groups, and members of the public can make arguments and provide evidence to NIRB board members in person. After the hearing, NIRB issues a final report, in which it recommends whether or not the project should proceed. At the end of the day, the federal government still makes the final decision. The minister responsible for northern development can accept NIRB's recommendations, reject NIRB's recommendations, or send the proposal back to NIRB for further review. If NIRB recommends a project not be approved, the minister can override NIRB's recommendation if the minister believes the project is in the "national or regional interest."[7]

Mines and exploration camps in Nunavut also require a water licence from the Nunavut Water Board (NWB). The Nunavut Agreement gave the NWB powers over the "regulation, use, and management" of water in Nunavut.[8] It is illegal to use water or dispose of waste water without a licence from the NWB. However, the NWB process is highly technical and focused on Western science. This leaves little room for community participation in decision making. As a result, I don't have as much experience with the NWB and don't discuss it much in this book.

Without a doubt, this co-management framework looks pretty good on paper. There appear to be many opportunities for community participation, and several checks and balances to protect our environment. However, my community's experiences with gold and uranium mining show that our ability to influence these processes is actually very limited. Ultimately, this system leaves most real power in the hands of the mining companies.

The Meadowbank Gold Mine

In the 1980s, a junior mining company called Asmara Minerals discovered gold deposits north of Baker Lake. The rights to these deposits were eventually acquired by another junior company called Cumberland Resources.[9] In 2003 Cumberland submitted a proposal for a gold mine 110 kilometres north of Baker Lake, to be called Meadowbank. Cumberland's proposal included several open pit operations, a mill, and an all-weather road connecting the mine to the community of Baker Lake.[10]

Cumberland's proposal was sent to the Nunavut Planning Commission for a conformity review. Because the Keewatin Regional Land Use Plan (the land use plan for the Kivalliq Region) did not contain any specific restrictions on mining in the Meadowbank area, the NPC issued a positive determination. Next, the proposal was sent to the Nunavut Impact Review Board for a preliminary screening. NIRB recommended a full environmental review of the Meadowbank project. The federal minister of Indian Affairs and Northern Development accepted this recommendation and directed NIRB to conduct the review.[11] Cumberland's proposal slowly worked its way through the review process. After several years of technical meetings, community information sessions, and written submissions, NIRB held public hearings in Baker Lake, Chesterfield Inlet, and Rankin Inlet in March 2006.

There was a lot of support for the Meadowbank proposal at the public hearings. The Hamlet of Baker Lake,[12] KIA,[13] and the GN[14] gave presentations that supported the approval of the project. Residents of Baker Lake, Chesterfield Inlet, and Rankin Inlet also spoke positively about the project, and many asked questions about Inuit employment and training.[15] The only serious environmental concern came from hunters and Elders in Chesterfield Inlet—they were worried (rightfully so) that increased shipping activity associated with the project could disturb marine mammal hunting.[16]

Aside from these issues with marine life, we believed that our concerns with the project would be taken care of by the NIRB process. It appeared that the proposal had been thoroughly reviewed by so many different experts that it would be deemed environmentally acceptable. We did not foresee how many conflicts and other problems the gold mine would create in our community.

Five months after the hearings, NIRB issued its report for the Meadowbank proposal.[17] The report recommended the project should proceed as proposed. This recommendation was accepted by Jim Prentice, then minister of Indian and Northern Affairs Canada, and authorizations for the project were issued. NIRB then released a Project Certificate for the Meadowbank mine, containing various terms and conditions that the mining company must follow.

Not long after the proposal was approved, the Meadowbank project was acquired by a much larger mining company called Agnico Eagle Mines Limited. Agnico Eagle is headquartered in Toronto and has operations in Canada, Finland, Mexico, and the United States. Construction of the Meadowbank mine began in 2007 and commercial production started in 2010. Operations at Meadowbank were originally scheduled to end in 2019. However, Agnico Eagle began work on a satellite mine called "Whale Tail" in 2018. This new project, which uses the mill at Meadowbank to process ore, is scheduled to continue production until at least 2026.

The Benefits and Impacts of the Meadowbank Mine

No one can deny that the Meadowbank gold mine brought some benefits to my community. The project employed many Baker Lake Inuit who otherwise would have been unemployed. Some business owners living in Baker Lake managed to secure lucrative contracts with Agnico Eagle. NTI, KIA, and the GN all collected revenues from the project. Agnico has also provided financial support for many community initiatives over the years, including the construction of a new baseball diamond in Baker Lake.[18]

However, Inuit were not the major beneficiaries of the Meadowbank mine. Most of the economic benefits still went to non-Inuit living outside of our territory. For example, the profits were collected by Agnico Eagle and its shareholders, whom are based outside of Nunavut.[19]

As far as employment goes, most jobs still went to non-Inuit. The exact proportion of Inuit to non-Inuit employees varied over time, but tended to range from 30 to 40 percent Inuit employees. We also have to consider the types of jobs Inuit were hired for. Most of the "unskilled" and "semi-skilled" positions were filled by Inuit, while almost all "skilled" and "professional" jobs were filled by non-Inuit. Inuit made up almost all of the temporary and on-call workers at the mine.[20] In other words, Meadowbank had an "ethnically stratified workforce" where *qablunaat* held almost all highly paid jobs with authority, while Inuit worked almost all of the lower-paid labour positions.[21]

As I mentioned earlier, the GN, NTI, and KIA all collected revenues from the Meadowbank project. The mine was especially lucrative for NTI and KIA because of its location on Subsurface Inuit Owned Lands. This meant Agnico needed to pay royalties to NTI, as well as negotiate an impact and benefit agreement with KIA.

Even so, we haven't seen many local benefits from these payments. Part of the problem is that our community was left out of negotiating the original impact and benefit agreement. KIA negotiated this agreement privately with Agnico

Eagle, without meaningfully involving our community. As a result, our needs weren't really addressed.

While most of the benefits from Meadowbank went to non-Inuit, we were left to suffer the negative environmental and social consequences. Unsurprisingly, Agnico Eagle denies that its mine has caused any "significant" effects on our environment. It claims that project impacts to caribou are not "significant." This claim is based on reports from its consultants. However, the biologists working for these consulting firms clearly have no idea what is significant to me.

Hunters and Elders from my community observed changes to caribou migrations since the Meadowbank mine came into operation. Before the mine was built, we saw a lot of caribou close to our community. After the mine had operated for a few years, the caribou started shifting their migration routes farther and farther away. This made it more difficult for us to hunt, and resulted in many hunters coming home empty-handed. Many of us consider these changes "significant."[22]

Another environmental effect that I think is significant is the amount of dust the mine road threw up into our air, which was then deposited on our land. According to the project certificate for the Meadowbank mine, Agnico Eagle was required to suppress dust on all roads related to the project. However, when the mine went into operation, Agnico didn't use any dust suppression on the 110-kilometre access road between Baker Lake and the Meadowbank mine site.[23]

Dust from the mine road was very upsetting for our hunters and Elders. The huge trucks that drove back and forth kicked up a lot of dust. It accumulated on the land, making it impossible for caribou to graze in the area. And, even though we can't observe it directly, the dust probably accumulated in lakes and rivers north of Baker Lake. It was also difficult to cache caribou meat in the area because most of the rocks were covered in a layer of dust. As a result, we had to travel quite far away from the mine road to cache caribou. Dust spoiled our enjoyment of the land, too—it's very frustrating when you're making tea or preparing food, only to have a truck pass by and spoil it with dust. Most concerning, though, is the potential health impacts from people and wildlife inhaling this dust. I know some people who won't hunt north of Baker Lake because they're worried about inhaling so much dust. For the first few years the mine was in operation, whenever there was a local meeting about mining—even if it had nothing to do with Meadowbank—Elders would talk about their concerns with road dust.

NIRB backed up our Elders. Every year, in its annual monitoring reports for the Meadowbank mine, NIRB told Agnico Eagle that it was violating its project certificate by failing to suppress dust on the access road. These reports also directly instructed Agnico Eagle to use dust suppression measures.[24] However, Agnico Eagle dismissed our concerns and ignored NIRB's instructions—they claimed project monitoring data showed that the dust wasn't having a "significant" impact on the environment.[25]

After years of NIRB and Elders pressing Agnico Eagle about this issue, the company gradually began to suppress dust on some small sections of the road. In 2011, Agnico Eagle started suppressing dust in high-traffic areas along the access road, between its exploration camp and the Meadowbank mine site. In 2013, it began to suppress dust on the areas of the road that are closest to the community of Baker Lake.[26] In 2016, it began to suppress dust at additional locations near important hunting and fishing areas.[27]

However, I know a lot of people aren't really satisfied with these efforts. I still hear hunters complain that dust from the road is disturbing their enjoyment of the land. NIRB, too, continues to voice concerns about the lack of dust control at the Meadowbank mine. For example, NIRB's 2019 annual monitoring report noted that Agnico continued to violate its project certificate by failing to suppress dust on the entire access road, which Agnico still uses to supply the Whale Tail mine. NIRB also found, in Agnico's monitoring data, that the amount of dust created by the road sometimes violates air quality standards. NIRB's report also argued that Agnico's monitoring program may have underestimated the amount of dust produced by the road because the company was not following standard practices for air quality monitoring.[28]

Another environmental impact of Meadowbank has to do with marine shipping. Just as the Elders from Chesterfield Inlet predicted, the increased shipping associated with Meadowbank has disturbed marine mammals, making it more difficult for Inuit to hunt seals and whales. At many different regulatory meetings, hunters and Elders from Chesterfield Inlet and Baker Lake have testified to witnessing a serious decline in marine mammals in the Chesterfield Inlet area after the Meadowbank project began operations.[29]

The Meadowbank mine also brought negative social effects to our community. Needless to say, the mine didn't benefit everyone financially. While some Inuit workers and a handful of Inuit business owners are better off than they were before Meadowbank, many other Baker Lake Inuit continue to live in poverty. Gold mining hasn't really benefitted Baker Lake as a whole. Instead, it created more inequality within our community.[30]

There were a lot of conflicts on the job site between Inuit and *qablunaat* workers. For example, language use in the workplace was a big source of tension when the mine first opened. Inuit workers complained they were told to speak English, not Inuktitut, while they were at work. Even so, they noted some *qablunaat* workers—who were mostly French Canadians and weren't too keen on being forced to speak English either—were able to speak French on the job.[31] Some Inuit also reported generally being treated poorly, compared with their *qablunaat* coworkers.[32]

The Meadowbank mine also caused a lot of problems for families in Baker Lake. The mine operates on a "two-weeks-on, two-weeks-off" rotation, which means workers are away from their families for two weeks at a time. This time apart puts a lot of stress on families and caused some relationships to fall apart.[33]

Inuit women tend to experience the worst of these negative social impacts. With regard to rising levels of inequality, many women weren't able to participate in project benefits as easily as men. Because many jobs in the mining industry are considered "masculine," women tend to get stuck in low-paying positions such as housekeepers and kitchen helpers. At home, women are usually responsible for child care. This makes it impossible for many mothers to work the two-week shifts at the mine site.[34]

It is now well known that resource extraction can expose Indigenous women to violence and harassment, both on and off the job site.[35] Inuit women from Baker Lake told researchers that sexual harassment and assault were problems at the Meadowbank mine, and that some Inuit women had quit their jobs because of these issues.[36] The stress from rotational shift work, combined with rising rates of substance abuse, may have also led to increased domestic violence in Baker Lake.[37]

My biggest social concern with gold mining has to do with its inevitable end: What will happen when the gold runs out? While the Whale Tail mine has allowed Agnico Eagle to continue operating near our community long after mining activities at Meadowbank were complete, it too will come to an end someday. Like many other people in Baker Lake, I'm worried that a sudden spike in unemployment could be a disaster for community well-being. Among other things, it could cause problems related to food security, mental health, and family relationships. All this could lead to even more violence in our community.[38]

The negative environmental and social effects of gold mining near Baker Lake are serious. I'm not convinced that a handful of "unskilled" and "semi-skilled" jobs will make up for all of the impacts we've suffered. I suppose it depends on who you talk to.

The Amaruq Exploration Project and Access Road

Agnico Eagle never intended to stop with the Meadowbank gold mine. Cumberland Resources' original Meadowbank proposal in 2003 included ongoing exploration work near the mine. Since acquiring Meadowbank from Cumberland, Agnico Eagle has conducted a lot of exploration in the Baker Lake area. The area they focused on the most is the Amaruq deposit, located fifty kilometres northwest of Meadowbank.

Agnico Eagle acquired the Amaruq property in 2013 and soon began an aggressive and constantly expanding exploration program.[39] In 2014, Agnico applied to build an eighty-kilometre winter road to connect the Meadowbank mine with the Amaruq site. This proposal was approved in early 2015 without a full environmental review.[40] As soon as the winter road was approved, Agnico applied to upgrade it to a sixty-five-kilometre all-season road following a different route.[41]

As part of its consultation requirements for developing the upgraded all-season road, Agnico held several meetings with the Baker Lake HTO. By this point I was working as the HTO's secretary manager, so I took part in this process. The Elders on our board repeatedly asked Agnico to change the route of the road because it would disturb important heritage sites and wolf dens. The entire proposed road followed an esker that Inuit used as a traditional travel route.

The company wouldn't budge! At these meetings, Agnico representatives just evaded our questions and ignored our comments by changing the topic of conversation. The Baker Lake HTO ended up writing to NIRB to request that a different route be chosen.[42] Despite our protests, the original proposed road route was approved in the fall of 2015 without a full environmental review.[43]

Around the same time, Agnico Eagle applied to expand its exploration activities in the Meadowbank and Amaruq areas. In response, the Baker Lake HTO submitted comments to NIRB expressing serious concerns with the effects that Agnico's operations were having on wildlife. The HTO believed gold mining and exploration were already disturbing caribou migrations, and that these impacts would only worsen if stricter protection measures were not imposed. The HTO also expressed concern with the amount of dust being created by the roads associated with the Meadowbank and Amaruq projects, and recommended stricter enforcement of dust control measures.[44] Despite the HTO's concerns, the proposal was approved in early 2016 without an environmental review.[45] That spring, Agnico applied to further expand its exploration program at Amaruq. This time, it wanted to build an underground ramp to allow for deeper drilling. Once again, the proposal was approved without a full environmental review.[46]

In the end, NIRB did impose some conditions on the Amaruq project in response to the HTO's comments about dust control and disturbance to caribou. However, these terms and conditions have done very little to address our concerns over the long term. As with the Meadowbank project, Agnico Eagle has failed to properly mitigate dust on the road between Meadowbank and Amaruq.[47] What's more, as I will explain later in this chapter, the measures to protect caribou from this new road are at risk of being removed.

The Whale Tail Gold Mine

It wasn't long before Agnico Eagle developed plans for a new mine at the Amaruq site. In early 2016 it submitted a proposal for a gold mine called Whale Tail. The Whale Tail project included creating an open pit mine and widening the access road between Meadowbank and Amaruq. More importantly, Agnico's proposal also included trucking raw ore from the Whale Tail site to the Meadowbank site, to be processed at the Meadowbank mill. The new mine would extend Agnico Eagle's operations near Baker Lake for only four years.[48]

NIRB began an environmental review of the Whale Tail proposal later the same year. After numerous technical meetings, community information sessions, and requests for written submissions, NIRB held final hearings in the fall of 2017. By this point I had retired from my job at the Hunters and Trappers Organization, but I attended some meetings as a member of the public.

Like many other Baker Lake residents, I had serious concerns with the proposal to use the Meadowbank mill to process ore from the Whale Tail mine. Because Agnico needs to constantly haul ore from the Whale Tail site to the Meadowbank mill, there is much more traffic on the Whale Tail haul road than on the original Meadowbank access road. This makes the Whale Tail project more disruptive, and puts our caribou herds at much greater risk.

However, the conversation about the Whale Tail proposal was rushed. The company said they needed quick approval for the new mine so they could avoid laying off Inuit workers. This created a lot of concern in town. The Hamlet of Baker Lake urged NIRB to ensure there were no delays in approving the new mine, in order to protect local jobs.[49] In November 2017, NIRB recommended the Whale Tail project be approved.[50] The federal government issued approvals for the project in March 2018.

Shortly after the Whale Tail gold mine was approved, Agnico applied to expand the mine's operations. The "Whale Tail Expansion Project" called for additional open pit and underground operations at the Whale Tail site, as well as an expansion of the existing Whale Tail pit. NIRB began a review of the expansion proposal in the fall of 2018.[51] After a year of more technical meetings, community information sessions, and written submissions, NIRB held final hearings in August 2019.

Submissions from the Baker Lake HTO stated that hunters and Elders were concerned with the ongoing effects of Agnico Eagle's activities on caribou, and recommended imposing stricter protection measures.[52] Again, Agnico Eagle used the threat of layoffs to shut down our demands for better caribou protection. At the community hearings, Agnico staff said the existing protection measures for caribou were already threatening the profitability of the Whale Tail mine. They claimed that the project would not be economically viable if stricter protection measures were introduced—which would force them to shut down the project and lay off most of their workers, including many Inuit from Baker

Lake.[53] Later that fall, NIRB wrote to the federal government, recommending the expansion be approved.[54]

You can be sure Agnico Eagle will come to us with more proposals for "expansions" and "modifications" of its projects in the Baker Lake area. Whale Tail is only one part of the Amaruq property, and I would be surprised if Agnico didn't propose more mines there in the future.

Caribou Protection at the Whale Tail Mine

NIRB did not include specific protection measures for caribou in the terms and conditions for the Whale Tail mine. Instead, NIRB allowed Agnico Eagle to be flexible, so the protection measures can be modified to adapt to changing circumstances and new information.

The Whale Tail mine's project certificate requires Agnico Eagle to maintain a Terrestrial Ecosystem Management Plan that includes protection measures for caribou. Agnico is allowed to modify this management plan through something called a Terrestrial Advisory Group—a committee with representatives from Agnico Eagle, the GN, KIA, and the Baker Lake HTO.[55] According to the terms of reference for the advisory group, it is supposed to operate by consensus and Agnico Eagle is supposed to follow the advice of the group.[56]

According to the protection measures in place when the Whale Tail expansion was assessed in the summer of 2019, the haul road must be closed to everything except "essential" vehicles if significant numbers of caribou are near the road during spring and fall migrations. In the spring, the road closes if twelve or more caribou are nearby. In the fall it closes for 110 or more caribou.[57]

However, in November 2019 Agnico Eagle told a meeting of the Terrestrial Advisory Group that these provisions for closing the road were making the project unprofitable. They explained that the road had been closed for sixty days in 2019, due to a combination of caribou protection and extreme weather. The company wanted to limit road closures for caribou to only eighteen days each year—twelve days in the spring and six days in the fall. Other members of the advisory group—the Baker Lake HTO, the GN, and KIA—all said they needed more information and evidence before they would support making such changes to caribou protections.[58] As subsequent letters from the Baker Lake HTO and

KIA make clear, their requests for more information, further research, and public consultations were not addressed by Agnico Eagle.[59]

Agnico Eagle decided to try to make these changes unilaterally, even though it is supposed to follow the recommendations of the advisory group. On April 22, 2020—near the beginning of the COVID-19 pandemic when our community organizations could not operate at full capacity—it submitted an updated Terrestrial Ecosystem Management Plan to NIRB. This updated plan contained serious changes to caribou protection. The thresholds for shutting down the road were raised. According to the new management plan, the road would only close in the spring if seventy-five or more caribou were nearby (previously, it would be shut down for twelve caribou during spring migrations). For fall migrations, the threshold was raised from 110 to 1,000.[60]

The Baker Lake HTO wrote to NIRB, informing it that these changes had been made unilaterally and against the advice of the advisory group.[61] NTI,[62] KIA,[63] and the GN[64] subsequently wrote to NIRB and confirmed that Agnico Eagle's changes to caribou protections were made without the participation of the advisory group and without sufficient evidence that these changes would be safe for caribou. Several of these submissions expressed serious concern that Agnico Eagle's actions violated the terms and conditions of its Project Certificate.

Agnico Eagle seems to have backed off for now. It responded to these criticisms by telling NIRB it wanted more time to discuss proposed changes with the advisory group before they are implemented.[65] However, it doesn't seem as though they've faced any consequences for so blatantly ignoring the terms and conditions they are supposed to abide by. You can also be sure that Agnico Eagle will continue to pressure the Terrestrial Advisory Group to reduce the protection measures for caribou on the Whale Tail haul road.

Mining companies always claim they come to Nunavut to create jobs and help "develop" the North. They tell us environmental protection is their top priority, and that they want to work in partnership with Inuit communities. But a corporation's first responsibility is to its shareholders. As our experiences with the Whale Tail mine shows, at the end of the day, profits take precedence over everything else.

Conclusions

Agnico Eagle's track record with my community shows that mining in Nunavut is still a form of colonialism. Even with the Nunavut Agreement, mining mostly benefits *qablunaat*, key decisions are mostly made by *qablunaat*, and negative impacts mostly affect Inuit (especially Inuit women). Colonialism is the term that best describes the relationship of power between mining companies and Inuit communities.

Our experiences with the Meadowbank and Whale Tail gold mines also show that many of my community's concerns about uranium mining are well-founded. As I explained in Chapter 4, one of our biggest concerns with Urangesellschaft's proposed Kiggavik mine was that one uranium mine would inevitably lead to more. Baker Lake is surrounded by uranium ore deposits. If one uranium mine was to be built, complete with a mill and an access road, the uranium industry could save money by using this infrastructure to support additional uranium mines. My community's ability to influence this sprawling uranium economy would be extremely limited. If we said yes to one uranium mine, it would be politically impossible for us to effectively oppose additional mines in the future.

Some people suggested we were blowing things out of proportion. They said that the threat of this "induced development" was minimal, and that future proposals for uranium mining would have to go through additional environmental assessments.[66] However, Agnico Eagle's mining operations show that our fears were well-founded. As soon as one gold mine was built, Agnico Eagle immediately began searching for additional gold deposits nearby. Once it identified a second major ore body, the company decided to maximize its profits by using the existing Meadowbank mill to process ore from the Whale Tail mine. Our hunters and Elders had many concerns with the route of the haul road and its effects on caribou. However, we were rushed into making a decision about the project because the company threatened to lay off Inuit workers if the project wasn't approved quickly.

Once it had its approvals for Whale Tail, Agnico began pressuring our community to reduce protection measures for caribou so it could increase its profits. So far, we have managed to resist this pressure and keep protection measures in place. But with significant numbers of Baker Lake Inuit working at the Whale Tail mine, I'm not sure we can hold the company back for long. Our economic dependence on Agnico Eagle gives them so much power over us; we are in no position to refuse their requests. When you think about it, my community's relationship with Agnico Eagle is similar to the relationship between Inuit and the federal government in the 1950s—the company has so much power over us that many Baker Lake Inuit feel too *ilirahungniq* (intimidated) to talk back.

CHAPTER 6

Uranium Policy in Nunavut

Shortly after the Nunavut Land Claims Agreement was signed in 1993, two policies were issued prohibiting uranium mining in our new territory. Nunavut Tunngavik Incorporated—our Nunavut-wide representative Inuit organization—prohibited uranium mining on Inuit Owned Lands (the lands that Inuit obtained collective ownership of through the Nunavut Agreement). The Keewatin Regional Land Use Plan—a planning document that guides mining and other land uses in the Kivalliq region—also prohibited uranium mining. The land use plan was developed by the Nunavut Planning Commission and approved by the Government of Nunavut and Government of Canada. In effect, there was an Inuit-led moratorium on uranium mining in our territory.

However, this moratorium didn't last. After the price of uranium spiked in 2005, the mining industry began to lobby Inuit leaders to change their position. A company called AREVA Resources acquired Urangesellschaft's abandoned Kiggavik project, and in 2006 it began to prepare an updated and expanded proposal for the Kiggavik mine. In 2007, Nunavut Tunngavik Incorporated and the Government of Nunavut adopted policies supporting uranium mining. In 2009, the planning commission lifted the ban on uranium mining under our land use plan.

In response to this chain of events, in late 2009 a new Nunavut-based non-governmental organization was formed called Nunavummiut Makitagunarningit ("The People of Nunavut Can Rise Up").[1] Its mission was to foster public debate about uranium mining and pressure our representative organizations to reconsider their pro-uranium positions. It was initially composed of people living in Iqaluit, but I soon joined this group along with several other residents of Baker Lake. We tried, unsuccessfully, to pressure the Government of Nunavut to hold a public inquiry into uranium mining. Despite our efforts, the Government of Nunavut and our Inuit organizations did not change their positions and continued to support uranium mining.

In this chapter, I tell the story of how the organizations created by our land claim came to lift the moratorium on uranium mining. I focus on attempts—by myself and others—to stop this change in position and keep the moratorium in place. I draw on my personal experiences as a spokesperson for the Baker Lake Concerned Citizens Committee, as a board member for the Baker Lake Hunters and Trappers Organization, and as vice-chair of Nunavummiut Makitagunarningit. These changes in uranium policy show just how disconnected our Inuit organizations and territorial government are from the reasons we negotiated the Nunavut Agreement in the first place: our traditional values and beliefs about protecting our land and animals.

A Moratorium on Uranium Mining

In the 1990s, the issue of uranium mining in our territory slowly faded into the background. The Kiggavik mine proposal had been shelved. Our political leaders were preoccupied with first finalizing and then implementing the Nunavut Agreement. The price of uranium was also very low, so mining companies weren't exactly clamouring to open a uranium mine in the Arctic. However, even though the issue faded into the background, it had not disappeared completely. Inuit still had many serious concerns about the industry. As a result, our territory's representative Inuit organization and an important co-management body placed a moratorium on uranium mining in Nunavut.

Nunavut Tunngavik Incorporated (NTI) prohibited exploration and mining for uranium on Inuit Owned Lands in Nunavut. This policy only applied to lands where we owned mineral (subsurface) rights because these were the only areas under NTI's full jurisdiction. Even though the policy prohibiting uranium mining only applied to about 2 percent of Nunavut, it covered some of the most promising uranium deposits in the territory. NTI's policy didn't make it impossible for the uranium industry to continue operating in Nunavut, but it certainly didn't make it easy, either.

The Nunavut Planning Commission (NPC) implemented a land use plan that placed a temporary ban on uranium mining in the Kivalliq region. The Keewatin

Regional Land Use Plan was drafted by the NPC in the 1990s, and was approved by the Government of Canada and the Government of Nunavut in 2000. It contains two provisions related to uranium mining. Term 3.5 states: "Uranium development shall not take place until the NPC, NIRB, the NWB, and the NWMB have reviewed all of the issues relevant to uranium exploration and mining. Any review of uranium exploration and mining shall pay particular attention to questions concerning health and environmental protection." Term 3.6 states: "Any future proposal to mine uranium must be approved by the people of the region."[2] These provisions were a major obstacle for the uranium mining industry because all proposals for major development in Nunavut must conform with land use plans.

Climate Change and the "Nuclear Renaissance"

The price of uranium remained low after Nunavut was created in 1999. For the next few years mining companies showed very little interest in our uranium resources. The Kiggavik project remained inactive, and many companies working in our territory shut down their exploration projects. However, it wasn't long before things began to change. The nuclear industry had begun rebranding itself as a source of energy that was cheap, environmentally safe, and necessary to solve the problem of climate change.

Climate change is a huge problem that we must take seriously. In fact, it is a crisis. That fact is very clear to most Inuit. As Sheila Watt-Cloutier explained in her book *The Right to Be Cold*, we have already witnessed serious changes in our weather, land, and wildlife. If these changes continue, they may put our hunting way of life at risk.[3]

I first understood how serious a problem climate change is in 2001, when I worked on a research project. A *qablunaaq* researcher named Darren Keith and I were hired by the Government of Nunavut to interview Elders in Arviat and Baker Lake about their experiences with climate change. The Elders described many changes they had observed in the Arctic climate, such as warmer year-round temperatures, changes in the length of seasons, changes in the direction of prevailing winds, less rainfall and snowfall, and reduced water levels in lakes and rivers.

The Elders also explained how these changes were causing serious problems for Inuit hunters. Travelling on the land was becoming much more dangerous. Traditional methods of predicting the weather were no longer working. The land around Arviat is very flat and it is easy to get disoriented in the winter. Hunters used to find their way by looking at the snowdrifts, but changes in the direction of the prevailing wind meant that this traditional navigation technique no longer worked. Low water levels in lakes and rivers had made some traditional camping and hunting spots inaccessible.[4] I had heard about climate change before, but interviewing these Elders really opened my eyes to how serious and urgent a problem it really is.

However, I am not convinced that the nuclear industry offers an acceptable solution to the climate crisis. Research shows that nuclear power is costly and it takes a very long time to design and build new reactors—as a result it's unlikely to help us make the rapid changes necessary to minimize dangerous climate change.[5] Nuclear power poses serious risks to the environment and public health,[6] nuclear waste is a burden we have no solution for, and nuclear power and nuclear weapons are closely connected.[7] In fact, the former heads of the U.S., German, and French nuclear regulatory agencies and a former Secretary to the UK government's radiation protection committee issued a clear and powerful statement that "nuclear is neither clean, safe or smart; but a very complex technology with the potential to cause significant harm. Nuclear isn't cheap, but extremely costly. Perhaps most importantly nuclear is just not part of any feasible strategy that could counter climate change."[8]

Despite all of these problems with nuclear power, governments around the world started buying into the idea that it could help solve our climate crisis. By the late 1990s, many world leaders had announced plans to use nuclear power to curb carbon dioxide emissions. Some people started to talk about a "nuclear renaissance." Because of this renewed support for nuclear energy, in 2003 the price of uranium began to skyrocket (see Figure 13).

Uranium Exploration Boom

Before long, the uranium industry was back at our door, eager to search for uranium on our lands. In 2005, companies began submitting large number of applications to explore for uranium near Baker Lake. In many of these

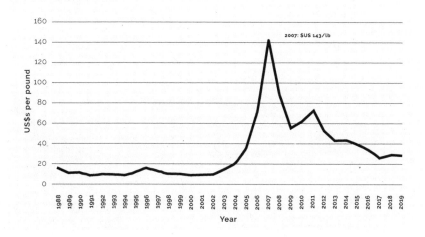

Figure 13. Price of Uranium, 1989–2019 (USD per pound, highest price per calendar year). Source: Raw data from Trading Economics, https://tradingeconomics.com/commodity/uranium.

applications, exploration was to take place in the calving and post-calving grounds of the Beverly and Qamanirjuaq caribou herds.

At this point, I sat on the board of directors for the Baker Lake Hunters and Trappers Organization. In January 2006, the HTO wrote to the federal government, requesting a one-year moratorium on issuing new mineral exploration permits west of Baker Lake. The area for the proposed moratorium included the calving and post-calving grounds of the Beverly caribou herd. It also covered the Kiggavik project.

We asked for this moratorium because we wanted a chance to take stock of our situation. We needed time to prepare for, and better respond to, the piles of applications for mineral exploration in our hunting grounds. At the time, we simply lacked the capacity to meaningfully consider the number of applications that were forwarded to us. We had only one full-time employee, many other responsibilities under the land claim, and no funding to hold meetings to engage

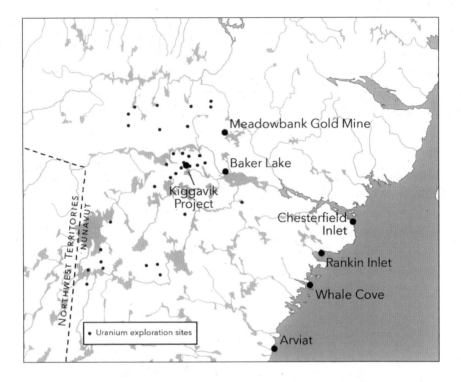

Figure 14. Map showing active uranium exploration projects in the Kivalliq region in 2008. Raw data from Indian and Northern Affairs Canada, Nunavut Overview 2008. Map design by Julie Witmer.

with our membership. The H T O board felt we needed time to discuss what areas required protection and what areas could be open for mining.

Unfortunately, the government rejected our proposal. Apparently the HTO's request for a moratorium arrived too late; we sent it only one week before the federal government had planned to announce new mineral permits for the year.[9] As a result, the H T O became overwhelmed and was unable to provide responses to the many permits being issued in our hunting grounds. By 2008, our lands had been overrun by uranium exploration companies, with over twenty exploration projects in the calving and post-calving grounds of the Beverly caribou herd (see Figure 14).

AREVA Reactivates the Kiggavik Project

After we defeated Urangesellschaft's proposal for the Kiggavik mine in 1990, the project lay dormant for many years. Kiggavik was eventually acquired by AREVA Resources, the Canadian subsidiary of the French nuclear corporation AREVA. It was a multinational giant—by far the biggest nuclear company in the world. Amid the uranium exploration frenzy, AREVA began to reactivate the Kiggavik project.

In 2006 AREVA opened an information office in Baker Lake and began to hold meetings with Baker Lake residents. It hired William Noah as a community liaison worker to staff its Baker Lake office. Noah is an Inuit artist and former politician who helped organize the Baker Lake court case against uranium exploration in the 1970s. Barry McCallum, AREVA's manager of Nunavut affairs, made regular visits to Baker Lake to promote the Kiggavik project in our community.

Looking back, there were some major differences in the ways Urangesellschaft and AREVA approached our community. As I mentioned earlier, Urangesellschaft's public-relations efforts were sometimes laughably bad, and members of their staff were unable to connect with the people of Baker Lake. AREVA, in comparison, had a much more effective approach. Barry McCallum was a smooth operator. He was skilled at connecting with people on a human level, and quickly befriended some very influential people in Baker Lake. This made AREVA a much more dangerous adversary.

Shortly after opening its information office, AREVA formed a community liaison committee made up of representatives from different local councils and interest groups, including the Hamlet Council, the Hunters and Trappers Organization, and the youth committee. AREVA claimed the community liaison committee was a way for the community to "provide advice" to the company regarding its Kiggavik project. While AREVA probably did receive a great deal of useful advice from our people, the committee was also a way for AREVA to manipulate our community members into supporting uranium mining. It allowed Barry McCallum to spend time with influential people from our community, pay them large honoraria for participating in meetings, and slowly convince them to support the Kiggavik project. The liaison committee helped AREVA direct criticism of its project into a forum that it controlled.

AREVA also held many "community engagement" meetings. These meetings included long presentations by AREVA staff and consultants, who tried their best to convince us that uranium mining could be done safely in Nunavut. The meetings included draws for door prizes, some of which were very expensive. In a small community where many people live in poverty, gifts like laptop computers and coupons for gasoline can be very persuasive and manipulative.

AREVA put a lot of time and energy into getting support from our Elders. Sometimes they took advantage of our cultural values, by giving Elders nice meals and honoraria. I think a lot of people felt they owed AREVA something in exchange for this generosity. By far, one of the most manipulative things AREVA did was its "homeland visits" program. AREVA representatives used a helicopter to take Elders and their families to see the places where they had once lived on the land. For some of the Elders, this was the first time they had seen their homelands since they were forced to move to Baker Lake in the 1950s and 1960s. I can't put into words how emotional these visits were for Elders, and how manipulative it was for AREVA to operate this program.

Some AREVA representatives played with people's emotions in other ways. They accused Elders who opposed uranium mining of being uninformed. They put a really big emphasis on how uranium is used in some medical procedures, including cancer treatments. This made some people feel like they were supporting cancer if they opposed uranium mining. They also said people who smoked cigarettes were hypocritical if they opposed uranium mining for health reasons. These types of arguments take advantage of people's vulnerability and play on their insecurities. This subtle pressure contributed to some Elders feeling *ilira-hungniq* (intimidated). I think it played a big role in keeping people quiet.

Slowly, AREVA gained the trust of some influential Elders in Baker Lake. This had a big impact on public discussions about uranium mining in our community. It is a very important Inuit value to not talk back or publicly contradict Elders. Once Barry McCallum managed to get a few Elders from big families on his side, a lot of people stopped speaking out against uranium mining in public, even though they still had concerns.

Many of us continued to oppose uranium mining. However, our community was no longer united in our opposition as we had been in the 1970s, 1980s, and

1990s. Even worse, many of the people who still opposed uranium mining felt unable to speak out.

NTI's Draft Policy Supporting Uranium Mining

The uranium industry found sympathetic ears in the Lands departments of Nunavut Tunngavik Incorporated, which released a draft uranium mining policy in 2006. The draft policy was very supportive of uranium mining. It gave several reasons for this support, which are summarized below:

- Uranium mining would, the policy claimed, bring substantial economic benefits to Inuit, especially where Inuit own mineral rights.

- By allowing uranium mining, Inuit would allegedly be helping stop climate change.

- While uranium mining was environmentally destructive and harmful to human health in the past, advances in technology and new regulations apparently ensure that "modern" uranium mining is safe for the environment and human health.

- International agreements and treaties ensure that uranium mined in Nunavut would not contribute to nuclear weapons.

I don't believe that any of these arguments really hold up to critical scrutiny. Uranium mining might bring some short-term economic benefits to our community, such as jobs. However, most of the economic benefits from existing mines in Nunavut are realized outside of our territory. As I discussed in Chapter 5, most of the economic benefits from the Meadowbank gold mine did not go to residents of Baker Lake. I don't see why a uranium mine would be any different in terms of local employment and other benefits. Also, as I explained previously, nuclear energy is not a viable solution to climate change, uranium mining poses significant health and environmental risks, and the nuclear power industry is closely tied to the production of nuclear weapons.

I became very disheartened when I learned that N T I was developing a pro-uranium policy. I wrote a letter to *Nunatsiaq News* in June 2006 to express my concerns and frustrations.[10] I explained that I felt defeated because N T I—an organization that is supposed to protect Inuit rights—was publicly endorsing uranium mining without consulting the Inuit communities it is supposed to represent. This decision was, in my opinion, totally irresponsible, unethical, and uninformed. I urged Nunavut residents, especially Inuit, to establish an independent group to fight uranium mining in our territory because N T I was no longer representing our interests on the matter.

Reactivating the Baker Lake Concerned Citizens Committee

Together with my brother Hugh Ikoe, I decided it was time to consider reactivating the community group I had formed in 1988 to fight Urangesellschaft's Kiggavik proposal: the Baker Lake Concerned Citizens Committee (B L C C C). The B L C C C had essentially been disbanded after the Kiggavik proposal was withdrawn in 1990. Our funding to participate in the environmental review ran out, we gave up our office space, and ceased meeting regularly.

In November 2006, Hugh and I held a call-in show over Baker Lake radio. We asked residents how they felt about the direction in which our new territory was headed, and if they wanted us to revive the B L C C C. The show lasted for an hour and half. Thirteen callers were Elders, full-time hunters who spent most of their lives on the land. Together, their combined age totalled 890 years—that is a *lot* of combined experience. All thirteen were unhappy with the negative impacts of exploration on their hunting grounds, and all complained that low-flying aircraft and other activity was disturbing caribou herds. They also complained that their perspectives were not being seriously considered when it came to decisions about mining and exploration. We received twelve callers from the younger generation (aged thirty to forty-five) as well. All of these callers supported reactivating the B L C C C. They wanted us to set up an office where people could voice their complaints and concerns, and where they could obtain information from independent sources.

A few days later, I wrote a letter to NTI and KIA, requesting funding to help us reactivate the BLCCC. On January 26, 2007, I received a response from NTI, rejecting my request. Their letter explained that there were official channels for us to report our concerns, particularly the Kivalliq Inuit Association.

I decided to go back on community radio, to see what direction other concerned residents wanted me to take. Once again, callers suggested we reactivate the BLCCC, even though we had zero funding. By the end of January, eight members were elected to a new board for the BLCCC.

I continued to write letters to our official organizations. I wrote to NTI, requesting that a BLCCC representative give a presentation at an upcoming NTI annual general meeting. The draft policy supporting uranium mining was on the agenda, and we wanted to express our concerns directly to NTI delegates. I didn't receive a response. I wrote to NTI and KIA, requesting funding for a BLCCC representative to attend public hearings in Lutsel'ke. The Lutsel K'e Dene were opposing a uranium exploration project in their homelands, and we wanted to learn what their concerns were. Again, I didn't receive a response. It was very disheartening to be treated this way by our Inuit representative organizations. The BLCCC was a grassroots group representing Indigenous people who were concerned about the future of their lands. It was so disappointing that our leadership would discourage us from participating in these discussions. Regardless, we continued to do our best to help Baker Lake residents express their concerns with uranium mining, even though we had no funding and paid for everything out of our own pockets.

NTI Supports Uranium Mining

NTI held a consultation meeting about its draft policy supporting uranium mining in late May 2007 in Baker Lake. The meeting was, in my opinion, very poorly conducted. Its structure and agenda made it feel like NTI was primarily concerned with selling the idea of uranium mining to Inuit, rather than genuinely discussing the issue with us. They certainly didn't seem interested in allowing us to come to our own decision on the issue, which would have required providing us with information about uranium mining from a variety of perspectives and committing to have meaningful dialogue with us.

Only twenty-seven residents attended the meeting. Late May to early June is one of the busiest hunting and fishing seasons in Baker Lake. Anyone who has worked in Nunavut knows that late May is probably the worst time to hold a consultation meeting and expect a serious turnout, especially if you want avid hunters to participate.

The meeting was dominated by long presentations by representatives from uranium mining companies, industry consultants, and government regulators.[11] There was very little time set aside to discuss community concerns. Community discussion about the "big picture" issues did not begin until the end of the night, after many people had already gone home.

The information provided at the meeting seemed biased. Every presentation implied that we should support uranium mining. AREVA promised us huge benefits—employment, royalties, tax revenue—if we supported uranium mining in Nunavut. SENES Consulting (a firm that has taken contracts from both Urangesellschaft and AREVA) reassured us that modern uranium mining was safe for human health and the environment because of new regulations and advances in technology. The Canadian Nuclear Safety Commission (CNSC) also focused on reassuring us that the nuclear industry was environmentally safe and morally acceptable. All presenters repeated the claim that the nuclear industry will solve the problem of climate change, implying that we would be "doing our part" to stop climate change by allowing uranium mining on our lands.[12]

It was only at the end of the evening when NTI representative presented the draft policy supporting uranium mining, and only afterwards were we asked for our opinions on the matter. By this point, it was past 10:00 p.m., and many people had already given up and gone home. According to NTI's meeting minutes, only three residents of Baker Lake (including myself) are on record giving any feedback whatsoever.[13] My brother Joseph Scottie complained that the presentations proceeded too quickly, and that one night of consultation was not enough. Another woman from the community asked if Inuit would be permitted to hunt on the proposed road to the Kiggavik project, or if the road would be for private use only.[14]

I presented on behalf of the Baker Lake HTO because I was a board member at the time. We requested that NTI's uranium policy include a chapter showing areas that Baker Lake hunters and Elders want protected from uranium mining.

We wanted to give our membership the opportunity to select lands where uranium mining would be prohibited, including important caribou habitat, important hunting grounds, and areas that are important to our culture and heritage. We suggested that caribou calving grounds, as well as the Kazan and Thelon rivers and their many water crossings, were areas that Baker Lake hunters would probably support protecting.[15]

A few months later, in September 2007, NTI released a final policy supporting uranium mining. The policy used the same weak arguments that appeared in the 2006 draft. It made no mention of the Baker Lake HTO's request to map areas where hunters and Elders want uranium mining to be banned.

Before long, NTI entered into agreements with uranium exploration companies. It signed a deal with Forum Uranium to explore for uranium on Inuit Owned Lands close to AREVA's Kiggavik project. This deal promised NTI huge royalties if Forum's project proceeded into the construction of a mine.[16] NTI also inked a deal with Kaminak Gold Corporation to explore for uranium in the southern Kivalliq region close to Yathkyed Lake. This led to the creation of a new uranium exploration firm called Kivalliq Energy. As a part of the exploration agreement, NTI received shares in Kivalliq Energy.[17] The conflict of interest created by these agreements is substantial. How can we trust NTI to represent our interests and safeguard our hunting rights, if these projects go through an environmental assessment in the future?

At this point it became obvious to me that our supposedly "representative" Inuit organizations no longer served us. As I explained in another letter to *Nunatsiaq News*, they were only thinking about filling their wallets by selling our traditional lands—the root of our culture and traditions—to foreign companies.[18] As far as I was concerned, they had totally given up on our traditional values and beliefs.

Government of Nunavut Supports Uranium Mining

As I explained in Chapter 5, the Government of Nunavut (GN) does not have jurisdiction over mining in our territory. This is because the federal government holds jurisdiction over Crown lands. However, the GN still participates in decisions about mining in several ways. Because it has jurisdiction over some wildlife resources, including caribou, the GN plays an important role in the environmental assessment of proposed exploration and mining in Nunavut. The GN Department of Economic Development also works to promote mining in our territory.

On June 4, 2007, a few days after NTI held its uranium policy consultation meeting in Baker Lake, the GN announced that it supported uranium mining in Nunavut. Businessman David Simailak, the former mayor of Baker Lake, had become the MLA for Baker Lake as well as the minister of Economic Development. He read the new government policy in the legislative assembly. It was brief, and read in its entirety:

> The Government of Nunavut regards mining, including uranium mining, as an important source of jobs for Nunavummiut and for revenues to meet the needs of our growing population.
>
> The Government of Nunavut recognizes that uranium development places special responsibilities on government because of the nature of uranium and its byproducts, the history of its use for both peaceful and non-peaceful purposes, and its potential risks to human health and the environment.
>
> Uranium development must have the support of Nunavummiut, especially in communities close to development.
>
> The Government of Nunavut will support uranium development in Nunavut provided that the following conditions are satisfied:
>
> Health and safety standards are issued for workers.
>
> Environmental standards are assured.
>
> Nunavummiut must be the major beneficiaries of uranium development.
>
> The Government of Nunavut believes that nuclear power will be an important part of meeting global energy needs while limiting greenhouse gas emissions.

The Government of Nunavut believes that Canadian Law and
international agreements provide assurance that uranium mined in
Nunavut will be used for peaceful purposes.[19]

The GN had not conducted any sort of consultation or other public engagement with Baker Lake Inuit before adopting this position. This decision was
also made months before NTI had formally adopted its policy supporting
uranium mining.

Nunavut Planning Commission Uranium Workshop

The NPC held a uranium workshop in Baker Lake in early June 2007. This
was shortly after NTI held its consultation meeting in Baker Lake, and shortly
after the GN had announced its support for uranium mining. The meeting
was supposed to address Term 3.5 of the Keewatin Regional Land Use Plan,
which forbade uranium mining until the NPC, NIRB, and other advisory
boards created by the Nunavut Agreement were able to review issues related
to uranium mining. I was appointed to give short presentations by both the
BLCCC and Baker Lake HTO.

The NPC uranium workshop was, hands down, one of the lousiest meetings
I have ever attended. The NTI meeting in May had been ruined by long presentations by uranium industry supporters. The NPC workshop, in comparison, was
ruined by providing so little time for each organization and community member
to present. We have to speak slowly and pause frequently at public meetings in
Nunavut, to allow time for proper interpretation between English and Inuktitut.
But the NPC limited our presentations to only five minutes!

In my presentation for the BLCCC, I hardly had time to describe the group's
purpose and recent struggles with funding before I was cut off. My brother Hugh
Ikoe and I had taken a lot of time to carefully write a longer presentation. We
wanted to articulate our biggest concerns with uranium mining and explain
why we were upset with the way communities were being "consulted" about
it. We didn't get to address any of this, however, and Hugh didn't even have an
opportunity to speak.[20]

In my presentation for the Baker Lake HTO, I was likewise cut off before I could finish describing the HTO's mandate. The HTO board wanted me to explain the recommendation I had made at the NTI uranium policy consultation meeting: that uranium mining should not proceed until Baker Lake hunters and Elders have the opportunity to select lands for protection. However, I was unable to state our position, let alone explain it, in the time provided.[21]

The NPC released its report for the workshop in October 2007. The report included an NPC resolution declaring that its board believed that Term 3.5 of the land use plan had been satisfied by the Baker Lake event. In my opinion, the workshop had been too poorly organized to satisfy anything. I was not the only one who thought so. In May 2008, the chairs of the other co-management boards in Nunavut—NIRB, NWMB, and NWB—wrote an extraordinary joint letter to the NPC regarding its workshop report:

> We are in receipt of the email from your Executive Director, providing or directing, apparently on our behalf, the Uranium Workshop Report to Ministers and many other interested parties.
>
> We were surprised with the correspondence, because, among other things, we had not seen the report; as such, it did not come from us; nor did we fully participate at the workshop—other than giving a very brief overview presentation.[22]

However, the letter made no difference. The NPC did not reconsider Term 3.5 of the Keewatin Regional Land Use Plan. They were one step closer to lifting the moratorium on uranium mining in Nunavut.

NPC Lifts the Moratorium on Uranium Mining in Nunavut

By this point, the only thing keeping the moratorium in place was Term 3.6 of the land use plan, which required that uranium mining be supported by the people of the region. Many of us understood this to mean that there would be a public vote, similar to the 1990 plebiscite, where all residents could decide whether or not uranium mining should take place on our lands. However, the

NPC saw things differently. It decided that uranium mining could proceed if the KIA and the Hamlet Councils in the Kivalliq region supported it.

Beginning in 2006, the KIA and the Hamlet Councils quietly passed resolutions supporting an environmental assessment of AREVA's proposed Kiggavik mine.[23] In my opinion, these resolutions did not really show that our municipal councils, let alone the people of the region, had agreed to lift the moratorium on uranium mining. They did not clearly indicate support for the Kiggavik project. Most of them simply voiced support for a full environmental assessment of the proposal. The Hamlet councillors and KIA representatives who voted in favour of these resolutions may have done so because they believed an environmental assessment would be the best way to make a responsible decision, not because they supported uranium mining.

Further, it is not clear that they understood that these motions would be used as evidence of support from the "people of the region" to overturn Term 3.6 of the land use plan and lift the moratorium on uranium mining. For example, the motions from Baker Lake, Coral Harbour, and Repulse Bay all state that they "support [the NPC's] efforts to *clarify* [emphasis added] the conditions in the Keewatin Regional Land Use Plan respecting uranium development." The motions from Coral Harbour and Repulse Bay also indicate that they "support the regulatory principle which states 'any future proposal to mine uranium must be approved by the people of the region.'" These statements suggest that Hamlet councillors may have assumed that public support would be determined later, once further details of the project were available.

In 2008, AREVA submitted a formal proposal for the Kiggavik uranium mine to federal regulators. The KIA and Hamlet Council motions were appended to the proposal, which was forwarded to the NPC. In January 2009, the NPC released its conformity determination, which found that AREVA's proposal complied with the land use plan for the Kivalliq region. The determination stated that the requirement for support by the people of the region had been satisfied by the motions discussed above.

The moratorium on uranium mining in Nunavut—the result of countless hours of our hard work back in the late 1980s and 1990s—was lifted after a few biased meetings. I was deeply frustrated with our leadership. It made me so angry to see our people being manipulated in this way. This was also a very difficult time for my family, as my son-in-law, Philip Tagoona, had been diagnosed with cancer. Because I could not imagine defeating AREVA under these circumstances, I decided to take a break from activism. Before long, the BLCCC disbanded.

Around this time, AREVA held another one of its community engagement meetings in Baker Lake. Some important officials were in town that day, from the company's head office in France. I didn't want to go to the meeting because I felt absolutely defeated. It was a beautiful spring day. I went to get some fresh water from the river for my son-in-law because he wasn't able to do so on his own. I remember Phillip was so happy that I brought him fresh water. He asked if I was going to attend the meeting. When I said no, he really encouraged me to go.

I showed up to the meeting a half hour late. They were offering bottled water to everyone right when I arrived. I asked them, "You're handing out bottled water today. After you pollute our lakes and rivers, will you give us bottled water every day?" They didn't have much of an answer for me. I started to walk out just as they started giving out T-shirts. One of AREVA's representatives chased after me, insisting that I take a T-shirt. I tried saying no but he wouldn't let it go. Eventually I grabbed one and said, "Thanks, I'll use it to scrub my floors!"

Looking back, I'm glad I took my son-in-law's advice and gave those people a piece of my mind. However, at the time, I was ready to give up the fight for our land. I felt absolutely defeated. By this point I couldn't imagine that it would be possible to defeat such a huge and powerful nuclear corporation. Luckily, there were other strong and outspoken Inuit women who took up our cause and kept our movement alive.

Nunavummiut Makitagunarningit

Nunavummiut Makitagunarningit ("The People of Nunavut Can Rise Up") was formed in September 2009 by three young lawyers in Iqaluit. Two of the three, Sandra Inutiq and Siobhan Arnatsiaq-Murphy, were Inuit. It made me so happy to see young educated Inuit standing up for our rights. They invited Jack Hicks, who had moved to Iqaluit in 1994, to join the new group.

The group was often called "Makita" for short. Makita's goal was to stimulate debate about uranium mining and challenge the way that decisions about uranium mining were being made in our territory. They wanted to pressure the

Figure 15. Sandra Inutiq of Nunavummiut Makitagunarningit speaks during a public meeting about uranium mining in Iqaluit on 28 November 2009. Photo courtesy Chris Windeyer.

Government of Nunavut and our representative organizations to reconsider their pro-uranium positions. Most importantly, Makita wanted an inclusive and democratic approach to decisions about uranium mining, where all residents of Nunavut could meaningfully participate.

Sandra Inutiq became the chair and leading spokesperson for Makita. Her demeanour, her thoughtfulness, and her commitment to Inuit values made her a very compelling public figure. Makita soon reached out to Baker Lake residents who were concerned with uranium mining. I joined and became vice-chair of the group. My brother Hugh Ikoe and daughter Hilu Tagoona also became members of Makita, along with several other Baker Lake residents.

Our first major campaign was to petition the GN to hold a public inquiry into uranium mining in Nunavut. In a position statement that was published in *Nunatsiaq News* we argued that a public inquiry would be the most responsible and inclusive way to make the decision about whether or not uranium mining should be allowed in our territory. The entire position statement is included as an appendix at the end of this book. We gave several reasons why an environmental assessment by Nunavut's regulators should not be used to make the decision:

A public inquiry is more transparent, flexible and democratic than a regulatory process is.

A public inquiry is important because Nunavut's organizations [had] already shown themselves incapable of protecting the public interest in matters of uranium.

Our land claims institutions are not equipped to deal with the complex long-term and cumulative effects of a nascent uranium industry in the territory.[24]

One of our biggest concerns was that environmental assessments were designed to make decisions about single projects, not to address major political questions about the nuclear sector:

Why shouldn't we let Nunavut's regulators make the decision? For one, a determination on a single project cannot address the magnitude of the decision. It simply isn't appropriate or fair to "use" a regulatory process intended to review individual projects to make decisions about an entire sector of the mining industry.

When it comes to uranium, a public inquiry creates the accountability that a regulatory process (including an environmental assessment process) cannot.

We concluded by stating:

> So far our elected leaders have been asleep at the switch and the tough questions still wait to be answered. Unless a public inquiry is called, we will never know whether uranium mining is the right choice for Nunavut.
>
> The effects of uranium mining will last for thousands of years. Do we not owe it to ourselves, to our children and to our grandchildren to take enough time and care to make sure that we have it right?

Makita members heard from many people who, even if they didn't necessarily agree with our position, were pleased that we had initiated public debate and were challenging our elected political leaders. There was clearly a sense that too many discussions were being had, and decisions being made, behind closed doors.

Our petitions were tabled in the legislative assembly by Baker Lake MLA Moses Aupaluktuq and Quttiktuq (High Arctic) MLA Ron Elliott. Unfortunately, Nunavut premier Eva Aariak refused our request for a public inquiry. Instead, she announced that the GN would hold public forums on uranium mining and that it would, at some point, develop a uranium policy.

The GN hired a consulting firm called Golder Associates to conduct background research for the public forums. Golder Associates is a company that makes most of its money doing work for mining companies, including AREVA.[25] They were hardly an impartial choice. The fact that they had been hired to advise the GN on uranium mining was an indication of just how much influence non-Inuit, pro-mining officials had within our territory's government.

The GN held public forums in Iqaluit, Baker Lake, and Cambridge Bay in early 2011. Unsurprisingly, they were mostly dominated by supporters of the uranium industry. A journalist from *Nunatsiaq News* commented, "A panel composed mostly of mining industry spokesmen, regulators and a Nunavut Tunngavik employee said little to reassure the fears of those Nunavut residents who have already decided for themselves that uranium mining is bad for Nunavut."[26] However, Makita managed to make sure that at least some critical information about the nuclear industry was presented. Ramsey Hart from MiningWatch Canada—an Ottawa-based NGO with significant expertise on mining issues—attended the meetings at the request of Makita.

In her speech at the Iqaluit meeting, Sandra Inutiq raised some very important questions about the direction in which our territory was headed. She said,

> We must focus on how we as a people have come to this displaced place where we now are so desperate that even one of the most destructive mining practices in the world has now become appealing to us. We must address issues of decolonizing and ultimately work to believe in ourselves and the more sustainable choices we can make; that we can have an analytically thinking society that is not only reliant on damaging our lands in order to have an economy. We haven't even started the process of exploring innovative ways in which we as a people can become self-reliant. Let us not be in haste to only go this route before we destroy the very land which has sustained us for millennia.

Sandra also called for a territory-wide referendum on uranium mining in Nunavut: "The Nunavut Land Claims Agreement foresaw that Inuit would be included in the decision-making processes, Inuit would be included in important discussions. The Kivalliq Land Use Plan stated the people of Kivalliq would decide whether uranium mining should happen or not. Given the history of resistance to have uranium mining, this means a vote. Let's settle the matter once and for all and have a vote for Nunavut!"[27] Sandra's call for a public vote became a second key campaign for Makita. We published another position statement in *Nunatsiaq News*, explaining why a territory-wide referendum was needed.[28] In a letter to the editor, Sandra explained that "a democratic vote is the only way to know for sure how people feel—no corporate spin or backroom deals, just you, your conscience, and a ballot."[29]

Unfortunately, our call for a public vote was ignored. The GN released a "new" uranium mining policy in the summer of 2012. It was almost identical to the six-point policy it had issued in 2007. The process had been carefully engineered to obtain a desired result.

Makita had done other things to raise public awareness of the problems with the nuclear industry. For example, in November 2010 we held public meetings in Baker Lake and Iqaluit. We flew in guest speakers who had experience fighting the nuclear industry. My old friend Gordon Edwards, who had spoken at public meetings I helped organize in 1990, delivered a message that was as clear and powerful as ever. Dr. Isabelle Gingras, a psychiatrist from Sept-Îles, Québec, also made a big impact on the audience. Isabelle had made national news in December 2009 when she and more than twenty other doctors had threatened to quit their jobs and leave their communities unless the provincial government banned uranium mining—which the doctors called a threat to public health—near their towns. The speakers' presentations made it very clear that there was more to the story than what the government and the nuclear industry were telling us.

On the surface, it might look like Nunavummiut Makitagunarningit had been defeated on every front. However, our work made a big difference. We did a lot of important consciousness-raising work. We showed everyone that it was possible to stand up to the nuclear industry, its allies in the bureaucracies, and careerist politicians who were trying to shove uranium mining down our throats. Furthermore, we made it clear that we weren't going to let these decisions remain in the "back room" any longer. No matter what, decisions about uranium mining were going to be subjected to intense public scrutiny.

I feel the same way about my attempts to revive the Baker Lake Concerned Citizens Committee. We used the same tactics we had used twenty years earlier. Even though we often felt defeated, and sometimes people attacked us personally, we kept going. That alone is a major victory, as far as I am concerned.

In hindsight, while we may have lost a number of battles, we were positioning ourselves to win important victories in the future. I am very proud of the work that Makita did, and very thankful for the contributions Sandra Inutiq and others made to debates about uranium policy in Nunavut. If it wasn't for their hard work and dedication, I might have a uranium mine in my backyard today.

CHAPTER 7

Kiggavik Round 2: The AREVA Proposal

In the previous chapter, I discussed how the Government of Nunavut (GN) and Nunavut Tunngavik Incorporated (NTI) adopted policies supporting uranium mining. As a part of that story, I explained how AREVA Resources acquired and reactivated the Kiggavik project. In this chapter, I tell the story of how we defeated AREVA's proposal in an environmental review.

In 2008 AREVA Resources submitted a revised and expanded proposal for the Kiggavik mine to government regulators. AREVA's proposal included plans for four open pits and one underground mine, milling infrastructure, and the storage of radioactive tailings in perpetuity. The site would be serviced by an airstrip and an access road to Baker Lake. Personnel would be transported to the site by aircraft, while materials would be brought to Baker Lake by barge and then trucked to the mine site. The uranium concentrate (known as yellowcake) would be transported by air to northern Saskatchewan for further processing and enrichment.

From 2009 to 2015 the Nunavut Impact Review Board (NIRB) conducted an environmental assessment of AREVA's proposal for the Kiggavik uranium mine. During the review I worked as the manager of the Baker Lake Hunters and Trappers Organization (HTO). In my role as manager, part of my job was to keep the HTO board up to date on the review process and to prepare our submissions to NIRB. As part of his graduate research, Warren Bernauer volunteered with the HTO to help support our participation in the review of the Kiggavik proposal. Together with HTO board members and local hunters, we read over technical documents, drafted written submissions to the review board, and gave oral presentations at public meetings. The HTO board eventually resolved to oppose the mine, and it became our job to stop AREVA's proposal.

Nunavummiut Makitagunarningit (Makita), the environmental group I joined in 2010, also participated in NIRB's assessment of AREVA's proposal. Sandra Inutiq, Hilu Tagoona, Hugh Ikoe, and Eric Ukpatiku were spokespeople for Makita during the NIRB review. Jack Hicks provided important technical and organizational support. They wrote letters, presented at public meetings, and shared our concerns with the media. Makita consistently opposed the Kiggavik proposal and argued that a public inquiry and public vote, instead of an environmental assessment, should be used to make decisions about uranium in Nunavut.

The NIRB assessment progressed slowly. After a preliminary screening in 2009, a full environmental review began in 2010. NIRB issued a scope and guidelines for the review later that year. AREVA released a final Environmental Impact Statement in 2014. It concluded, rather unsurprisingly, that the project would not have any significant negative effects on Nunavut's environment. Neither the HTO nor Makita accepted this conclusion. In written submissions and public hearings, both groups urged NIRB to reject AREVA's proposal.

NIRB issued its final report in May 2015. It recommended that AREVA's proposal for the Kiggavik project should not be approved. The following year the federal government announced that it accepted NIRB's recommendation and closed the file on the Kiggavik proposal. For a second time in my life, my community took on the nuclear industry and won.

However, our victory certainly did not come easily. As I explained in Chapter 6, NTI and the GN issued policies supporting uranium mining in 2007. Both NTI and the GN, along with the Kivalliq Inuit Association (KIA), were supportive of the Kiggavik proposal throughout the NIRB review. AREVA was also a much more aggressive and dangerous adversary than Urangesellschaft had been. Moreover, the NIRB process was not very accommodating because it was highly technical and difficult to participate in. Sometimes I still can't believe we won under these conditions.

Our experiences show that an NIRB review was not a very good way to decide whether we should allow uranium mining in Nunavut. There were many systematic barriers to Inuit participation. Our biggest concerns with uranium mining in Nunavut—contamination, induced development, and moral concerns with the nuclear industry—were not satisfactorily addressed by the review. The final result was also not a total victory. While AREVA's proposal was not approved at this time, both NIRB and the federal government left the door open for the proposal to be resubmitted sometime in the future. If, or rather when, the question of uranium mining in Nunavut comes back, I hope Nunavummiut (the people of Nunavut) will deal with it in a more democratic and critical way.

Even so, our experiences also show that regular Inuit were able to use this system to win an important strategic victory. We organized our opposition through community organizations like HTOs and grassroots citizens' groups that are independent from the GN and corporate Inuit organizations like NTI and KIA. We worked together with people from all across the world to develop technical comments and other interventions that led to AREVA's proposal being rejected, at least for the time being. I hope our experiences might help others who are trying to use environmental assessments to protect Indigenous peoples' rights.

Screening

The first step in a Nunavut Impact Review Board assessment is a preliminary screening. A screening determines whether or not a proposed project requires a full environmental review. NIRB circulates the project proposal to government departments, Indigenous organizations, and other interested parties. The proposal is also made available to the public through NIRB's online public registry. All parties are invited to submit comments on the proposal. After receiving written comments, NIRB releases a screening report that recommends whether or not the project requires a full environmental review.

The NIRB screening of AREVA's proposal began in early 2009, before Makita was formed. At the time, I was working as the Secretary Manager for the Baker Lake HTO. The HTO offered to help community members submit written comments, as this would give us an idea of how the public felt about the proposal. We held a public meeting one evening and invited anyone who was interested to come fill out a comment card. I worked with Thomas Elytook, an HTO board member, to scan their comments, translate them into English if necessary, and submit them to NIRB via email.

Even though our community had become divided on the question of uranium mining, many people still opposed it passionately. The written comments we sent to NIRB made this very clear.[1] Eighty-four residents of Baker Lake provided comments. Forty-four, the majority, explicitly opposed the Kiggavik project. Thirty-one residents supported the proposal, and nine were undecided.

The comments opposing AREVA's proposal showed that some Baker Lake residents remained dead set against uranium mining. Timothy Tunguaq, a hunter who grew up on the land near the Kiggavik site, wrote, "I believe that uranium mining can never be 100 percent safe and I don't want uranium mining close to my community." His wife, Joan Tunguaq, wrote, "Fifteen years ago we said 'no' to uranium mining. We still say 'no.'"

As usual, the women in my family were strong spokespeople for protecting our land. My mother, Lucy Qaunnaq, wrote, "Uranium mining and all the revenues is not worth our cultural and traditional life—we have too much to lose." My sister, Susan Toolooktook, wrote, "Go look for uranium somewhere else!" My daughter, Hilu Tagoona, wrote, "Uranium mining will hurt Inuit in so many ways. The community is downwind and downstream. The exploration phase is already driving away the caribou herds and further development will make this worse. The mine will do irreversible damage to our land, air, water, and animals, which will in turn affect our health. The community is being bombarded with exploration and development and NIRB is supposed to look out for the interests of the Inuit of Nunavut. I recommend that NIRB deny development of the AREVA proposal in the Baker Lake area. Uranium mining is *not* safe."

As part of my attempts to revive the Baker Lake Concerned Citizens Committee (BLCCC), I submitted written comments on the committee's behalf. I outlined all the reasons why Baker Lake residents opposed uranium mining in the 1990s, and explained that these were still valid and important concerns today. These reasons included:

Our belief that once one uranium mine is opened in the Kivalliq it will be politically impossible to stop the development of future uranium mines in the region.

Our belief that all these future uranium mines, plus gold mines and possibly others as well, will have a very serious negative impact on the Beverly and Qamanirjuaq caribou herds upon which we depend as an essential food source—and upon which our culture as Caribou

Inuit is based. They will impact on human health, on traditional activities, on our environmentally friendly economic alternatives for the future, on community infrastructure, and on social issues in the communities. They will also have significant transboundary impacts on other Aboriginal peoples living in the Northwest Territories, Saskatchewan and Manitoba.

Our belief that there are very serious moral issues associated with uranium mining, nuclear power, nuclear weapons, and the storage of radioactive waste for countless generations to come.

The BLCCC's comments included our perspective on NTI's and KIA's support for uranium mining:

> We are well aware that Nunavut Tunngavik Inc. and the Kivalliq Inuit Association have already given their approval in principle to uranium mining in our region. They paid no attention to our concerns, and we feel that their decisions were made on the basis of one-sided information. We want you to know that we do not feel that we have been adequately consulting during the development of these positions, and that these organizations do not speak for us in this regard. The fact that several political organizations have already made their minds up does not mean that the people of the region have.

We also explained our position that the process the Nunavut Planning Commission had used to lift the moratorium on uranium mining was illegitimate:

> We will also be asking the Minister of Indian and Northern Affairs to investigate the process by which the Nunavut Planning Commission claims to have met its responsibility under Term 3.6 of the Keewatin Land Use Plan—which states that "Any future proposal to mine uranium must be approved by the people of the region"—before granting land use plan conformity for the project. As you may be aware, on March 26, 1990 the people of Baker Lake voted in a

plebiscite to oppose the proposed Kiggavik mine by a margin of 90.2 percent to 9.8 percent. Since when does a motion passed by a Hamlet Council trump the overwhelming results of a democratic public vote?

These comments were one of my last actions with the BLCCC. As I mentioned in Chapter 6, the group disbanded later that year.

Unfortunately, submissions from Inuit representative organizations did not reflect the fact that many residents of Baker Lake (perhaps the majority) continued to oppose uranium mining. NTI and KIA sent a joint submission that reaffirmed their conditional support for uranium mining and recommended a full review of AREVA's proposal. The GN's submission likewise expressed support for uranium mining in principle and recommended a full review of the proposed Kiggavik mine.

NIRB released its screening report in March 2009, recommending the project undergo a full environmental review. It took the federal government almost an entire year to respond. In February 2010 Chuck Strahl, the Conservative minister of Aboriginal Affairs and Northern Development, directed NIRB to conduct a full environmental review of AREVA's proposal.

Scope and Guidelines

The next step in an NIRB assessment is to determine the scope of the review. Based on input from various parties—including government departments, Indigenous organizations, and members of the public—NIRB issues a "scoping list." This document lists all of the issues that NIRB will consider during the review.

After the scope has been determined, NIRB develops guidelines to help the mining company write its Environmental Impact Statement (EIS). As I discussed in previous chapters, the EIS is a document prepared by the mining company that studies the potential environmental impacts of the proposed mine and explains how the company will mitigate the negative impacts. The guidelines provide a framework and tell the company what needs to be included in their EIS.

Taking part in such a process might sound boring, and it was. The documents were full of technical jargon and about as unexciting as you can imagine.

However, the development of the scope and guidelines is one of the most important stages of the review. If local residents' concerns were left out of these documents, they would be ignored later on when the final decisions were being made.

We found it very difficult to participate in the development of the scope and guidelines. A major problem was a lack of translation. The draft guidelines were only available in English. Both Makita[2] and the Baker Lake HTO[3] requested that NIRB suspend the review until these important documents could be translated. Unfortunately, our requests were denied. Even though we had a land claim agreement, co-management boards, and our own territory and government—all created with the goal of allowing Inuit to participate in decisions—the review went ahead without the full participation of unilingual Elders.

Several of our biggest concerns were left out of the final scope and guidelines. At NIRB's public meetings in April 2010, Kivalliq residents asked moral and political questions about the different possible end uses of uranium—for example, to make nuclear weapons, to treat cancer, or to help stop climate change. People also discussed the problem of induced development—if we allowed AREVA to move forward with the Kiggavik mine, many more uranium mines would inevitably follow.[4] Makita twice recommended that NIRB include these issues in the scope and guidelines.[5]

However, when NIRB issued the final scope and guidelines in May 2011, there was no mention of the end uses of uranium, or the many mines that would likely follow Kiggavik.[6] Two of our biggest concerns were "off the table" for the remainder of the review, as far as NIRB was concerned.

Draft Environmental Impact Statement

After NIRB issued the final guidelines in 2011, AREVA began to develop its Environmental Impact Statement. AREVA released a draft EIS in 2012. It claimed that the Kiggavik mine would not have any significant negative impacts on the Arctic environment, and that it would provide net benefits for Nunavut. For the next two years, NIRB solicited written comments and held public meetings on AREVA's draft EIS.

As part of developing its EIS, AREVA hired Golder Associates to conduct an Inuit Qaujimajatuqangit (Inuit Knowledge) study about the area near the proposed Kiggavik project. I was highly suspicious of this research from the get-go. The mining industry has no business going around "collecting" Inuit Qaujimajatuqangit. Allowing them to do this research gave them power over us later in the process—if we complained that the mine was going to impact caribou hunting, they could say "Well, that's not what the Elders we interviewed said." Looking back, the HTO never should have agreed to let AREVA hire consultants to do this research. If anything, we should have demanded that AREVA provide us the funding to do the research ourselves.

When I turned sixty, I joined our local Elders' committee. AREVA invited members of the committee to a dinner at the Nunamiut Lodge—a nice hotel and restaurant in Baker Lake. AREVA's consultants presented their Inuit Qaujimajatuqangit research to us over dinner. They were hoping we would approve or support their report.

I asked the consultants which Elders they had interviewed, but they wouldn't tell me. Apparently, there were privacy concerns. This was a big problem for me. There are a lot of really poor quality Inuit Qaujimajatuqangit reports out there because the researchers didn't interview the right people. Not everyone in Baker Lake has expertise in the Kiggavik area. For all I know, they might have just interviewed random people on the street with no relevant knowledge or expertise. I asked the rest of the Elders in the room if they had been interviewed. Almost none of them put their hands up. I could tell AREVA's staff and consultants were really unhappy with me.

Meetings, Meetings, and More Meetings

For the next two years, from 2012 to 2014, NIRB held many public meetings and accepted written comments. A big technical meeting and pre-hearing conference took place in the spring of 2013. Along the way, AREVA also held many community engagement meetings where they asked Baker Lake residents what we thought about their proposed mine. On top of this, we continued to be invaded by consultants and university researchers who wanted to ask us about our perspectives on mining.

On the surface, it appeared as if we were being consulted very well. However, the truth of the matter is that these meetings were not an effective way for my community to participate in decisions about uranium mining. There were several barriers that prevented us from meaningfully participating.

The timing of important meetings was a major barrier to our participation. For example, NIRB held public information sessions in each community in the Kivalliq region in May 2012. Unsurprisingly, few Elders and active hunters showed up for the meeting in Baker Lake. As I explained in Chapter 6, late May is one of the worst times to host a meeting in Nunavut and expect a serious turnout. Spring is a busy time for people who continue to live a traditional lifestyle. It is still easy to travel on the lake ice, fishing is excellent, and caribou are starting to migrate through our hunting grounds. Best of all, there are no bugs! We explained very clearly to the NIRB staff-person that their meeting timelines conflicted with our traditional seasonal activities.[7]

However, despite our complaints, NIRB decided to schedule technical meetings and a pre-hearing conference for May 2013. These were important meetings that determined how the final hearings would be conducted, so community participation was especially important. Makita,[8] the North Slave Métis Alliance,[9] and the BQCMB[10] wrote to NIRB and requested that the meetings be rescheduled to avoid conflicts with traditional activities. However, despite all of our protests, the NIRB technical meeting and pre-hearing conference went ahead in late May and early June. As you might expect, it was difficult to find knowledgeable hunters and Elders to work with us during these meetings. They were too busy going out on the land to feed their families.

A second barrier to our participation had to do with the overwhelming number of meetings that were being held in Baker Lake. Our community suffered from something environmental assessment experts call "consultation fatigue." In plain language, we were being consulted to death! Many of us, myself included, were sick of going to meetings, having the same discussions over and over, and not seeing any results. Up until NIRB released its final report, there was no evidence that our participation was having any impact on the decision-making process. Most meetings were focused on explaining plans that had already been set in motion, rather than genuinely allowing us to participate in decisions. When we raised concerns, we were given answers that had been prepared well in advance. It seemed like these meetings were essentially opportunities for us to "blow off steam" and get our frustrations off our chests. The fact that NIRB failed to translate key documents into Inuktitut and ignored our concerns about the timing of important meetings reinforced the feeling that our participation was having no measurable impact on the process. It's therefore not surprising that many Baker Lake residents eventually gave up and stopped attending public meetings, as it seemed like a huge waste of time.

A third barrier to our participation in the NIRB review was *ilirahungniq*, or intimidation. There are several reasons why some Inuit felt too intimidated to speak out at public meetings. The "expert" nature of the environmental review was a source of intimidation for many people. The process is complicated, and it's difficult to understand how to influence it. It is also highly technical, and deals with concepts that are difficult (sometimes impossible) to translate into Inuktitut. The key documents are also very long (AREVA's EIS was over ten thousand pages!) and only available in English. At the end of the day, it is difficult to participate if you don't have a university education. This left most Inuit at a huge disadvantage.

In addition, some people were worried that speaking out would have repercussions for their employment prospects. AREVA's proposal had the support of several Baker Lake business owners who stood to benefit financially from the mine. Their employees would have had legitimate reasons to avoid publicly going against their employers. Other people may have worried that they, or their family members, might not be able to obtain employment in the future. If the mine were to go ahead, AREVA might be hesitant to hire someone whose family members vocally opposed Kiggavik.

Another challenge we faced was the misinformation we received from government regulators and AREVA. At one public meeting, a community member asked if there was any way to prevent uranium mined in Nunavut from ending up in nuclear weapons in countries like India. A representative from the Canadian Nuclear Safety Commission (CNSC) replied that there was nothing to worry about because India is a signatory to the Nuclear Non-Proliferation Treaty (NNPT). Jack Hicks, who was representing Makita at the meeting, stood up and challenged her. India is *not* a signatory to the NNPT, and it was shocking that a CNSC employee would not know that. Later in that same meeting, an AREVA employee said that uranium from Kiggavik was necessary to ensure a continued supply of radioactive isotopes for treating cancer. Again Jack interjected, stating that what the employee had said was simply not accurate. Red-faced, Barry McCullum took the microphone and acknowledged that Jack was right. It was a clear example of how representatives of both the nuclear industry and federal regulators make misleading statements to try to convince the public to support uranium mining.

AREVA's Final Environmental Impact Statement

AREVA submitted its final Environmental Impact Statement in the fall of 2014. It wasn't all that different from the original draft EIS that AREVA had released in 2012. It claimed that the Kiggavik mine would not have any significant negative effects on our environment.

There was, however, one key difference: there was no clear timeline identified for the project. The original 2008 proposal said that AREVA intended to begin construction of the Kiggavik mine in 2012. The draft EIS pushed that date back to 2017. The final EIS, however, did not contain an estimated start date for the project. It acknowledged that the price of uranium was too low for the project to be profitable, and that AREVA would begin construction on the project if and when markets improved.[11]

When AREVA submitted its original Kiggavik proposal in 2008, the world price for uranium was high enough that the mine would have been profitable. But by the time AREVA released its final EIS, the world price for uranium had fallen to the point that Kiggavik would not have been profitable. At least in the short to medium term, the project no longer made economic sense. AREVA therefore had to make a strategic decision. It had three options:

It could withdraw the proposal and terminate the review process.

It could forecast that the price of uranium would rise, and estimate a start date on that basis, but opponents like us could have noted that many industry analysts believe that the price of uranium will remain low for the foreseeable future. It just wouldn't have been credible.

It could acknowledge that the proposal wasn't currently economically viable but express the belief that it will be at an unspecified time in the future—and proceed with the review process without providing an estimated start date.

AREVA chose the third option.

Kivalliq Hunters and Trappers Organizations Oppose Kiggavik

In January 2015 the Baker Lake HTO resolved to oppose the Kiggavik project.[12] The board gave two main reasons for its opposition. First, the fact that AREVA's proposal did not have clear timelines made it impossible to accurately predict how the Kiggavik mine would affect our environment and well-being. The board did not agree with conducting environmental reviews of projects without start dates in the reasonably foreseeable future—it was a waste of our time and resources, and left our community at a disadvantage.

The HTO's second major concern had to do with induced development. One of our biggest concerns with Kiggavik was that it would open the door for many more uranium mines in our hunting grounds. The HTO board decided it would only consider supporting Kiggavik if Inuit representative organizations, the government, and the mining industry worked together to create new protected areas that banned mining in caribou calving grounds and post-calving grounds. The HTO believed that a protected area strategy could help control the impacts of the many mines that were likely to follow in Kiggavik's footsteps. However, as I explain in Chapter 8, our calls to fully protect caribou calving grounds were falling on deaf ears.

We realized that the Baker Lake HTO had an uphill battle on our hands. AREVA was one of the biggest uranium mining companies in the world. What's more, it had the support of the Government of Nunavut and Nunavut Tunngavik Incorporated. If we were going to succeed, we were going to need allies.

The HTO used the Kivalliq Wildlife Board (KWB) to organize a regional alliance against Kiggavik. The KWB is a regional board created by the Nunavut Agreement. The chairs of the seven HTOs in the Kivalliq region sit on KWB's board. It is responsible for managing wildlife on a regional level. It can also be a very important organizing space to help Kivalliq HTOs coordinate their efforts to fight for Inuit hunting rights.

On February 23, 2015, the KWB passed a motion opposing AREVA's proposal. The KWB's position was based on the same concerns the Baker Lake HTO had raised about the lack of a project start date and induced development in caribou habitat. The motion resolved that "the Kivalliq Wildlife Board does not agree with approving the Kiggavik proposal at this time. The Kivalliq Wildlife Board is not necessarily opposed to Kiggavik, but it is firmly opposed to approving Kiggavik until: 1) A land use plan or government legislation bans mining and exploration in caribou calving and post-calving grounds, 2) AREVA further develops the Kiggavik proposal with firm and realistic project timelines, including a project start date."[13] Passing this motion might not seem like much, but it was politically very important. It allowed hunters from across the Kivalliq region to work together to fight AREVA's proposal at the upcoming final hearings.

Final Hearings Part 1: Technical Hearings

Public hearings were held in March 2015 in Baker Lake. The first week of the hearings were technical meetings that focused on presentations by AREVA and registered intervenors. The room was set up with long tables in a big square. One side was the NIRB board, to their left was AREVA's large technical team. The other two sides of the square were filled with NIRB staff and intervenors. Baker Lake residents were left sitting in an audience to observe. The way the room was set up—with most Inuit sitting in the crowd as passive observers, staring at the intervenors' backs—was not a good way to start things off.

NIRB's schedule had the first two days filled with presentations by AREVA. This was an opportunity for the company to try to convince Baker Lake residents and the NIRB board to support their proposed mine. The next four days were set aside for presentations by registered intervenors, mostly government departments and Inuit representative organizations. Based on previous meetings, I knew that these groups would not pose any serious challenges to AREVA's proposal. As I explained in Chapter 6, meetings that begin with long technical presentations can be alienating, especially for unilingual Elders. According to the schedule for this hearing, we would have to listen to almost a whole week of technical presentations before we could speak up.

The Baker Lake HTO decided to disrupt this schedule by tabling a motion at the very beginning of the meetings. The motion argued that the hearings should be cancelled because NIRB should not be reviewing proposed mines that do not have clear timelines and start dates. This caught a lot of people off guard and left them scrambling to figure out how to respond. The hearings were delayed by a whole afternoon while the different intervenor groups discussed our motion with their lawyers.

NIRB did not adopt the HTO's motion. However, the motion still changed the dynamics of the meeting. Instead of giving AREVA the platform first, the HTO managed to begin the meeting with a critical discussion. The motion made sure that the HTO's position and concerns (*not* AREVA's) were front and centre from the outset. The motion also helped set the tone for the rest of the meeting because it made space to challenge AREVA.

For the next two days, we listened to AREVA's presentations. As usual, they promised us that their big team of experts and their complicated technical studies—that they knew most members of the public couldn't fully understand—would make sure that the Kiggavik project would be safe.

After AREVA's presentations wrapped up, the intervenor presentations began. KIA, NTI, the GN, federal government departments, and the Hamlet of Baker Lake all took a similar approach. They did not explicitly support or oppose the project. They usually claimed they were "neutral" if we pressed them on the issue. Their presentations all focused on finding ways to reduce the negative impacts of AREVA's project, and increase the benefits that stayed in our region. None of them said anything to suggest that AREVA's proposal should not be approved.

Baker Lake HTO Chair Richard Aksawnee and Warren Bernauer explained the HTO's position opposing Kiggavik and its biggest concerns with AREVA's proposal. David Toolooktook and Timothy Tunguaq—two hunters who were born and grew up on the land close to the Kiggavik site—also presented as part of the HTO's delegation. They gave overviews of the history of Inuit land use in the area. Timothy and David also explained their personal connections to the land, to help people understand what was at stake for their families.

My daughter, Hilu Tagoona, presented for Makita. I was *so* proud to see her speak truth to power and stand up for our people's rights. Hilu explained that Makita shared the HTO's concerns with induced development and the lack of a project start date. She also explained that Makita's members were morally opposed to uranium mining because of its relationship with nuclear weapons and nuclear waste.

Paula Kigjugalik Hughson, an Inuk woman from Baker Lake, also presented. Paula had registered as an individual with intervenor status (in other words, she was not affiliated with any organization). Her mother, Betty Hughson, grew up on the land near the proposed mine site. Several years earlier, Paula had written a master's thesis about Inuit place names near the Thelon River. Paula's presentation raised serious concerns with the way decisions were being made about uranium mining in Nunavut. She was especially concerned with the lack of democratic participation when NTI and the NPC lifted the moratorium on uranium mining in Nunavut. Paula explained that she had been working with a Hamlet councillor named Silas Arngna'naaq to petition the GN to hold a public vote on the Kiggavik question. Unfortunately, their original petition had not gone ahead due to technical errors, and they were in the process of exploring other options for a community vote.

Two Dene groups also opposed the Kiggavik mine at the final hearings. Vice-Chief Joseph Tsannie explained that the Athabasca Denesuline were opposed to Kiggavik because of AREVA's plans to fly yellowcake from the Kiggavik mine site to northern Saskatchewan for processing. Elder August Enzoe and his daughter Terri Enzoe stated that the Lutsel K'e Dene First Nation was entirely opposed uranium mining anywhere within the Thelon River's watershed.

There was very little time or opportunity for community members to participate in this part of the hearing. Audience questions were permitted, but opinions were not. If we started to state an opinion on the project, the chair would interrupt and tell us to stick to questions.

Final Hearings Part 2: Community Round Table

After the intervenor presentations concluded, the hearings switched to a different format: the community round table. For this stage of the hearings, the intervenors sat in the audience. Taking their place at the table were representatives from each of the seven communities in the Kivalliq region. Eva Elytook and I sat as the representatives for Baker Lake.

In a lot of ways, the community round table was a repeat of the technical meetings. AREVA and registered intervenors repeated their presentations, only this time the community representatives sat around the table and asked questions (instead of intervenors). Again, we were only allowed to ask questions to the groups that had presented, and again the chair would cut us off if we started to express our opinions about the project. She reminded us that there was time scheduled for community comments at the end of the hearings.

However, even with these restrictions, some of us managed to slip in some critical comments. For example, Rebecca Kudloo said, "If this project is to be approved, how are we going to be assured that the Indigenous people, Inuit and our Dene friends, have had prior and informed consent? I have the same feelings as Paula Kigjugalik Hughson, who spoke yesterday. How did it get this far without us being consulted by our Hamlet Council and our Inuit organizations? Our Hamlet Council stated yesterday they are divided on the issue. If they had consulted the people of Qamani'tuaq [Baker Lake], whom they represent, it would have been clear as night and day as to what the people want."[14] I made an intervention after NTI's presentation. I explained how NTI was in a conflict of interest on questions related to uranium mining. I asked about the details of the exploration agreements NTI had signed with uranium companies, including one project operated by Forum Uranium located right next to Kiggavik.[15]

I also asked why NTI owned shares in a uranium exploration company called Kivalliq Energy. NTI representatives responded that the organization had recently sold its shares in Kivalliq Energy because of concerns from the public. However, this didn't really change NTI's conflicted position. If the Kiggavik mine were to be approved, KIA and NTI would likely profit handsomely from their exploration agreements with Forum Uranium.[16]

When the intervenor presentations were over, they *finally* made time for community members to express their comments. A few Baker Lake residents said they supported the project, including some AREVA employees and business owners that stood to benefit from the Kiggavik project. However, the majority of the people who spoke were clearly opposed to the project. Some Elders who had previously supported AREVA came out against the Kiggavik proposal. For example, John Nukik (my older brother), told NIRB, "When AREVA first started coming here, I was on the socio-economic committee, and I think I contributed in making suggestions. And it seems as though the company was getting more and more . . . into wanting to see their exploration camp open into a mine, and then I stopped going to the . . . committee meetings because I started to disagree with some of the things that they wanted to do . . . I think that's what most people see . . . I think it's very dangerous as to what they want to do."[17] Winnie Owingjayak said, "I used to be in favour of seeing them open, but now, today . . . I'm not in favour of seeing mining happen."[18]

However, it wasn't just Elders who spoke out—people of all ages came out against the Kiggavik project. For example, the Grade 11 social science class from Jonah Amitnaaq High School gave a presentation. Tanisha Noah and Michael Peryouar explained that their class saw both positive and negative aspects to the proposed mine. They asked very well-informed and thoughtful questions. Tanisha explained that her classmates had decided the mine was not in their best interests: "As a class we agreed that this project is good for the mine but not for the people because we want to protect our land, culture, and lifestyle."[19]

After audience comments wrapped up it was time for closing comments from the community representatives. We were told to prepare a recommendation for the review board. Each community was supposed to have one "vote" on whether or not the project should be approved.

Eva Elytook and I were so nervous as we sat there, waiting for each community representative to answer. Coral Harbour, Chesterfield Inlet, Naujaat, Rankin Inlet, and Whale Cove all recommended the project should not be approved at this time. Arviat gave a split recommendation: half of the community representatives supported the mine, but the other half opposed it.

I gave the final comments for Baker Lake. I began by explaining that our concerns were serious and quite real, as we have been negatively affected by mineral exploration since the 1970s. I also explained that it was very difficult for Baker Lake community representatives to make a recommendation because the Hamlet Council had not held a public vote or anything similar to gauge public support. However, the most recent discussions in the community—call-in shows on community radio, debates on community social media groups, and public comments at the NIRB hearings—showed mostly opposition to AREVA's proposed mine. Therefore, our recommendation was that the mine should not go ahead.[20]

After I presented our answer, Silas Arngna'naaq requested that NIRB allow the Hamlet of Baker Lake to hold a plebiscite before making a recommendation about Kiggavik.[21] The following day, the Baker Lake Hamlet Council tabled a motion requesting that NIRB keep its record open on the Kiggavik file until the Hamlet is able to hold a local plebiscite. However, the NIRB board rejected the motion.[22] As a result, my recommendation that AREVA's project should not proceed was Baker Lake's final closing statement at the community round table.

Final Hearings Part 3: Closing Comments from the Proponent and Intervenors

After the community round table wrapped up, it was time for intervenor groups to give their closing comments. NTI, KIA, the GN, and federal government departments all said AREVA had addressed all major issues. Any outstanding issues or disagreements were submitted as simple recommended terms and conditions for AREVA's project certificate. In other words, Nunavut's Inuit organizations, the GN, and the federal government would have been happy to see AREVA's proposal approved.

Baker Lake HTO Chair Richard Aksawnee read a "declaration of cooperation" signed by representatives of the Baker Lake HTO and the Lutsel K'e Dene First Nation, promising to work together to stop Kiggavik. The declaration concluded as follows: "We affirm that we will work together to stop this proposal, as we do not agree with the proposal as it is currently presented. We commit to standing together to protect the caribou herds that both of our communities depend upon for our traditional culture and economic well-being. We have to protect the environment for the future of our people."[23]

NIRB Report and Minister Decision

It felt like an eternity, waiting for NIRB to release its report and recommendation. The decision finally came out in late May 2015. On the afternoon the announcement was expected, my daughter Hilu was so stressed out that she went to play basketball. Jack Hicks was the first to see the email from NIRB announcing their recommendation that the project should not be approved. He immediately texted Hilu. Hilu burst into tears of joy in the middle of her game. She then phoned me, overwhelmed by emotion, to tell me the news. At first, I didn't believe her. I honestly expected we would lose, given that the Inuit representative organizations, the GN, and federal government all supported the project. She was so excited; I was sure she was mistaken or had misread something. However, once I read the announcement for myself, I realized that it was true. We had won!

Because we were so certain we would lose, Makita had drafted a media release saying that we were "profoundly disappointed" by NIRB's recommendation and that "Future generations of Inuit will view this decision as a mistake." We quickly changed it to say "Makita is overjoyed by the NIRB's decision" and "Future generations of Inuit will view this decision as responsible and just."

NIRB's recommendation was based on the argument—made by the Baker Lake HTO and others—that there was an unacceptable level of uncertainty in AREVA's impact predictions. As stated in their report, "The NIRB found that the absence of a definite project start date for the Project has compounded the uncertainties in the assessment of project effects . . . arising from the absence of baseline information. These uncertainties are such that, in the view of the Board, the onus of proof has not been met, and the Project should not proceed at this time."[24] However, the report left the door open for AREVA to resubmit its proposal later. It stated that NIRB did not "intend that this project not proceed at any time." It recommended the proposal be "resubmitted for consideration at such future time when increased certainty regarding the project start date can be provided."[25]

NIRB's recommendation was an important victory in the fight against Kiggavik. However, the final decision on the matter was really up to the federal government. At the time, Stephen Harper's Conservative Party was still in power. We were *very* concerned that he might not accept NIRB's recommendation because his government was notorious for its unwavering support for resource extraction, including in the Arctic.[26]

Shortly after NIRB's report came out, AREVA wrote to Bernard Valcourt, the minister of Aboriginal Affairs and Northern Development at the time, asking him to not accept NIRB's recommendation. In response we organized a letter-writing campaign. Valcourt received letters from several groups urging him to accept the NIRB recommendation and reject AREVA's proposal. These groups included the Baker Lake HTO, the Chesterfield Inlet HTO, the Kivalliq Wildlife Board, Makita, MiningWatch Canada, and the Beverly and Qamanirjuaq Caribou Management Board. Not surprisingly, neither the GN nor our Inuit organizations participated in our letter-writing campaign.

Valcourt had not responded to the NIRB recommendation, or any of the letters, before the 2015 federal election, which resulted in a Liberal government and the loss of Valcourt's cabinet position. Carolyn Bennett, the new minister of Indigenous Affairs and Northern Development, issued a decision in the summer of 2016. Bennett accepted NIRB's recommendation and rejected AREVA's proposal. AREVA responded with a letter to Minister Bennett, indicating that the company was "immensely disappointed" with the decision, as AREVA and its partners had spent over $60 million developing the Kiggavik proposal and participating in the review process. That summer, AREVA ceased exploration work at the Kiggavik site, and began transitioning the project to care and maintenance.

Next Time . . .

The NIRB review of AREVA's Kiggavik proposal shows just how much regular Inuit can accomplish when we work together and stand our ground. A small grassroots group of Indigenous people, with little funding and the help of a handful of volunteers, was able to stop one of the biggest nuclear companies in the world right in its tracks. This is certainly a very big accomplishment. Everyone involved in the campaign to stop AREVA—Inuit and non-Inuit alike—should feel proud of what was achieved by working together.

However, it's important that we don't look back on these experiences through rose-coloured glasses. As Makita has argued from day one, a NIRB review was not a good way to decide whether or not uranium mining should proceed in Nunavut. Some of our biggest concerns were left out of the scope of the review. Important documents were not translated into Inuktitut. Key meetings were held at times of the year when our community is busy hunting and fishing. The entire NIRB process was dominated by technical experts, leaving most Inuit at a big disadvantage.

I am not the only one who feels this way. In their presentation at the final hearings, the Grade 11 social science class from the local high school argued that the NIRB review was intimidating and prevented many people from speaking out. They said, "We are very concerned about the NIRB process because this setup is not welcoming to the average person. We think people in the community are not attending [meetings] because the language is difficult and hard to understand. Some don't care but many do not want the mine to happen. . . . Many are afraid of the process and don't think the board will listen to them . . . that our opinion doesn't matter and the decision has already been made."[27] Another Inuk from Baker Lake told a researcher that Inuit were excluded from important stages of the NIRB review because of the focus on technical expertise: "We need to be educated to understand the whole process, and the people at the hearing, the first round of intervenors, there were no Inuit there, there were experts at the table and I said that maybe once we are ready and we have Inuit at all those levels of expertise then it's time to make a decision about that."[28] An Elder told another researcher that he opposed uranium mining, but the focus on technical experts made it difficult for him to talk back and challenge the mining industry:

They keep telling you these good stories of products in your own home . . . as an example, TV gives off radiation or is made from some sort of radioactive material . . . so is your microwave . . . so is the clock . . . they give out radiation all over the place. They say, if that's safe . . . why shouldn't our products be safe? . . . [that] is the analogy they're using.

Obviously, it is hard to answer back when you are told that your TV produces radioactivity . . . As a real Inuk, you don't really know what else to say. But still, there are questions. It gets to the point where there may be issues that might come up, but given that type of answer it is difficult to try and talk back.[29]

Many of us clearly felt left out of the process, even though we won in the end.

My point is not to simply criticize the Nunavut Impact Review Board. I am sure its board members and staff did the best they could, given the circumstances. At the end of the day, I am happy that we have co-management boards with Inuit board members. If AREVA's proposal had been reviewed by a panel of *qablunaat* from southern Canada, the outcome might have been very different. But that doesn't change the fact that a single, limited, and project-specific environmental assessment was not a good way to make a decision about uranium mining—a decision that could open up an entire region to development by the nuclear industry.

If the question of uranium mining comes up again, I hope Nunavummiut will take a more democratic and critical approach. Because we have our own territory, we should be using our autonomy to make decisions that uphold our values and traditions. This means Elders must be meaningfully included. We need to make sure *all* Nunavummiut can access critical information about uranium mining. We also need to make spaces where our people feel comfortable speaking out and talking back. Finally, we need to make sure everyone can actually participate in these decisions. We don't just want to share our concerns with experts. We want to make our own decisions about our future.

A public plebiscite or territorial referendum would be a good way to make sure everyone has an opportunity to participate. However, a public vote alone is not enough. It would mean nothing if our people didn't have access to critical information beforehand. To be meaningfully included, we have to understand all aspects of the issue. We need to hear from people who are critical of the nuclear industry for moral and political reasons.

A public inquiry could provide space to discuss these issues and hear from critical voices. I still believe it would be a good way to stimulate public debate about uranium mining. If Nunavut held a public inquiry and referendum on uranium mining, it could help set a new democratic standard for implementing the principle of free, prior, and informed consent in Canada. Doing so would be in accordance with the United Nations Declaration of the Rights of Indigenous People (UNDRIP), which both the federal and territorial governments have committed to implement.

CHAPTER 8

Protecting Our Land and Caribou

Most people know about me because of my role in the struggles against uranium mining in Nunavut. However, I have been involved in many other struggles to protect our land and caribou from mineral exploration and mining. As a community researcher, board member for the Baker Lake Hunters and Trappers Organization, and (later) HTO manager, I was involved in several other campaigns to protect caribou habitat and other important places from the mining industry.

As I explained in Chapter 3, calving grounds and post-calving grounds are important habitat. Caribou are very sensitive to disturbance when they give birth and nurse their young. Caribou are also sensitive to disturbance when they swim across the water, and we have an extensive set of Inuit *pitqussiit* (Inuit rules, customs, and social norms) to protect water crossings. The crossings are also priceless heritage sites for inland Inuit because many families hunted and camped near them when Inuit still lived on the land.

In the early 1970s, the federal government allowed unrestrained mineral exploration in calving grounds and at water crossings. In response to protests from Baker Lake Inuit, including a landmark court case, the federal government developed Caribou Protection Measures in the late 1970s to protect caribou from disturbance. These measures did not ban mining and exploration in calving grounds, but instead imposed seasonal restrictions—all activity in calving grounds had to stop during the calving season. I was hired as a federal land inspector in the early 1980s, and part of my job was to enforce the protection measures. While these measures weren't ideal—there should be no exploration or mining in calving grounds—they did help reduce the impact of exploration on caribou.

After we signed the Nunavut Land Claims Agreement in 1993, I expected there would be a bigger focus on respecting Inuit *pitqussiit* regarding the land and wildlife. I thought that the Government of Nunavut (GN) and the Inuit representative organizations would push for stronger protection for caribou habitat than the federal Caribou Protection Measures. I was seriously mistaken. In many cases, the GN and Inuit organizations have sided with the mining industry and have stopped our attempts to protect important caribou habitat.

In a lot of ways, caribou protection has gone downhill since I worked for the federal government in the 1980s. The federal government cut its budget for calving grounds surveys in the 1990s, so we no longer have enough information about where the caribou give birth from year to year. There are some organizations that want to do away with the Caribou Protection Measures altogether, and replace them with more relaxed measures that are less rigorous for industry. Many exploration companies also violate the terms and conditions of their permits, including by failing to clean up camps and drill sites after their work is completed.

This chapter describes attempts by Baker Lake Inuit to protect caribou habitat after the Nunavut Agreement was signed. These stories show how hard many of us have worked to uphold our Inuit *pitqussiit* and protect sensitive caribou habitat from the mining industry. They show that the GN and Inuit organizations tend to side with industry instead of with Inuit hunters and Elders. The cases discussed in this chapter also show that mineral exploration and mining companies routinely ignore regulations with no serious consequences. The Nunavut Agreement has not lived up to my expectations that it would allow us to protect our hunting culture. In some ways, it put our traditions and values at greater risk.

A Trip to Mallery Lake with Government Officials

Before I get into our activism around caribou habitat protection, I want to tell you a story about a trip I took to the Mallery Lake area with some senior government officials. I hope it will help you appreciate how wrong it is to assume that my homeland is "barren" "empty" or "untouched," as *qablunaat* often do. It is very common to find evidence of caribou and human activity on the landscape, if you know what to look for. Unfortunately, there is also a growing legacy of garbage on our land from old exploration camps and drill sites.

In the summer of 2012, officials from the federal government asked the Baker Lake HTO to select representatives for a day trip to some uranium exploration sites in the Mallery Lake area. They wanted the HTO to appoint someone who understood the significance of the area to Inuit. The HTO board initially selected two Elders to go on the trip. However, there was limited room on the plane, and these Elders were unilingual and required an interpreter. At the last minute, the HTO board asked me to go instead because I was the only one available.

I was pretty stressed out about the trip. I wasn't too familiar with the Mallery Lake area—it's quite far from where I grew up and where I hunt today. I also had very little time to prepare. I talked to an Elder who grew up in the area named Thomas Qaqimat. He told me about the caribou migration routes and water crossings, as well as the places they would hunt, fish, and camp in the area. All of the information was a bit overwhelming, but I tried my best to understand what he was teaching me.

I was told we'd be visiting exploration sites operated by a company called Forum Uranium. Forum was a junior exploration firm that had acquired several mineral claims near AREVA's Kiggavik project.[1] It was one of the companies that signed exploration agreements with NTI to explore for uranium on Inuit Owned Lands (IOLs).[2] If AREVA's Kiggavik project had been approved, Forum would have probably made a *lot* of money selling these claims to a larger company.

The first stop on our trip was one of Forum's old work sites. We all travelled there in a fixed-wing airplane. I wasn't very impressed with what I saw when we arrived. The place was a huge mess with cigarette butts, oil cans, drill rods, and old cables littered across the land. It looked like Forum had tried to burn some of their garbage, but they didn't do a good job—there was a lot of half-burned garbage still on the ground. I don't think the government had done any site inspections in that area.

Our next stop was Forum's camp at Mallery Lake. We had to fly there by helicopter because the fixed-wing plane couldn't land at the camp. There were too many people to fit in the helicopter at the same time, so they had to make several trips. I was supposed to give my presentation after everyone arrived. I was pretty nervous. Sometimes *qallunaat* (non-Inuit of European descent) government officials can be very arrogant and talk to Inuit hunters like we don't know anything. I didn't want to give them the satisfaction of seeing me at a loss for words. Even though I had spoken to Thomas Qaqimat to prepare, I didn't know what I was going to say. Luckily, I was on the first helicopter trip to the camp, so I had time to figure something out.

I went for a walk and looked around. Before long, I found some tracks from a major caribou migration. I kept walking a little farther and found stones marking a fishing spot. A little farther away I found tent rings from an old camp. I now had the perfect things to talk about for my presentation.

I was relieved. For my presentation I took everyone for a walk and interpreted the landscape. I explained how we traditionally protected caribou migration routes, how we used stone markers for different things on the land, and the way our traditional camps would be set up. While it didn't change the government representatives' minds about promoting uranium mining in the area, it sure felt good to give them clear evidence that the area is important to Inuit.

Fall Caribou Crossing National Historic Site

One of my first experiences with creating protected areas to conserve caribou habitat was in the 1990s. Shortly after the Nunavut Agreement was signed, Parks Canada decided to create a national historic site around important caribou water crossings on the Kazan River—the homeland of the Harvaqtuurmiut Inuit. As part of this initiative, my friend Darren Keith conducted research into Inuit history and knowledge of the Kazan River area.[3] I worked with Darren as a local project coordinator and community researcher, helping him interview Elders and organize trips on the land.

Darren and I interviewed several Harvaqtuurmiut Elders to document their oral history and traditional knowledge. We discussed where they were born, the places they lived and camped, and the techniques they used for hunting. One theme that came up over and over was that caribou are especially sensitive to disturbance at water crossings. The Elders explained that Inuit had many *pitqussiit* to protect these sensitive places. For example, Elizabeth Tunnuq said, "Too much human activity would divert the caribou from crossing. Crossings are very sensitive places for caribou, we always watched our activities, trying

not to go to the sensitive areas, watching the direction of the wind and so on."[4]
Mary Nagniayuk Iksiktaaryuk said,

> Living at caribou crossings requires a lot of special advertence. There
> were times we were not allowed to utter a sound or move as long as
> there were caribou waiting to cross. Caribou tend to be most sensitive
> to noise, scent, and visually at crossings.[5]

> We would camp on the other side of the river [from] where the
> caribou would hit the water. The crossings were very scent sensitive,
> we were not even allowed to leave our footprints or foot scent on the
> beginning of the crossing where the caribou hit the water.[6]

Interestingly, archaeological studies of the area later confirmed what the Elders
were telling us—that they and their ancestors closely followed these rules when
camping near water crossings.[7]

The Elders also taught us many stories about the area, as well as a song about
the Kazan River. It is an ancient song, written long before any of the Elders we
interviewed were alive. It lists the places someone visited on their journey from
the coast to the inland of the Kivalliq region:

> Aye ya ya ya Aye ya, isn't it fun to go on top of my lookout hill
> Ukiliarjuk and imagine seeing the hills and wildlife to the south,

> Aularniarviglu, Inukhuliglu, Tirilujait, Itsarijat, Avilukit, Paninaat,
> Avarhiuvinaluglu,

> Kapinhinnarviglu-qa, Qalinilu, Itimnirlu, Amarujat, Shunakatlu,
> Iqumngat-qa, Qarlirlu-qa, Qimirjuaq,

> Naujatluima, Naujaaraajuit, Ungaluk-qa, Iqiliqtalik, Igjuartaq,

> Miluggijat, Hiurajuarlu-qa, Nurha'narlu-qa, Uviulu, Natsirviglu,
> Ikira'hak, Kangi&uklu, Mirjungnituarlu-qa, Tibjaliglu eemah,

> Umiivik-qa, Kalingujat, Pinnaajuk, Itqilitlu nunaatlu napaatut,

At the ocean I didn't have any luck with sea animals, I put aside three to take along. Ayae ye eh ya ye ya ya Aya.

Is there anyone else here besides me? Ayae ye ya ya Ayae ye ya ya Ayae ye ya ya Ayae ye ya ya Ayae ye ya ya.

Ayae ya aya is there someone else here? I am moving to other lands because no one is to be seen,

Piqqiqturlu, Qamaanaarjuglu, Siura'tuaq, Ukpiktujuk, Qangiuvik, Siluartaliglu, Kihimiajija, Nallurhiaq,

Kivaqattaqtalik, Qurluqturlu, Unahugiik, Nuillaglu, Piqqirlu-qa, Piqqiarjuk, Puarinaaq, Innitaaq, Itimnirlu,

Pigaarvik, Quukitruq, Ammiruqtuuq, Ammiriqivik, Qikita'tuaq, Qikihiturlirlu, Halluhinariituq,

Umingmaujartalik, Piluqugaajuk, Manikturlu, Utaqqivigjuaq, Angilutarjuaq, Panajuarlu-qa,

Qikitaruktitaq, Tutaaraaq, Qatutaarlu, Autuviglu, Nuvuksat, Papikarlu, Quuviiglu, Naharahugaluaq,

Naujatujurlu, Ningavik, Hulurarlu, Kingaalu, ayae ya ya ya, ayae ya ya ya, ayae ya ya ya, ya ye ya ya ya—aye ya ya ya—Harvaqtuuq![18]

Elizabeth Tunnuq had a recording of a Harvaqtuurmiut Elder named George Tatanniq singing the Kazan River song. By this point George had long since passed away, but for a long time he was the oldest Harvaqtuurmiut Elder in Baker Lake. The song itself doesn't have much of a melody. The lyrics are mostly spoken, quickly and rhythmically. In some ways it is similar to modern rap music.

One summer, as part of our research process, Darren and I went on a trip up the Kazan River with a Harvaqtuurmiut Elder named Luke Tunguaq. We hired Peter Tapatai, an Inuk businessman and former TV personality from Baker Lake, to take us up the river by boat. I had a great time. Darren did a lot of fishing along the way, so we ate a lot of fish on our trip. It was in early August and the tundra was very green and beautiful. There were holes all over the place, where grizzly bears had dug up the tundra looking for *siksiks* (ground squirrels). I was pretty worried about grizzly bears coming into our camp at night.

Darren and I sang the Kazan River song as we were travelling, always arguing about what the correct lyrics were. We tried to visit as many of the places in the song as we could, but we weren't able to travel farther than Thirty Mile Lake because the water levels were so low. It was very interesting visiting these sites with Elders as our guides. I learned a lot on that trip.

The Fall Caribou Crossing National Historic Site was officially created in 1995.[9] I was happy to see this important area protected. However, there are hundreds of other important water crossings, migration routes, and hunting areas across the Kivalliq region. In my opinion, they are all sacred places worthy of protection.

Thelon Wildlife Sanctuary and Special Management Areas

Another major debate about caribou habitat protection in the 1990s had to do with the future of the Thelon Wildlife Sanctuary—a protected area that straddles the current border between Nunavut and the Northwest Territories. It was created in 1927 to protect endangered muskox. The boundaries of the sanctuary were expanded in 1956. As a result of the creation and expansion of the sanctuary, several Inuit and Dene families lost access to important parts of their traditional homelands. They were no longer permitted to hunt, travel, or live in the areas they had used for generations.[10]

When the Nunavut Agreement was signed in 1993, a major question was how the Thelon Wildlife Sanctuary should be managed. Some representatives of the mining industry were pressuring Inuit to open the sanctuary to mineral exploration and mining. A lot of hunters from Baker Lake and the Lutsel K'e Dene First Nation wanted to protect additional areas near the sanctuary from the mining industry.[11]

The Government of the Northwest Territories developed a management plan for the sanctuary in the 1990s, before Nunavut became a territory. During consultations, both Inuit and Dene made it very clear that the sanctuary should stay in place and that mineral exploration and mining should be banned within its borders. There were extensive discussions about how to best protect important areas adjacent to the sanctuary, including the headwaters of the Thelon River (in Dene territory) and the calving grounds of the Beverly caribou herd (in Nunavut).[12]

The Thelon Game Sanctuary Management Plan was released in 2001. It recommended that mineral exploration and mining should remain prohibited inside of the sanctuary. It also recommended that federal and territorial governments create two proposed Special Management Areas adjacent to the sanctuary: one to conserve the headwaters of the Thelon River, and one to conserve the calving grounds of the Beverly caribou. Many of us hoped that a Special Management Area would allow us to protect the calving grounds from mineral exploration and mining.

The Baker Lake HTO conducted a research project to help inform the decision about the proposed Special Management Area north of Aberdeen Lake, inside the Beverly calving grounds. My friend David Pelly was hired to interview Elders who had once lived inside the proposed Special Management Area at a place called Hanningajuq (Garry Lakes). David worked with Hattie Mannik, an Inuk woman who has published her own book on inland Inuit culture and heritage.[13] Together, they interviewed twenty-six Elders, living in five different communities, to document the Inuit history and knowledge of the area.

Several of the Elders from Baker Lake told David and Hattie that they did not want mining or mineral exploration to take place in the Hanningajuq area. Others said that mining and exploration *might* be acceptable under special circumstances. Despite these differences of opinion, everyone seemed to agree that some sort of special protection was required for the area.[14]

Unfortunately, before the Baker Lake HTO was able to decide what sort of protection it wanted for the Special Management Area, the Beverly calving grounds were overrun by uranium exploration. As I mentioned in Chapter 6, there was a rush to explore for uranium in the Baker Lake area in the mid-2000s. A lot of this activity took place in the Beverly calving grounds. In 2006 the Baker Lake HTO requested a moratorium on issuing new permits in the Beverly calving and post-calving grounds, to give it time to decide what sort of special protection might be required for the area. However, our request was denied. By

2008 there were many active exploration camps in the calving and post-calving grounds of the Beverly herd.

Uravan's Garry Lakes Project

The question of uranium exploration in the Beverly calving grounds came to a head in the fight against the Garry Lakes project proposed by a junior mining company called Uravan Minerals.[15] In the spring of 2008, Uravan submitted a proposal to explore for uranium near Hanningajuq—right in the middle of the Beverly calving grounds. NIRB began a screening in early April and sent out a request for comments to government departments, Inuit organizations, and various other groups including the Baker Lake HTO and Hamlet Council.

We were only given twenty days to respond to NIRB's request for comments. As I mentioned earlier, the Baker Lake HTO simply lacked the resources required to participate in NIRB screenings for the many proposals for uranium exploration near Baker Lake at that time. With only one full-time staff-person and a mountain of applications for exploration in our hunting grounds, we were overwhelmed.

Only the GN Department of Environment and the Beverly and Qamanirjuaq Caribou Management Board (BQCMB) responded by the deadline. The GN expressed concerns with the cumulative impacts of so many exploration projects in the calving grounds, but recommended that Uravan's project be approved so long as it strictly followed the seasonal restrictions outlined in the Caribou Protection Measures.[16] The BQCMB recommended the project not be approved because it would be situated inside a caribou calving ground and the proposed Special Management Area. The BQCMB also recommended the federal government conduct a regional assessment to consider the cumulative impacts of the many active projects across the Beverly caribou range.[17]

NIRB sent out a second request for comments on May 23, 2008. This time NIRB included more groups, including those involved in developing the management plan for the Thelon Game Sanctuary. The Lutsel K'e Dene First Nation[18] and the Athabasca Denesuline Negotiating Team[19] submitted comments opposing the proposal. Like the GN and BQCMB, these Dene communities were concerned with the cumulative effects of so much exploration in the Beverly calving grounds.

Because of these concerns, NIRB recommended that Uravan's proposal undergo a full environmental review.[20] The federal government accepted this recommendation, and an environmental review began in the fall of 2008. It's uncommon for a simple exploration project to go through a full environmental review. In this case, however, NIRB's decision made sense. There were serious concerns about the cumulative impacts of the numerous projects operating in the Beverly calving grounds. It would have been very risky to approve another project in the area with only a simple screening.

Our Inuit organizations finally decided to speak up. Unfortunately, they sided with the mining company. KIA and NTI wrote to NIRB expressing disappointment that a full review was being conducted on an exploration project.[21] In a follow-up letter, KIA and NTI said that they would not support the proposed Special Management Area to protect the Beverly calving grounds. They stated, "There are Inuit Owned Lands in this area, some . . . where Inuit own the mineral title and where Inuit have the right to explore and mine."[22]

Uravan ended up abandoning their project without completing the review. They claimed the process was too onerous, and that they were being treated unfairly. However, that was not the end of our battle with Uravan. We soon learned that they had already been doing low-level exploration in the area that didn't require approval from NIRB. What's more, they had repeatedly violated the conditions of their permits and left behind a huge mess!

In August 2009 a federal government inspector discovered that Uravan had stored fuel barrels without the required authorizations. The company had jumped the gun and had started moving materials to a new work site, expecting that NIRB would approve their proposal. There were over one hundred fuel barrels improperly stored, several of which had together leaked an estimated one thousand litres of fuel onto the ground. Other garbage had been blown around by the wind. The government issued an order for Uravan to clean up the site by the end of September. Uravan responded that it was unable to finish by then because of poor weather. Instead of removing all of the fuel barrels, they decided to try to store them more securely. However, some of the barrels had frozen to the ground and therefore remained improperly stored. Uravan promised to finish the job in June 2010. The federal government responded in December 2009, ordering Uravan to complete the cleanup by May 15, so as to avoid disturbing caribou during the calving season.[23] Uravan responded two weeks later, explaining that cleanup prior to May 15 was not feasible because of winter weather, and that the final cleanup would have to wait until after calving season ended in July 2010.[24]

By the summer of 2012, Uravan still had not completed the cleanup of its Garry Lakes project. A federal government inspector found camp furniture, rotting tent pads, and empty fuel drums littered on the ground. There were also some improperly stored full fuel drums. The inspector gave Uravan thirty days to respond with a detailed plan explaining how it would clean up the site.[25] It took Uravan almost four months to respond. The company promised to clean up the site the following summer, in August 2013.[26] However, in September 2013 Uravan wrote to the federal government and explained that the site had yet to be cleaned up, again due to bad weather.[27]

The federal government did not confirm that the site had been cleaned up until the summer of 2015—*six years* after it first caught Uravan breaking the rules.[28] As far as I know, no charges were laid or penalties were issued. And people wonder why I don't trust mining companies when they tell me they will follow the rules and keep our land clean!

What Happened to the Beverly Caribou Herd?

While we were fighting to protect the Beverly calving grounds, biologists were reporting that the herd was declining. In 1994, biologists did a survey of the Beverly calving grounds and estimated that the herd had two hundred and seventy thousand adult caribou.[29] The next survey, in 2002, showed a very significant decline in the number of cows using the calving grounds. Further surveys from 2007 to 2011 showed an extremely rapid decline in the number of cows on the Beverly calving grounds, until the area had essentially been abandoned by the herd.[30]

I ended up working on one of these surveys in the spring of 2008. Two biologists from Yellowknife had contacted the Baker Lake H T O and asked us to select representatives to join them on the survey, to help make sure that the caribou were not being harassed or treated disrespectfully by the biologists. My nephew John Nukik Jr. was selected as an observer. The biologists also asked the HTO to help them find a cook. I couldn't find anyone for the cook position on short notice, so I decided to take the job myself. We camped at Sand Lake. I remember there was a lot of old equipment there from an abandoned mineral exploration camp. We planned to be there for ten days. Every morning the survey crew would take off at 7:00 a.m. and fly for ten hours looking for caribou.

I had a lot of free time every day while the survey crew was working, so I went for long walks and did some fishing. I expected to see a lot of caribou, since we were camping inside the Beverly caribou herd's calving grounds. I only saw one lone caribou the whole time. The survey crew didn't see any caribou at all. They ended up giving up and going home two days early. I was pretty unhappy—I was expecting to be paid for ten days of work but only ended up getting paid for eight. I was also unhappy about the lack of caribou in the area.

Biologists have given different explanations for the absence of caribou in the Beverly calving grounds. At first, they argued that the herd was declining because of overhunting. However, when they discussed their survey results with the Baker Lake HTO and Elders from our community, we told them that they might be wrong. We were pretty sure that mineral exploration activity is what drove the caribou away from their usual calving grounds. Even if the exploration camps shut down during the calving season, all of the disturbances to the landscape might have frightened the herd. Remember, when we lived on the land, we kept caribou migration routes very clean. We didn't leave any waste in those areas because we knew it might affect migration paths. As I explained in Chapter 1, when I was growing up on the land my father used rows of *aul'laqutit* (flags) to divert small groups of caribou and so they would be easier to hunt. Other families used to use rows of *inuksuit* (stone markers) to divert caribou in the direction they wanted them to go. The tents, trailers, vehicles, drill rigs, and fuel caches from mining exploration might have had a similar effect.

Before long, some of the radio collars biologists were using to monitor the Beverly caribou started showing up around the Queen Maud Gulf—250 kilometres north of the Beverly herd's calving grounds. This suggested that these caribou were giving birth near the calving grounds of the Ahiak caribou herd. A 2011 report published by the GN Department of Environment argued that the

Beverly herd had not necessarily declined, but rather shifted its calving grounds to the Queen Maud Gulf area.[31] However, some biologists argue that the Beverly herd's population declined so much that it is no longer a distinct herd, with the few survivors joining the Ahiak herd.[32]

Biologists speculate that the change in the Beverly caribou herd was caused by a combination of different things, including disease, insects, and changes in weather patterns, as well as increased predators and human activity (like mineral exploration) in the calving grounds.[33] Personally, I believe the mining industry is at fault. While caribou might be stressed and disturbed by multiple factors, there were numerous uranium companies operating in the calving grounds, and at least one of them was flagrantly and repeatedly breaking regulations. It would have been impossible for caribou to use the area undisturbed.

Anconia's Marce Lake Project

The next big conflict over caribou calving grounds came with the Marce Lake project. This project was proposed by another junior mining company, Anconia Resources. Anconia developed a proposal to explore for minerals right in the middle of the Qamanirjuaq caribou herd's calving grounds. NIRB began a screening for the proposal in late 2011. A request for comments was sent out on December 12, with a deadline one month later. As usual, the BQCMB submitted comments recommending the project not be approved. No comments were received from the GN, KIA, or NTI.

Unfortunately, the HTOs in the Kivalliq region did not find out what was going on until it was too late. By this time, I was working as a manager for the Baker Lake HTO, so I have some first-hand insight into how this happened. The screening process took place during the holiday season, and our office was already overwhelmed dealing with the proposed Kiggavik mine. The request for comments ended up in a big pile of backlogged paperwork. We didn't learn about the project until a government biologist informed the Baker Lake HTO about the Anconia's proposal. When the Baker Lake HTO learned that Anconia's proposed project would be in the Qamanirjuaq calving grounds, the HTO board passed a motion declaring that it would support whatever the Arviat and Whale Cove HTOs decided to do. These were the communities closest to the project.

The Arviat HTO passed a motion opposing Anconia's proposal, but not until after the NIRB deadline for comments had passed. NIRB released its decision in March 2012, recommending the project be approved without a full review.[34] Both KIA and the federal government issued permits, and Anconia set to work in the calving grounds that summer. The BQCMB and Arviat HTO had been ignored.

When the rest of the HTOs in the region found out about Arviat's position, we decided to voice our support for Arviat's position. Between June 2012 and March 2013, letters opposing Anconia's project were submitted by the Baker Lake,[35] Chesterfield Inlet,[36] Whale Cove,[37] and Rankin Inlet[38] HTOs. However, because permits had already been issued for the project, our letters had no immediate effect.

Just like Uravan, Anconia broke the rules and regulations many times. In September 2013, a federal government inspector found that Anconia had failed to send regulators required information about the project. Fuel was also being improperly stored at the project site.[39] Shortly afterwards Anconia temporarily shut down the Marce Lake project.

In January 2016, Anconia wrote to the federal government, announcing that it was no longer interested in the site and intended to let its permits expire. The letter claimed that the site had been cleaned up and remediated.[40] However, in the summer of 2016 a federal inspector found that the site had not been cleaned up properly. Many things had been left behind, including drilling equipment, propane cylinders, wooden pallets, and fuel. Garbage had blown around across the tundra, and the abandoned fuel was still improperly stored.[41]

Anconia also had neglected to send its wildlife monitoring reports to NIRB in a timely manner, as required by its permits. In fact, it didn't submit these reports until 2015, two years after project activities had stopped. It's difficult to take our regulators seriously when they let companies get away with this behaviour, especially when a project is right in the middle of the calving grounds.

The approval of Anconia's project was certainly a big letdown. However, one good thing came out of our conflict with Anconia. It provided an opportunity for several Kivalliq HTOs to work together to protect the calving grounds. Moving forward, this collaboration would prove to be very important politically.

Nunavut Planning Commission and the
Nunavut Land Use Plan

In 2007 the Nunavut Planning Commission (NPC) began developing a land use plan for Nunavut. Land use plans are similar to zoning regulations—they place restrictions on the types of activities permitted in certain places and during certain times. This new plan, when final, is intended to cover all of Nunavut and replace all existing land use plans in the territory. Based on meetings with and submissions from various groups—federal and territorial government departments, Inuit organizations, HTOs, and of course the mining industry—the NPC released Draft Nunavut Land Use Plans in 2012, 2014, and 2016.

By far the most controversial issue in this whole process has been the question of caribou calving grounds.[42] The mining industry, as usual, argues for relaxing the current Caribou Protection Measures that place seasonal restrictions on exploration activity. Submissions from the NWT and Nunavut Chamber of Mines recommend introducing new, "mobile" protection measures. According to this proposal, instead of using seasonal shutdowns, exploration companies could continue working in calving grounds during the calving season. However, if large numbers of caribou were to come close to their camp or work site, activity would have to stop. These are called mobile measures because they move with the caribou (rather than being limited to a specific area, like the existing Caribou Protection Measures).

These mobile measures would certainly be convenient for the mining industry. The problem is, they are much weaker than the existing seasonal restrictions. Based on my own experience and what Elders have told me over the years, I know that caribou usually see, smell, or hear you long before you see them. By the time mining companies spot the caribou and start to shut down operations, it will be too late, and the caribou will have already been disturbed.

Another problem is that these mobile measures depend almost entirely on industry monitors to make the call when work needs to shut down. After our experiences with companies like Uravan and Anconia, why should we trust the mining industry to monitor themselves?

Mobile protection also suffers from the same shortcomings as the seasonal restrictions in the existing Caribou Protection Measures. Both mobile measures and seasonal restrictions do very little to help us address cumulative impacts.

They might help a bit if there are only one or two projects inside a herd's calving grounds. However, they become less effective if there are multiple companies operating at the same time. The fate of the Beverly caribou herd is evidence of this.

Neither mobile measures nor seasonal shutdowns help us deal with actual mining in calving grounds. While these measures might help with small exploration projects, an actual mine—complete with big open pits, roads, tailings ponds, camps, mills, and other infrastructure—will disturb caribou even if activity is reduced during sensitive periods or when caribou are spotted nearby.

My community's experience with the Meadowbank gold mine has taught us that it becomes much harder to hold companies to account once a mine goes into operation. At that stage, mining companies are focused on maximizing production, even if it means relaxing some environmental protections. If we allowed an actual mine in the calving grounds, there's a good chance the mining company would eventually try to remove environmental protections that affected production. Meadowbank also showed us that once one mine is built, more usually follow, and it becomes very difficult for our communities to resist these additional mines. So, if we say yes to one mine in the calving grounds, we might as well be saying yes to several mines in the area.

HTOs from the Kivalliq region recommended that the new Nunavut Land Use Plan should prohibit mineral exploration and mining inside caribou calving grounds. We organized our intervention through the Kivalliq Wildlife Board (KWB). In Chapter 7 I explained that the KWB served as an important venue for Kivalliq hunters to coordinate our opposition to AREVA's Kiggavik proposal. The KWB played the same role in our fight to protect calving grounds.

At a meeting in February 2013, the KWB board unanimously passed a motion calling for a ban on mining and exploration in caribou calving grounds.[43] Several resolutions reaffirming this position were passed at later meetings. By developing a unified position and politically organizing on a regional basis, we were able to coordinate our efforts to protect the caribou. Letters calling for a ban on mining and mineral exploration in caribou calving grounds were subsequently sent to the NPC by HTOs from Baker Lake,[44] Naujaat,[45] Chesterfield Inlet,[46] Whale Cove,[47] and Arviat.[48] As a result of our campaign, the Nunavut Wildlife Management Board ended up supporting our position.[49]

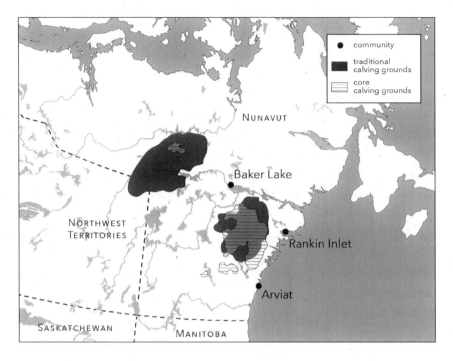

Figure 16. Locations of the calving grounds for the Beverly and Qamanirjuaq caribou herds. Map design by Julie Witmer.

Several Dene and Métis communities in the Northwest Territories, Manitoba, and Saskatchewan also called for a ban on mining and exploration in caribou calving grounds in Nunavut. The NPC received submissions recommending full protection for calving grounds from the Lutsel K'e Dene First Nation,[50] the Northwest Territories Métis Council,[51] the Fort Smith Métis Council,[52] the Athabasca Denesuline Negotiating Team,[53] the Northlands Dene First Nation,[54] and the Sayisi Dene First Nation.[55] These communities depend upon the migratory caribou herds that give birth in Nunavut. The Beverly and Qamanirjuaq Caribou Management Board also recommended full protection for caribou calving grounds.[56]

As usual, our Inuit organizations and territorial government ended up siding with the mining industry against hunters' rights. The GN's position flip-flopped.

In a May 2014 submission to the NPC, the GN recommended that mineral exploration and mining should be prohibited in "core" caribou calving grounds.[57] These core calving grounds are the most heavily used sections of the larger "traditional" calving grounds that the Baker Lake HTO and BQCMB originally tried to protect. The idea of focusing on protecting these core areas was an attempt by government wildlife biologists to compromise with the mining industry.[58] However, even this compromise position was short-lived. At an NPC technical meeting in March 2016, the GN announced that it had changed its position and no longer supported full protection in calving grounds.[59]

The Kivalliq Inuit Association was also initially hostile to our campaign to prohibit mineral exploration and mining in caribou calving grounds. In a 2013 submission to the NPC, KIA discouraged the creation of new protected areas.[60] In 2016, KIA responded to the push to protect calving grounds by recommending mineral exploration and mining be prohibited in some parts of the calving grounds, but allowing it to continue in parts of the calving grounds with high mineral potential.[61] This recommendation might seem confusing. That's because it doesn't make any sense. What's the point in protecting part of the calving grounds from mineral exploration, if you're going to allow it in the parts of the calving grounds that are of interest to the mining industry?

Luckily, the planning commission listened to the HTOs and wildlife boards. In June 2016 the NPC released an updated Draft Nunavut Land Use Plan. This new draft included full protection for calving grounds, post-calving grounds, and water crossings. This was a major victory for hunters, but the battle was not over yet. The NPC still had to hold more technical meetings and public hearings. More importantly, the plan had to be approved by the federal government, the GN, and NTI. Clearly, we had our work cut out for us.

At first, we made some good progress. In 2017 KIA sent comments to the NPC supporting full protection for core calving grounds.[62] This was another major victory and seemed to signal that we might be able to convince NTI to support our position. The years of hard work we had put into this issue were finally starting to pay off.

However, these gains were soon lost because of pressure from the mining industry. Mining companies used the NWT and Nunavut Chamber of Mines to coordinate a campaign to keep the calving grounds open for exploitation.

They threatened to use one of the most powerful weapons mining companies have at their disposal to strong-arm KIA into changing its position about calving grounds—an investment strike. In March 2018, the Chamber of Mines announced that projected expenditures on mineral exploration in Nunavut for the year had dropped 35 percent—a decrease of $58.6 million from the previous year. The Chamber of Mines blamed the proposed protection for caribou habitat in the Draft Nunavut Land Use Plan for driving away investment. It went on to urge our Inuit representative organizations to reconsider the proposed conservation measures, or else its economy would continue to suffer.[63]

Unsurprisingly, KIA caved into this pressure rather quickly. By the fall of 2018 it changed its position *again*. In a written submission to the NPC, KIA announced that it supported exploration and mining within caribou calving grounds.[64]

At this point, the land use planning process stalled. Instead of proceeding with final hearings, pressure from the mining industry forced the NPC to conduct more consultations and revise the plan. When I finished writing this book in early 2021, the planning process was still on hold, and calving grounds were still open to the mining industry.

It is very frustrating to see mining companies disturb caribou habitat. Even worse, our territorial government and Inuit representative organizations side with the mining industry time and again. However, one of the most frustrating things is the way the mining industry has disrespected my family's traditional homeland at Ferguson Lake.

Mineral Exploration at Ferguson Lake

Mineral exploration companies first arrived at Ferguson Lake—the place where I grew up—in the 1950s. Several different companies have explored the area on-and-off ever since, and have discovered significant nickel, copper, and platinum deposits. In 2006 I found out that a company called Starfield Resources was planning to expand its base camp on the shore of Ferguson Lake. However, instead of consulting with my family, Starfield had been discussing their project with the community of Rankin Inlet.

My extended family held a meeting in late January 2007 to discuss the situation at Ferguson Lake. I wrote down our concerns and submitted them to the Nunavut Impact Review Board. I explained how previous exploration companies had caused irreversible damage to the area, including an important caribou crossing. We were very worried that this would happen again. I also made clear that the company must work with my family to identify important heritage sites and caribou migration routes near Ferguson Lake, to ensure that they are protected.[65]

In response to our comments, Starfield reassured us that it would clean up and restore the land when its exploration work was completed. The company also agreed to meet with us to identify important wildlife habitat and heritage sites.[66] A few weeks later NIRB approved Starfield's proposal.[67] I expected the company would live up to its promises.

After several years of exploration, Starfield commissioned an economic assessment of the Ferguson Lake Project in 2011. The study found that a combined nickel, copper, and cobalt mine at Ferguson Lake would be very profitable.[68] However, Starfield soon found itself in financial trouble. In 2013 it declared bankruptcy and effectively abandoned its exploration project at Ferguson Lake.[69]

In the summer of 2016 *Maclean's* magazine wanted to run a story about the centre of Canada. According to the Canadian Cartographic Association, the geographic centre of Canada is located at Yathkyed Lake, two hundred kilometres south of Baker Lake. Reporter Meagan Campbell hired Boris Kotelewetz—a *qablunaaq* bush pilot and businessman who has lived in Baker Lake for a long time—to fly her and a photographer to Yathkyed Lake. My brother Hugh Ikoe and I were brought along as guides.

One of Boris's employees flew us to Yathkyed Lake in a small fixed-wing plane: Boris came along for the ride as a passenger. However, when we got to Yathkyed Lake, the pilot couldn't find a safe place to land. He did *try* landing at a few sites that turned out to be unsafe (and scared me half to death in the process!). Eventually he gave up and decided to land at Starfield Resources' abandoned airstrip at Ferguson Lake. His plan was to drop us off at Ferguson Lake, fly back to Baker Lake, and charter a helicopter to bring us to Yathkyed Lake. Regardless, I was excited to have an unexpected visit to my home.

However, what I saw when we arrived made me *very* upset. The place was a total mess. In her article, the reporter wrote that Starfield's camp looked like a "junkyard" filled with "depressing shelters, sprawling roads, mouldy fridges, [and] soggy Harvest Crunch in boxes."[70] She wasn't wrong. Old rotting food, machinery, and fuel barrels littered my homeland.

Because Starfield's abandoned camp is located on Inuit Owned Lands, the Kivalliq Inuit Association is the responsible authority. It is KIA's job to monitor exploration activity and ensure that companies follow regulations and live up to their commitments. I wrote to KIA requesting funding so I could travel to Ferguson Lake and clean the area up myself. I even offered to pay half of the costs, which was rather generous. I didn't receive a response.

Both KIA and Nunavut Tunngavik Incorporated love to give away our Inuit Owned Lands to mining and exploration companies. When we object, their staff always tell us that our concerns are unfounded, and that KIA and NTI will hold these companies to account. However, they sure don't seem to be doing any better than the federal government at keeping my homeland clean. In some ways, they are even more frustrating to deal with.

Environmental Protection in Nunavut

In my opinion, environmental protection has gone downhill since we signed the Nunavut Agreement in 1993. Some problems have to do with changes in the mining industry. When mining and mineral exploration companies first started coming to our homeland, they would do most of their work themselves. Today, a lot more work is contracted out. Even if big mining companies follow the rules, sometimes their subcontractors don't. When we complain about rules not being followed, companies often try to blame it on subcontractors.

The federal government has also reduced its role in monitoring and enforcement, and no one has picked up the slack. It delegated responsibility for caribou monitoring to the Government of Nunavut. Unfortunately, the GN doesn't do nearly as much monitoring as the federal government did when I worked as a federal land use inspector in the 1980s. I also don't think the federal government does as many site visits to exploration camps today as I did back then.

I certainly wouldn't have let all these companies flagrantly break the rules with no consequences.

KIA and NTI assumed responsibility for monitoring and enforcing regulations on the Inuit Owned Lands in the Kivalliq region. Unfortunately, KIA looks at our land with tunnel vision—it seems all they see is mining potential, and they are blind to how the land is the root of our culture. It is frustrating, but not surprising, that this has happened. Some of the politicians and staff who run these organizations own businesses that benefit financially from the mining industry. Many of the non-Inuit staff who work for these organizations used to work for the mining industry, so they are more likely to be sympathetic to mining interests.

Perhaps the biggest problem is that these organizations want to make money, and royalties and other revenue from mining on our Inuit Owned Lands is the easiest way for them to do so. As organizations, they are in a huge conflict of interest. When the Nunavut Agreement was negotiated, most of the Inuit Owned Lands were selected by communities because of their cultural and heritage value—we chose our traditional camps and hunting grounds. Now KIA can make a lot of money by agreeing to allow mining on these same lands.

There are problems with transparency within these organizations. Members of the public can look up federal site-inspection reports for exploration projects on Crown lands—the reports are all available through the Nunavut Water Board's online public registry. In comparison, reports from KIA about projects on Inuit Owned Lands are not publicly available. I am honestly not convinced that they have been doing site visits at Ferguson Lake at all.

It's difficult for me to explain how disheartening all of this is. Even though my community has stopped a uranium mine twice in my lifetime, sometimes I can't help feeling defeated.

Conclusion

Until I was twelve years old, I lived on the land with my family at Ferguson Lake. Our lives back then were not perfect. I fundamentally disagree with some of our historical practices, including the way some women were treated in traditional Inuit society. However, that does not change the fact that many aspects of our culture should be celebrated. We do not need to romanticize our history to see that it holds important lessons for the present.

In my opinion, our traditional knowledge of the Arctic environment is one of the most important parts of our culture. Growing up on the land with my parents, we lived like other inland Inuit, depending on caribou for food, clothing, and other necessities of life. We were able to thrive because we inherited the knowledge of countless generations, passed down by Elders in our traditional stories and *pitqussiit* (Inuit rules, customs, and social norms). We had many rules to follow to protect the caribou and ensure the herds returned each year. These *pitqussiit* should be the basis for environmental regulations and resource management in the Arctic.[1] When we negotiated the Nunavut Land Claims Agreement, I supported it because I thought it would allow us to turn our traditional rules into modern laws and regulations.

Unfortunately, I was mistaken. Mineral exploration and mining still disturb caribou migration routes and calving grounds, just like before the land claim. The fact that the Government of Nunavut (GN) and Nunavut Tunngavik Incorporated (NTI) issued policies supporting uranium mining shows that these organizations do not take our traditional values seriously.

Looking back on my community's decades-long struggle against uranium mining, I feel like we have a lot to celebrate. Stopping the Kiggavik uranium mine twice is certainly quite an accomplishment. In both cases, even though we had support from allies across the world, the nuclear proponents were denied approval for their proposals because regular Inuit like me refused to be intimidated, stood up for their rights, and said NO to uranium mining in our hunting grounds. I take pride in these victories, as should everyone who fought alongside us.

However, at the same time, I cannot help but feel defeated. Both the GN and NTI still have policies in place that support uranium mining in Nunavut. The Nunavut Impact Review Board's (NIRB) report, which recommended the Kiggavik mine not be built, also left the door open for the proposed mine to be reconsidered sometime in the future. We have been unable to stop mineral exploration in caribou calving grounds or implement our *pitqussiit* to protect migration routes. If our traditional values and rules were respected, there would be no exploration in these sensitive areas. The current protection measures for caribou habitat are totally inadequate compared with the traditional rules we followed when hunting and travelling near caribou migration routes and water crossings. What's worse, many companies break these protection measures with no serious repercussions. This is all extremely disappointing.

Sometimes I feel defeated for other reasons as well. It can be very difficult to be outspoken in a small community like Baker Lake. I have certainly made my fair share of enemies over the years. After we stopped the first Kiggavik proposal in 1990, it was almost impossible for me to find employment in Baker Lake. Some local business owners who supported uranium mining—and who had managed to control our municipal government—effectively blacklisted me because of my activism.

In any case, it is important to learn from the history of resistance documented in this book. Our victories and failures have important lessons for other Inuit communities—and Indigenous peoples more broadly—who are fighting to defend their land from industries such as mining, hydroelectric development, and oil and gas extraction.

One lesson is that we must approach bureaucratic processes such as environmental assessment with caution. My community managed to use the environmental assessment process to our advantage in both of our campaigns against the Kiggavik project. When Urangesellschaft's proposal was being reviewed by a federal assessment panel in the late 1980s, our written submissions helped raise the bar for what was required of the company. This resulted in the company shelving the project because it could not satisfy the more extensive requirements we helped establish. When the NIRB reviewed AREVA's Kiggavik proposal twenty years later, we persuaded the review board to dismiss the project on a technicality—A R E VA did not have a firm start date for its mine, which created unacceptable levels of uncertainty for the assessment.

However, we didn't limit ourselves to participating in these assessment processes. In both cases we did a lot of political campaigning and conscious-ness-raising work, as well. For example, we petitioned elected officials, presented our arguments to the media, and provided critical information about the nuclear industry to Baker Lake residents. This dual strategy was important because environmental assessment was not the right forum to decide whether or not we should open our territory to the uranium industry. As Nunavummiut Makitagunarningit explained, a process designed to consider a single project should not be used to make decisions about an entire industry. Our moral concerns with nuclear weapons and waste were ignored in the review process, as was our political concern that approving Kiggavik would lead to proposals for more uranium mines that we would be powerless to stop. The entire process was intimidating and dominated by non-Inuit "experts," leaving many Baker Lake residents unable to meaningfully participate. If Nunavut is confronted with another proposal for uranium mining in the future, I hope we will choose a more democratic way to make these decisions.

In the Qikiqtani region of Nunavut, there is a lot of controversy over offshore oil and gas extraction. As we prepare this book for publication in 2021, there is a debate about whether or not the federal government's moratorium should be lifted, allowing the oil and gas industry back into our territory. Whatever decision Qikiqtani Inuit come to, they should learn from our experiences with uranium mining. Using a project-specific environmental assessment to determine if oil and gas development is right for Nunavut would not allow the full and fair participation of Inuit.

A second lesson from Baker Lake's experience with uranium mining is that the Government of Canada has consistently supported the expansion of the uranium industry into the Arctic. In fact, the conflicts over uranium explora-tion and mining discussed in this book probably never would have happened without the Canadian government's support for uranium mining. It was the federal government that enabled uranium exploration companies to invade our hunting grounds in the 1960s and 1970s by providing tax incentives and other subsidies for Arctic mineral exploration, participating in a secret and illegal uranium cartel to drive up the global price of uranium, and ignoring my community's pleas to put a halt to exploration activity. When northerners were debating Urangesellschaft's proposal for the Kiggavik uranium mine in the late 1980s, the federal government organized a "uranium workshop" where representatives from the nuclear industry and regulatory organizations both tried to reassure us that uranium mining would not pose a serious risk to our health or the Arctic environment. When uranium exploration companies returned to our territory in the early twenty-first century, the federal government dismissed the Baker Lake HTO's request for a moratorium on uranium exploration west of Baker Lake. During the debate about AREVA's proposal for the Kiggavik uranium mine, federal regulators again went out of their way to reassure us that uranium mining near Baker Lake would be perfectly safe. At the end of public hearings for the environmental review of AREVA's proposal, government representatives announced that they had no significant outstanding concerns with the project, implying that the proposed uranium mine should be approved, despite obvious opposition from Baker Lake Inuit.

The fact that we cannot rely on our territorial government or representative Inuit organizations to defend our hunting way of life is a third lesson from our experiences. These institutions have completely embraced the idea that mining should be the main driver of our economy, and they have supported risky types of extraction such as uranium mining and allowing mining activities in caribou calving grounds. Just as the federal government did in the 1980s, both the GN and NTI spent significant time and resources organizing "consultation" meetings that focused on reassuring us that uranium mining near Baker Lake would not cause any harm. This situation is not unique. In other regions of Canada[2] as well as internationally,[3] modern treaties and land claims have tied Indigenous organizations to "extractivist" development strategies. This has led to conflicts between the corporate Indigenous organizations created by land claims and the Indigenous communities that remain tied to land-based lifestyles, similar to the conflicts between Hunters and Trappers Organizations and NTI in Nunavut.

However, we also cannot depend entirely on community organizations like HTOs. In all my years organizing against uranium mining, I have always believed that involving regular people, not just our formal organizations, is very important politically. We can elect the best leaders, but if our communities do not push them in the right direction, they will not have much power at the negotiation table. Baker Lake's experience with the Meadowbank and Whale Tail gold mines shows that mining companies hold most of the power in these negotiations. This is one of the reasons I have always put so much time and effort into building and supporting grassroots groups like the Baker Lake Concerned Citizens Committee and Nunavummiut Makitagunarningit. These organizations helped give regular people a voice in these debates, by providing them with critical information that empowered them to speak out.

The need to build alliances with non-Inuit is a fourth lesson from our experiences fighting uranium mining. There is a lot of debate around the role of environmental organizations and non-Inuit activists in Nunavut politics. Many Inuit are hesitant to involve outsiders in our struggles, out of concern that they might try to manipulate our communities for their own purposes. This concern is understandable, especially when large environmental organizations are involved—they played a driving role in the anti-fur and anti-sealing movements that seriously harmed the Inuit hunting way of life. They also have their own agendas and reasons for wanting to protect the Arctic environment.

That said, there are a growing number of non-Inuit environmentalists who are genuinely interested in helping to protect our hunting culture. In our fight against the Kiggavik mine, we worked closely with many people and organizations from across the world that supported our struggle, including Gordon Edwards (Canadian Coalition for Nuclear Responsibility), Rosalie Bertell (International Institute of Concern for Public Health), Jim Harding (University of Regina), Ramsey Hart and Jamie Kneen (MiningWatch Canada), and of course my co-authors Warren and Jack. However, when working with non-Inuit allies, even if their intentions are genuine, we need to ensure that they work under Inuit leadership.

At the end of the day, the most important alliances are the ones we form with other Indigenous communities. In our struggles against uranium mining and to protect caribou habitat, we benefitted from the support of many different First Nations and Métis groups. In both cases, the Beverly Qamanirjuaq Caribou Management Board provided an important forum for Inuit, First Nations, and Métis from different communities to share perspectives and concerns, and develop common positions on important issues. I also think we need to work more with Indigenous peoples from other countries. Mining is a global industry, and we need to work with communities facing similar struggles to develop effective strategies and solutions.

Finally, the way my father resisted *qablunaat* authority shows that Inuit do not always have to be passive and deferential. By talking back to the *qablunaat* and refusing to send his children to school, my father taught me to stand up for myself and say "no" to things I disagree with. Our culture places a high value on political harmony, and as a result most Inuit are very uncomfortable with open conflict. While this approach might have worked well when we lived on the land, it is not always appropriate in the present context. There are some forces in the Arctic—including the uranium and oil industries—whose goals and interests are totally incompatible with ours. In these cases, a more aggressive approach is necessary.

There is no way of knowing what challenges future generations of Inuit will face. But it's safe to assume that communities will, from time to time, continue to find themselves dealing with proposals for non-renewable resource development that are not in their long-term best interests—projects like the Kiggavik mine, which would have made other people rich but would have left Inuit with radioactive tailings that would have to be managed in perpetuity, and projects that could irreparably damage natural treasures like caribou calving grounds, which are essential to our culture and our well-being.

My hope for this book is that it will show future generations of Inuit and other Indigenous peoples that they *can* fight proposals for unwanted development on their traditional territories. You'll have to be grounded, well-informed, agile, and tenacious; it won't be easy, and there will be days when the odds against you seem overwhelming; you'll have to sustain ridicule and attacks from people you know and people you don't know; and you'll need allies; but if you always keep the long-term best interests of the ordinary people of your community and your natural environment in your heart and mind and you don't lose hope . . . YOU CAN WIN!

Like we did.

Acknowledgements

Numerous individuals and organizations helped make this book happen.

First and foremost, the authors would like to acknowledge the invaluable assistance provide by Joan's daughter, Hilu Tagoona, who helped us identify important information, translated material into English, and reviewed and commented on several draft manuscripts. Hilu also deserves recognition for dealing with the authors' many quirks and eccentricities over the years. There is no way this book would have been written without your help.

The authors would like to thank the people at the University of Manitoba Press who helped bring this book into production, including David Larsen, Glenn Bergen, and Jill McConkey. Your guidance, advice, and patience were invaluable. The suggestions and feedback from our copy editor (Mary Lou Roy) and two anonymous peer reviewers was similarly indispensable. The authors would also like to thank Julie Witmer for producing the maps for our book.

Several people deserve recognition for providing feedback on draft manuscripts, suggestions for relevant information and photographs, and/or otherwise providing advice and support during the development of this book, including: Alanna Makinson, Alexander Zahara, Alex Levant, Anna Zalik, Arn Keeling, Brandon Laforest, Christopher Trott, Clayton Tartak, Darren Keith, David Hugill, David Pelly, Elizabeth Lunstrum, Emilie Cameron, Ezra Greene, Frances Abele, Frank Tester, Gabrielle Slowey, Glen Hostetler, Gordon Edwards, Hugh Ikoe, Jamie Kneen, Jerry Natanine, John Sinclair, John Thompson, Jonathan Peyton, Laura Lepper, Lori Hanson, Megan Youdelis, Monte Hummel, Natalie Marchand, Nathan Prier, Nettie Wiebe, Peter Braun, Peter Kulchyski, Peter Usher, Ramsey Hart, Robert del Tredici, Robin Roth, Sandra Inutiq, Shari Fox, Tyler McCreary, Tyler Shipley, and William Payne.

Joan Scottie would like to acknowledge the support and guidance she has received over the years from Baker Lake Elders. During her community's struggles against uranium mining, Elders provided a foundation for Joan's activism. Their passion for protecting the Inuit homeland provided her with the strength and resolve to keep fighting when things seemed impossible. Moreover, Joan's knowledge of Inuit culture and history is based on teachings from Baker Lake Elders.

Jack Hicks would like to acknowledge the many friends, allies, fellow campaigners, and comrades—across Nunavut, across Canada, and around the world—who shared their insights and expertise with us, and who helped keep our spirits up during two long struggles.

Some sections of this book draw on research Warren Bernauer conducted as a graduate student in Geography at York University and Native Studies at the University of Manitoba. Most of the work Warren did editing the manuscript and preparing it for production was completed while he was a postdoctoral fellow at the University of Manitoba (Environment and Geography / Natural Resources Institute). He would like to acknowledge the support, advice, and feedback provided by academic supervisors, committee members, and the faculty, staff, fellow students, and others who took the time to discuss his research with him. He would also like to say a sincere thank you to his family and friends who provided him with emotional and other support during his studies.

Some sections of this book include substantially reworked material that was originally published in *Canadian Journal of Development Studies*,[1] *Canadian Journal of Native Studies*,[2] *Polar Record*,[3] and *Studies in Political Economy*.[4]

The Government of Nunavut Department of Culture and Heritage provided financial support for this project. The authors would also like to recognize the assistance from the Baker Lake Hunters and Trappers Organization and Pauktuutit Inuit Women of Canada for supporting funding applications associated with this project.

And last but certainly not least, Joan, Jack, and Warren want to thank Dr. Gordon Edwards, president of the Canadian Coalition for Nuclear Responsibility, for his support and expert advice from the very beginning of our struggle to the very end of it. Gordon's knowledge and experience in understanding and challenging the nuclear industry is unsurpassed, and irreplaceable. He was there for us whenever we needed him, answered our many questions, and spoke at our events and at hearings. We honour and celebrate his many, many contributions towards a cleaner and safer world, free of nuclear weapons, nuclear power reactors, and uranium mines. Thank you so much, Gordon!

Why Nunavut Needs a Public Inquiry into Uranium Mining—A Position Statement from Nunavummiut Makitagunarningit

This position statement was released on 29 June 2010, and was published in its entirety in *Nunatsiaq News*.

A petition initiated by Nunavummiut Makitagunarningit has been tabled in the Legislative Assembly calling for a public inquiry on whether or not to open Nunavut to uranium mining.

Nunavut is in danger of being on the receiving end of one of the biggest snow jobs in its history. The uranium industry has come to town, and the elected leaders of our public government may be willing to let bureaucrats in Nunavut and Ottawa decide whether or not its arrival is in our public interest.

Some other jurisdictions in Canada have concluded that it is not in their best interest. In British Columbia, Nova Scotia and the City of Ottawa, elected leaders and citizens have debated the wisdom of uranium mining and nuclear power. They have decided that the risks outweigh the rewards, and they have banned uranium exploration and mining in their jurisdictions.

Similarly, the new government in Greenland banned uranium mining in the country as one of its first acts upon taking office last November.

Contrary to the messaging coming from the heads of land claims organizations and some senior government officials, Nunavummiut Makitagunarningit believes that a uranium industry in Nunavut would pose serious risks to the environment, to public health and safety, and to Inuit traditions and practices.

For whatever reasons, the elected leaders of our public government have not been willing or able to publicly acknowledge those risks—or examine whether Nunavut is ready to deal with them.

Those who would have us believe Nunavut's regulatory system can protect us against the risks of a project like Kiggavik say: "The company must prove it can build and operate its project in an environmentally and socially responsible manner."

But this is not about a single project—it is about an entire industry. As a hunter in Baker Lake recently told the Nunavut Impact Review Board: "Everyone knows that this review is not really about the Kiggavik proposal, yes or no. This review is about opening the Kivalliq—and Nunavut as a whole—to uranium mining, yes or no. . . . In 20 years there could be several or many mines, with several or many roads between them, and everything else that comes with additional mines."

Some other jurisdictions in Canada have decided they are comfortable with the uranium industry polluting their lands. Saskatchewan is, and so is Ontario. Both of these jurisdictions have pitched their future health and wellbeing on their ability to regulate the uranium industry. And both of them made their decisions openly, through public inquiries.

Nunavut, on the other hand, is about to leave the decision to a regulatory process led by bureaucrats and federal politicians.

Why does this matter? Why shouldn't we let Nunavut's regulators make the decision? For one, a determination on a single project cannot address the magnitude of the decision. It simply isn't appropriate or fair to "use" a regulatory process intended to review individual projects to make decisions about an entire sector of the mining industry.

When it comes to uranium, a public inquiry creates the accountability that a regulatory process (including an environmental assessment process) cannot.

There are three reasons why Nunavut needs a public inquiry. First, a public inquiry is more transparent, flexible and democratic than a regulatory process is.

- The members of the Nunavut Impact Review Board (NIRB) are not elected, and so are not directly accountable to the public.

- The impact review process is highly technical and difficult for the public to understand, so it cannot properly gauge public acceptability.

- The scope of NIRB's process is defined by the Nunavut Land Claims Agreement—which requires the Board to focus on the environmental and socio-economic effects of a single project rather than the impacts of an entire industry.

- A public inquiry would force Nunavut's experts to come out and say what they think about uranium mining. Does Nunavut's Chief Medical Officer of Health think uranium mining is safe? If he does, what evidence did he use to make his decision? (Especially when the City of Ottawa's Chief Medical Officer of Health does not.) The public deserves to know this.

- In a public inquiry, Nunavut's elected representatives would be responsible for framing the issues, setting the scope of inquiry and calling evidence. Rather than leaving the decision in the hands of federal bureaucrats (and a few from Nunavut), our own elected MLAs would examine the issues on behalf of all Nunavummiut.

Second, a public inquiry is important because Nunavut's organizations have already shown themselves incapable of protecting the public interest in matters of uranium.

- Representative Inuit organizations have overturned their long-standing opposition to uranium mining without involving beneficiaries in the decision-making process, putting in place a policy that absolves them from responsibility by leaving regulators to decide on their behalf.

- Without public consultation or research, the Government of Nunavut has implemented essentially the same policy.

- The Nunavut Planning Commission has already determined that the people of the Kivalliq region support the Kiggavik project, allowing the project to proceed to an environmental assessment without regard for the democratic standard set in Baker Lake by a public plebiscite conducted by the Hamlet in 1990. At that time, just over 90 per cent of votes cast in Baker Lake were against the Kiggavik project.

- Today, the same project may be developed because a very small group of politicians have decided behind closed doors that it should proceed.

Third, our land claims institutions are not equipped to deal with the complex long-term and cumulative effects of a nascent uranium industry in the territory.

- The health and safety of animals and people depends on government's capacity to enforce regulations, build infrastructure and implement programs to support the industry. Programs might include socio-economic monitoring, job training, social programs and collaborative wildlife monitoring. Are these programs in place? Are they enough?

- Nunavut's regulatory process is proponent driven. A public inquiry is not. It is not in the proponent's interest to criticize government regulations if they are inadequate for protecting the environment. Are we confident our regulations are adequate?

- What about infrastructure? Are we going to trust AREVA Resources to tell us whether the Kivalliq region has the necessary medical infrastructure to deal with the possible results of uranium mining?

- Let us be clear. The NIRB is not a regulator or policy maker. Its primary role is to provide advice to government on environmental decisions. The NIRB does not control purse strings or decide how much to spend on inspection and enforcement or other programs and services.

So far our elected leaders have been asleep at the switch and the tough questions still wait to be answered. Unless a public inquiry is called, we will never know whether uranium mining is the right choice for Nunavut.

The effects of uranium mining will last for thousands of years. Do we not owe it to ourselves, to our children and to our grandchildren to take enough time and care to make sure that we have it right?

Under the rules of the Legislative Assembly, the Government of Nunavut has until Aug. 6 to respond to the MLA for Baker Lake, who along with the MLA for Quttiktuq tabled signed copies of the petition in the Assembly.

We urge the Premier and Cabinet to choose transparency and democratic accountability, and call a public inquiry. If they do not, future generations will judge them harshly.

Abbreviations

AECB	Atomic Energy Control Board	**KRC**	Keewatin Regional Council
AECL	Atomic Energy of Canada Ltd.	**KRHB**	Keewatin Regional Health Board
BLCCC	Baker Lake Concerned Citizens Committee	**KWB**	Kivalliq Wildlife Board
BQCMB	Beverly and Qamanirjuaq Caribou Management Board	**KWF**	Keewatin Wildlife Federation
		Makita	Nunavummiut Makitagunarningit
CNA	Canadian Nuclear Association		
CNSC	Canadian Nuclear Safety Commission	**MLA**	Member of the Legislative Assembly
FEARO	Federal Environmental Assessment and Review Office	**NAUC**	Northern Anti-Uranium Coalition
GN	Government of Nunavut	**NIRB**	Nunavut Impact Review Board
HTA	Hunters and Trappers Association	**NPC**	Nunavut Planning Commission
HTO	Hunters and Trappers Organization	**NTI**	Nunavut Tunngavik Incorporated
ICC	Inuit Circumpolar Council	**RCMP**	Royal Canadian Mounted Police
IOL	Inuit Owned Lands		
		TFN	Tunngavik Federation of Nunavut
ITC	Inuit Tapirisat of Canada		
ITK	Inuit Tapiriit Kanatami		
KIA	Kivalliq Inuit Association (called "Keewatin Inuit Association" prior to 1993)		

Notes

Introduction

1 Ross, "Whaling, Inuit and the Arctic Islands"; Ray, *The Canadian Fur Trade.*

2 Brody, *The People's Land*; Tester and Kulchyski, *Tammarniit (Mistakes).*

3 Merritt, Fenge, and Jull, *Nunavut: Political Choices and Manifest Destiny.*

4 Hicks and White, "Nunavut: Inuit Self-Determination."

5 Cater and Keeling, "'That's Where Our Future Came From.'"

6 Tester, Lambert, and Lim, "Wistful Thinking."

7 Green, "'There Is No Memory of It Here.'"

8 McPherson, *New Owners in Their Own Land*; Tester, *Socio-economic and Environmental Impacts.*

9 Wilt, "'The Ice Can Be Conquered.'"

10 Bernauer, "Producing Consent."

11 Brody, *The People's Land*; Usher, "The Class System"; Dacks, *A Choice of Futures.*

12 Johnson et al., "Community Actions to Address Seismic Testing"; Rodgers and Ingram, "Decolonizing Environmentalism."

13 Bernauer, "Producing Consent."

14 Bernauer, "The Nunavut Land Claims Agreement and Caribou Habitat Management"; McPherson, *New Owners in Their Own Land.*

15 Bernauer, "The Nunavut Land Claims Agreement and Caribou Habitat Management"; McPherson, *New Owners in Their Own Land.*

16 Bowman, "Sealing the Deal"; Göcke, "Uranium Mining in Nunavut"; Scobie and Rodgers, "Contestations of Resource Extraction"; Rodon, "Institutional Development."

17 Bernauer, "Land Rights and Resource Conflicts"; Metuzals and Hird, "'The Disease that Knowledge Must Cure.'"

18 For a book written in a similar manner, see Manuel and Derrickson, *Unsettling Canada.*

19 Duffy, *The Road to Nunavut*; Brody, *The People's Land*; Tester and Kulchyski, *Tammarniit (Mistakes)*; Mitchell, *From Talking Chiefs*; Qikiqtani Truth Commission, *QTC Final Report: Achieving Saimaqatigiingniq*; Cameron, *Far Off Metal River.*

20 Kulchyski and Tester, *Kiumajut (Talking Back)*; Wachowich, *Saqiyuq.*

21 Bowman, "Sealing the Deal"; Göcke, "Uranium Mining in Nunavut"; Scobie and Rodgers, "Contestations of Resource Extraction"; Rodon, "Institutional Development"; Bernauer, "Land Rights and Resource Conflicts"; Metuzals and Hird, "'The Disease that Knowledge Must Cure.'"

22 Peterson, "Community Experiences of Mining"; Maksimowski, "Well-being and Mining"; Jones and Bradshaw, "Addressing Historical Impacts"; Rixen and Blangy, "Life after Meadowbank"; Blangy and Deffner, "Impacts of Mining Development"; Nightingale et al., "The Effects of Resource Extraction."

Chapter 1. Growing Up on the Land

1 Royal Canadian Mounted Police, *Conditions Amongst Eskimos Generally, Annual Report— Period Ending December 31, 1959 Baker Lake District NWT*, Division File TA 1491-2-1-2 (59), 11 January 1960.

2 Royal Canadian Mounted Police, *Camp Conditions—General—Baker Lake Detachment Area*, 25 February 1960. Keewatin is the historical name for the Kivalliq region.

3 Lucy Qaunnaq, interview conducted as part of a midwifery research project undertaken by Pauktuutit in 1992–93.

4 In the late 1980s, Bessie Iquginnaq Scottie told these stories to researcher and writer David Pelly, which he later published in paraphrased form. See Pelly, *The Ancestors Are Happy*.

5 The Inuit Broadcasting Corporation is a television production company that creates Inuit content in Inuktitut.

6 The song was transcribed and translated into English by Hilu Tagoona.

7 Ekho and Ottokie, *Childrearing Practices*, 28.

8 Lucy Qaunnaq, interview conducted as part of a midwifery research project undertaken by Pauktuutit in 1992–93.

9 Pelly, *The Ancestors Are Happy*.

10 Ibid., 151–52.

Chapter 2. Qablunaat, Moving to Town, and Going to School.

1 Brody, *The People's Land*.

2 Harper, *In Those Days*.

3 Trott, "Mission and Opposition in North Baffin Island."

4 Tester and Kulchyski, *Tammarniit (Mistakes)*.

5 Abele, "Canadian Contradictions."

6 Tester and Kulchyski, *Tammarniit (Mistakes)*.

7 Ibid.

8 Qikiqtani Truth Commission, *Illinniarniq: Schooling in Qikiqtaaluk*; Truth and Reconciliation Commission of Canada, *Canada's Residential Schools: The Inuit and Northern Experience*.

9 Royal Commission on Aboriginal Peoples, *Looking Forward, Looking Back*; Qikiqtani Truth Commission, *Nuutauniq: Moves in Inuit Life*.

10 Frank Vallee provides a useful discussion of the dynamics between Inuit and *qablunaat* in the community of Baker Lake in the 1950s. See Vallee, *Kabloona and Eskimo*. See also Brody, *The People's Land*.

11 Brody, *The Other Side of Eden*, 43.

12 Watt-Cloutier, *The Right to Be Cold*, 72–73.

13 Aglukark, "Ilirasungniq."

14 Aglukark, "A Culture of Inertia."

15 Kuptana, "Ilira, or Why it Was Unthinkable," 7.

16 Qikiqtani Truth Commission, *Paliisikkut: Policing in Qikiqtaaluk*, 183.

17 Brody, *The Other Side of Eden*, 43.

18 Hicks, "On the Application of Theories"; Harper, "The Answer the White Man Expects"; Kennedy Dalseg, "Seeing Like a Community."

19 Kulchyski and Tester, *Kiumajut (Talking Back)*.

20 Truth and Reconciliation Commission of Canada, *Canada's Residential Schools: The Inuit and Northern Experience*.

21 Watt-Cloutier, *The Right to Be Cold*, 41. The Truth and Reconciliation Commission's report on Inuit and Northern First Nations' experiences with school came to similar conclusions about the Churchill Vocational Centre. In survivors' stories, the Churchill Vocational Centre is "often cited for the positive [role it] played in developing and encouraging a new generation of Aboriginal leadership in the North" and that many Inuit who attended "would go on to play leading roles in the creation of the new Territory of Nunavut in 1999." Truth and Reconciliation Commission of Canada, *Canada's Residential Schools: The Inuit and Northern Experience*, 4.

Chapter 3. Uranium Exploration, Petitions, and a Court Case

1 Interdisciplinary Systems Ltd., *Effects of Exploration and Development*, v.

2 McPherson, *New Owners in Their Own Land*, 42–55.

3 "Survival of the Inuit Culture vs Mining," *ITC News*, September 1979.

4 Kulchyski and Tester, *Kiumajut (Talking Back)*.

5 Freeman, *Inuit Land Use and Occupancy Study*.

6 Harding, *Canada's Deadly Secret*.

7 Keeling, "'Born in an Atomic Test Tube'"; Mawhiney and Pitblado, eds., *Boom Town Blues*.

8   Harding, *Canada's Deadly Secret.*

9   Edwards, "Canada's Nuclear Industry."

10 Ibid.

11 Ibid.

12 "Tea and Biscuits," *Inuit Monthly*, May/June 1974, 49.

13 Ibid.

14 "ITC Calls for Land Freeze," *Inuit Today*, March/April 1977, 13.

15 Ibid.

16 "Prospecting Deferred in Keewatin," *Inuit Today*, June/July 1977, 23.

17 Interdisciplinary Systems Ltd., *Effects of Exploration.*

18 Robertson et al., "Territorializing Piquhiit," 9. See also: Ljubicic et al., "Inuit Approaches to Naming and Distinguishing Caribou."

19 The traditional prohibition on hunting the first caribou in a herd has also been documented by anthropologists and Inuit community historians. See Laugrand and Oosten, *Hunters, Predators, and Prey*; Mannik, ed., *Inuit Nunamiut / Inland Inuit.*

20 Hunting caribou at water crossings has been documented and discussed at length by numerous anthropologists and archaeologists. See Birket-Smith, *The Caribou Eskimos*; Rasmussen, *Observations on the Intellectual Culture*; Burch, "The Caribou Inuit"; Arima, *A Contextual Study*; Clark, "The Development of Caribou Eskimo Culture."

21 Contemporary use of water crossings has been documented in several land use studies. See Welland, "Inuit Land Use"; Riewe, ed., *Nunavut Atlas.*

22 Geert van den Steenhoven documents traditional songs about hunting at water crossings. See Steenhoven, *Leadership and Law.*

23 References to water crossings in Inuit toponyms have been examined by several scholars, including Paula Kigjugalik Hughson, an Inuk woman from Baker Lake. See Hughson, "Our Homeland." See also Stewart, Keith, and Scottie, "Caribou Crossings and Cultural Meanings"; Keith, "Caribou, River, and Ocean."

24 The rules regarding the proper use of water crossings have been documented and discussed by academics and community researchers. See Stewart, Keith, and Scottie, "Caribou Crossings and Cultural Meanings"; Keith, "Inuit Place Names and Land-Use History"; Mannik, ed., *Inuit Nunamiut / Inland Inuit*; Webster, *Harvaqtuurmiut Heritage.*

25 For example, Justice Berger's report on the proposed Mackenzie Valley Pipeline recommended that no pipeline be built across northern Yukon because it would disturb the calving grounds of the Porcupine caribou herd. See Berger, *Northern Frontier, Northern Homeland.*

26 The Beverly and Qamanirjuaq Caribou Management Board has produced significant literature explaining the sensitivity of caribou during the calving and post-calving seasons. See Beverly and Qamanirjuaq Caribou Management Board, *Protecting Calving Grounds.*

27 "Inuit Seek Court Protection for Baker Lake," *Inuit Today*, April/May 1978.

28 "ITC General Meeting," *Inuit Today*, April/May 1978.

29 Baker Lake Hamlet Council, Special Meeting Minutes, 7 April 1978.

30 Ibid.

31 Ibid.

32 *The Hamlet of Baker Lake v. The Min. of Ind. Aff. and North. Dev.*, [1979] 1 FC 487.

33 Ibid.

34 Ibid.

35 "Survival of the Inuit Culture vs Mining," *ITC News*, September 1979, 6.

36 Ibid.

37 Ibid., 7.

38 Ibid.

39 Ibid., 8.

40 Ibid., 12.

41 Ibid., 15.

42 *The Hamlet of Baker Lake v. The Min. of Ind. Aff. and North. Dev.*, [1980] 1 FC 518.

43 Gunn, "A Review of Research."

Chapter 4. Kiggavik Round 1: The Urangesellschaft Proposal

1 "Reindeer meat with Cs-137 concentrations of 300 becquerels (Bq)/kg or higher was declared unfit for human consumption and thrown into pits or ground into fodder for animals on fur farms. To save herders from economic ruin and to buttress the Saami culture—so locally dependent upon the continuation of reindeer herding—the Swedish state instituted wide-ranging compensation policies." Beach, "Pereptions of Risk, Dilemmas of Policy," 729.

2 Edwards et al., "Uranium: A Discussion Guide."

3 Loo, "Political Animals."

4 Kendrick, "Community Perceptions of the Beverly and Qamanirjuaq Caribou Management Board."

5 Proctor, "Uranium, Inuit Rights, and Emergent Neoliberalism."

6 "Inuit Want Uranium Ban in North," *ITC News*, April 1980.

7 Keske et al., "Waste Management in Labrador"; Abele, "Canadian Contradictions."

8 Lynge, *The Right to Return.*

9 Lichen has no root system and obtains nutrients from the atmosphere rather than the earth. One of the key nutrients it absorbs from the atmosphere is the mineral potassium. The element cesium is an analogue of potassium, which means it has physical and chemical properties similar to those of potassium. Because lichen can't tell the difference between the two, it absorbs cesium the way it normally absorbs potassium. While cesium isn't radioactive,

cesium-137 is an artificial radionuclide that is a product of the nuclear fission of uranium and other isotopes in nuclear reactors and weapons.

10 Tracy, "Radiocesium Body Burdens."

11 Ibid.

12 O'Neill, *The Firecracker Boys.*

13 "Soviet Nuclear Satellite Crashes in Canadian North." CBC radio documentary, 27 January 1978, https://www.cbc.ca/archives entry/1978-soviet-nuclear-satellite-crashes-in-canadian-north.

14 Rand, "Falling Cosmos."

15 Ibid.

16 "Inuit Circumpolar Conference," *Inuit Today*, September 1977, 28.

17 "ICC Resolutions," *Inuit Today*, February 1984; "Inuit Protest War's Madness," *Inuit Today*, February 1984.

18 Lynge, *Inuit: The Story of the Inuit Circumpolar Conference.*

19 Simon, *Inuit: One Future—One Arctic*; Simon, "Militarization and the Aboriginal Peoples."

20 Tagak Curley, open letter to Dennis Patterson, government leader of the Northwest Territories, 22 November 1988.

21 Keewatin Inuit Association, Resolution #6-89 "Proposed Baker Lake Uranium Mine," Annual General Meeting, 1989.

22 Northwest Territories, Legislative Assembly, *Hansard*, 9th Assembly, 4th Session, 1981.

23 Northwest Territories, Legislative Assembly, *Hansard*, 10th Assembly, 7th Session, 19 June 1986.

24 Tagak Curley, open letter to Dennis Patterson, government leader of the Northwest Territories, 22 November 1988.

25 Wray spoke of people weeping at public meetings, and stated, "We knew we had lost control when that happened." He did not explain why or how the Government of the Northwest Territories felt "in control" of the FEARO process. Hicks, "The Other Side of Kiggavik."

26 "The Kiggavik Controversy," *Focus North*, CBC Television, 1990.

27 McKay, "Snow Job."

28 Northwest Territories Legislative Assembly, Motion #05-90(1) "Opposition to Exploration and Mining of Uranium in the NWT," 1990.

29 Smellie, "Motion Opposing Kiggavik Stalled."

30 Hamlet of Baker Lake, untitled media release, 15 February 1990.

31 Garry Smith, open letter to M. Stuart, executive vice-president of Urangesellschaft Canada, 3 April 1990.

32 Urangesellschaft Canada untitled press release, 5 July 1990.

Chapter 5. The Nunavut Agreement and Gold Mining near Baker Lake

1　For an overview of the terms of the Nunavut Land Claims Agreement, see Hicks and White, "Nunavut: Inuit Self-Determination."

2　For an overview of the Government of Nunavut, including the process by which it was designed, see Hicks and White, *Made in Nunavut.*

3　This is a question Paula Kigjugalik Hughson, an Inuk woman from Baker Lake, discusses in her master's thesis. See Hughson, "Our Homeland."

4　McPherson, *New Owners in Their Own Land.*

5　Several scholars have examined conflicts between corporate Inuit organizations and community-based organizations in light of the structures created by the Nunavut Agreement. See Bowman, "Sealing the Deal"; Göcke, "Uranium Mining in Nunavut"; Scobie and Rodgers, "Contestations of Resource Extraction"; Kulchyski and Bernauer, "Modern Treaties, Extraction and Imperialism"; Rodon, "Institutional Development"; Bernauer, "Land Rights and Resource Conflicts."

6　For a discussion of northern co-management boards, including the challenges they face in incorporating Indigenous culture and values into their operations, see White, "Cultures in Collision"; Nadasdy, *Hunters and Bureaucrats*; Dokis, *Where the Rivers Meet.*

7　*Nunavut Land Claims Agreement*, 12.5.7.

8　*Nunavut Land Claims Agreement*, 13.2.1.

9　Côté-Mantha et al., "The Amaruq Deposits."

10　Nunavut Impact Review Board, Final Hearing Report for the Meadowbank Gold Project, NIRB File No. 03MN107, August 2006.

11　Ibid.

12　Ibid., vol. 2, p. 481.

13　Ibid., vol. 2, pp. 404–24.

14　Ibid., vol. 3, pp. 497–523.

15　Ibid., vol. 2, p. 325; vol. 3, p. 487; vol. 4, p. 572.

16　Ibid., vol. 5, pp. 790–69; vol. 6, pp. 1053–55.

17　Nunavut Impact Review Board, Final Hearing Report for the Meadowbank Gold Project, NIRB File No. 03MN107, August 2006.

18　Peterson, "Community Experiences of Mining"; Maksimowski, "Well-being and Mining."

19　Bernauer, "The Limits to Extraction"; Aglu Consulting, Agnico Kivalliq Projects 2019 Socio-Economic Monitoring Report, NIRB File No. 03MN107, March 2020.

20　Ibid.

21　Brody, *The People's Land*; Usher, "The North."

22　These observations have been documented by several university researchers. See Maksimowski, "Well-being and Mining"; Blangy and Deffner, "Impacts of Mining Development"; Bernauer, "The Uranium Controversy in Baker Lake."

23 Nunavut Impact Review Board, 2013–2014 Annual Monitoring Report for the Meadowbank Gold Project, NIRB File No. 03MN107, 2014.

24 Nunavut Impact Review Board, 2015–2016 Annual Monitoring Report for the Meadowbank Gold Project, NIRB File No. 03MN107, 2016.

25 Ibid.

26 Ibid.

27 Nunavut Impact Review Board, 2017–2018 Annual Monitoring Report for the Meadowbank and Whale Tail Projects, NIRB File No. 16MN056, 2018.

28 Nunavut Impact Review Board, 2018–2019 Annual Monitoring Report for the Meadowbank and Whale Tail Projects, NIRB File No. 16MN056, 2019.

29 Nunavut Impact Review Board, Preliminary Hearing Conference Decision Concerning the Kiggavik Proposal (p. 18), NIRB File No. 09MN003, 2013; Nunavut Planning Commission, Report on Public Consultation on the Draft Nunavut Land Use Plan in Chesterfield Inlet, November 2014; Nunavut Impact Review Board, Final Hearing Transcript for the Meliadine Gold Project (pp. 689–90, 981, 1066), NIRB File No. 11MN034, August 2014; Nunavut Impact Review Board, Final Hearing Transcript for the Kiggavik Project (pp. 1252, 1512, 1615, 1880), NIRB File No. 09MN003, March 2015.

30 Blangy and Deffner, "Impacts of Mining Development"; Jones and Bradshaw, "Addressing Historical Impacts."

31 Peterson, "Community Experiences of Mining"; Nightingale et al., "The Effects of Resource Extraction."

32 Ibid.

33 Peterson, "Community Experiences of Mining"; Blangy and Deffner, "Impacts of Mining Development"; Jones and Bradshaw, "Addressing Historical Impacts"; Nightingale et al., "The Effects of Resource Extraction"; Pauktuutit, *The Impact of Resource Extraction*.

34 Nightingale et al., "The Effects of Resource Extraction"; Pauktuutit, *The Impact of Resource Extraction*.

35 National Inquiry into Missing and Murdered Indigenous Women and Girls, *Reclaiming Power and Place*; Hall, *Refracted Economies*.

36 Nightingale et al., "The Effects of Resource Extraction"; Pauktuutit, *The Impact of Resource Extraction*.

37 Peterson, "Community Experiences of Mining"; Blangy and Deffner, "Impacts of Mining Development"; Jones and Bradshaw, "Addressing Historical Impacts"; Nightingale et al., "The Effects of Resource Extraction"; Pauktuutit, *The Impact of Resource Extraction*.

38 Rixen and Blangy, "Life after Meadowbank."

39 Côté-Mantha et al., "The Amaruq Deposits."

40 Nunavut Impact Review Board, Screening Decision Report for the Amaruq Winter Access Road, NIRB File No. 11EN010, 10 February 2015.

41 Nunavut Impact Review Board, Screening Decision Report for the Amaruq Exploration Access Road, NIRB File No. 11EN010, 4 November 2015.

42 Baker Lake Hunters and Trappers Organization, Comments on Proposal Amaruq All-Season Road, NIRB File No. 11EN010, 2015.

43 Nunavut Impact Review Board, Screening Decision Report for the Amaruq Exploration Access Road, NIRB File No. 11EN010, 4 November 2015.

44 Nunavut Impact Review Board, Screening Decision Report for the Amaruq, Meadowbank, and White Hills Exploration Project, NIRB File No. 15EN050, 15 January 2016.

45 Ibid.

46 Nunavut Impact Review Board, Screening Decision Report for the Amaruq Advanced Exploration and Bulk Sample Project, NIRB File No. 11EN010, 5 October 2016.

47 Nunavut Impact Review Board, 2018–2019 Annual Monitoring Report for the Meadowbank and Whale Tail Projects, NIRB File No. 16MN056, 2019.

48 Nunavut Impact Review Board, Final Hearing Report for Agnico Eagle's Whale Tail Pit Project, NIRB File No. 16MN056, November 2017.

49 Nunavut Impact Review Board, Final Hearing Transcript for the Whale Tail Proposal, NIRB File No. 16MN056, 2017.

50 Nunavut Impact Review Board, Final Hearing Report for Agnico Eagle's Whale Tail Pit Project (vol. 4, p. 680), NIRB File No. 16MN056, November 2017.

51 Nunavut Impact Review Board, Reconsideration Report and Recommendations for the Whale Tail Pit Expansion Project, NIRB File No. 16MN056, October 2019.

52 Baker Lake Hunters and Trappers Organization, Technical Review Comments for the Whale Tail Expansion Project, NIRB File No. 16MN056, April 2019.

53 Nunavut Impact Review Board, Final Hearing Transcript for the Whale Tail Expansion Project (vol. 3, pp. 518–23), NIRB File No. 16MN056, 2019.

54 Nunavut Impact Review Board, Reconsideration Report and Recommendations for the Whale Tail Pit Expansion Project, NIRB File No. 16MN056, October 2019.

55 Nunavut Impact Review Board, Project Certificate for the Whale Tail Mine, NIRB File No. 16MN056, 15 March 2018.

56 Agnico Eagle, Terrestrial Advisory Group Terms of Reference, NIRB File No. 16MN056, 24 October 2018.

57 Agnico Eagle, Terrestrial Ecosystem Management Plan for the Whale Tail Mine, Version 7, NIRB File No. 16MN056, 2019.

58 Kivalliq Inuit Association, Review of KIA Involvement in the Development of TEMP Version 8, NIRB File No. 16MN056, 21 May 2020.

59 Ibid.; Baker Lake Hunters and Trappers Organization, Re: The March 26th Letter from Agnico Eagle, NIRB File No. 16MN056, 10 April 2020.

60 Agnico Eagle, Terrestrial Ecosystem Management Plan for the Whale Tail Mine, Version 8, NIRB File No. 16MN056, 2020.

61 Baker Lake Hunters and Trappers Organization, Changes to Agnico Eagle's Terrestrial Ecosystem Management Plan, NIRB File No. 16MN056, 30 April 2020.

62 Nunavut Tunngavik Incorporated, Clarification on Agnico Eagle TEMP Version 8, NIRB File No. 16MN056, 13 May 2020.

63 Kivalliq Inuit Association, Review of KIA Involvement in the Development of TEMP Version 8, NIRB File No. 16MN056, 21 May 2020.

64 Government of Nunavut, Changes to the Whale Tail Project's TEMP, NIRB File No. 16MN056, 22 May 2020.

65 Agnico Eagle, Terrestrial Ecosystem Management Plan Responses, NIRB File No. 16MN056, 13 July 2020.

66 McPherson, *New Owners in Their Own Land*.

Chapter 6. Uranium Policy in Nunavut

1 See https://makitanunavut.wordpress.com/.

2 NPC, *Keewatin Regional Land Use Plan*, 61.

3 Watt-Cloutier, *The Right to Be Cold*.

4 Government of Nunavut, *Inuit Qaujimajatuqangit of Climate Change in Nunavut*.

5 For further discussion of the inability of the nuclear industry to help significantly reduce carbon emissions in an effective timeframe, see Muellner et al., "Nuclear Energy—The Solution to Climate Change?"; Ramana, "Small Modular and Advanced Nuclear Reactors"; Froese et al., "Too Small to be Viable?"; Green, *Nuclear Power's Economic Crisis*.

6 For more information about the environmental and health risks associated with nuclear power generation, see Sovacool, "Critically Weighing the Costs."

7 For more information about the relationship between nuclear power and nuclear weapons, see Harding, *Canada's Deadly Secret*; Edwards, "Canada's Nuclear Industry."

8 Jaczko et al., "Former Heads of US, German, French Nuclear Regulation."

9 Bell, "Baker HTO Worried."

10 Scottie, "Is NTI Irresponsibly Endorsing Uranium Mining?"

11 Nunavut Tunngavik Incorporated, "Uranium Consultation Meeting Minutes," NIRB File No. 09MN003.

12 Ibid.

13 Ibid.

14 Ibid.

15 Baker Lake Hunters and Trappers Organization, "Presentation to NTI Uranium Consultation Meeting," NIRB File No. 09MN003.

16 Nunavut Tunngavik Incorporated, *NTI and Forum Uranium Corp. Sign MOU*, media release, 8 December 2008.

17 Nunavut Tunngavik Incorporated, *NTI Grants Uranium Rights to Kaminak Gold*, media release, 7 February 2008.

18 Scottie, "NTI, Inuit Associations Do Not Serve Inuit."

19 Nunavut, Legislative Assembly, *Hansard*, 2nd Assembly, 4th Session, 4 July 2007, 1480–81.

20 Nunavut Planning Commission, NPC Uranium Workshop Transcript, 5–7 June 2007, 156–59.

21 Ibid.

22 Arragutainaq et al., letter to NPC Chairperson Ron Roach, 6 May 2008.

23 Copies of these motions are appended to AREVA's 2008 proposal for the Kiggavik project. See AREVA Resources, The Kiggavik Project, NIRB File No. 09MN003, 2008.

24 Nunavummiut Makitagunarningit, "Why Nunavut Needs a Public Inquiry."

25 Golder Associates wrote sections of AREVA's Environmental Impact Statement for the Kiggavik project.

26 Bell, "Nunavut Uranium Forum."

27 "Makita Co-President Sandra Inutiq's Speech," Nunavummiut Makitagunarningit (Makita), https://makitanunavut.files.wordpress.com/2012/03/inutiq_gn_forums.pdf.

28 Nunavummiut Makitagunarningit, "Nunavut Voters Should Decide."

29 Nunavummiut Makitagunarningit, "In Defense of Emotionalism."

Chapter 7. Kiggavik Round 2: The AREVA Proposal

1 All comments submitted for the screening of AREVA's Kiggavik proposal are included in Appendix B of the NIRB Screening Decision Report. See Nunavut Impact Review Board, SDR for AREVA's Kiggavik Proposal, NIRB File No. 09MN003, 2009.

2 Nunavummiut Makitagunarningit, "Makita Says the NIRB's Failure to Translate Draft EIS Guidelines Shows Flagrant Disregard for Inuit Rights," media release, 18 November 2010.

3 Baker Lake Hunters and Trappers Organization, Comments on the Draft Guidelines for AREVA Resources' Proposed Kiggavik Project, NIRB File No. 08MN003, 27 February 2011.

4 Nunavut Impact Review Board, Public Scoping Meetings Summary Report, NIRB File No. 09MN003, June 2010.

5 Nunavummiut Makitagunarningit, Comments on the Draft Guidelines for AREVA Resources' Proposed Kiggavik Project, NIRB File No. 08MN003, 24 January 2011; Nunavummiut Makitagunarningit, Comments on the Revised Draft Guidelines for AREVA Resources' Proposed Kiggavik Project, NIRB File No. 08MN003, 2 March 2011.

6 Nunavut Impact Review Board, Final EIS Guidelines for the Kiggavik Project, NIRB File No. 09MN003, 3 May 2011.

7 The Nunavut Impact Review Board's report from the meeting acknowledges that many of us were frustrated with the timelines for the review. See Nunavut Impact Review Board, Public Information Sessions Summary Report, NIRB File No. 09MN003, June 2012.

8 Nunavummiut Makitagunarningit, NIRB Timelines for Kiggavik Project Review, NIRB File No. 09MN003, 3 December 2012.

9 North Slave Métis Alliance, Re: Makita Letter to the NIRB Regarding Review Timelines, NIRB File No. 09MN003, 6 December 2012.

10 Beverly and Qamanirjuaq Caribou Management Board, Scheduling the Technical Meeting and Pre-Hearing Conference for the Kiggavik Technical Review, NIRB File No. 09MN003, 25 February 2013.

11 AREVA Resources, Final Environmental Impact Statement for the Kiggavik Project, NIRB File No. 09MN003, 2014.

12 Baker Lake Hunters and Trappers Organization, Technical Review Comments on AREVA Resources Inc.'s Proposed Kiggavik Mine, NIRB File No. 09MN003, 14 January 2015.

13 Kivalliq Wildlife Board, Motion Regarding Proposed Kiggavik Mine, Final Hearing Exhibit No. 59, NIRB File No. 09MN003, 23 February 2015.

14 Nunavut Impact Review Board, Final Hearing Transcript for the Kiggavik Project (vol. 7, pp. 1663–64), NIRB File No. 09MN003, March 2015.

15 Forum Uranium Corp., "Forum to Explore Nutaaq Rare Earth Property in Nunavut," media release, 23 June 2011.

16 Nunavut Impact Review Board, Final Hearing Transcript for the Kiggavik Project (vol. 8), NIRB File No. 09MN003, March 2015.

17 Ibid., vol. 10, p. 2221.

18 Ibid., vol. 10, pp. 2209–10.

19 Ibid., vol. 10, p. 2176.

20 Ibid., vol. 10.

21 Ibid.

22 Ibid., vol. 11.

23 Ibid., vol. 11, p. 2352.

24 Nunavut Impact Review Board, Final Hearing Report for AREVA's Kiggavik Proposal (p. 289), NIRB File No. 09MN003, 2015.

25 Ibid., p. 1.

26 Peyton and Franks, "The New Nature of Things"; Sincalir and Doelle, "The New IAA in Canada."

27 Nunavut Impact Review Board, Final Hearing Transcript for the Kiggavik Proposal (vol. 10, p. 2176), NIRB File No. 09MN00, March 2015.

28 Quoted in Metuzals and Hird, "'The Disease that Knowledge Must Cure,'" 11.

29 Bernauer, *Mining and the Social Economy in Baker Lake, Nunavut.*

Chapter 8. Protecting Our Land and Caribou

1 Forum Uranium Corp., "Forum Consolidates North Thelon Properties by Acquiring 100% of Agnico Eagle's Claims Adjoining AREVA's Kiggavik Uranium Deposit," news release, 6 February 2014.

2 Nunavut Tunngavik Incorporated, "NTI and Forum Uranium Corp. Sign MOU," news release, 8 December 2008.

3 This research also formed the basis of Darren Keith's master's thesis and several journal articles. See Keith, "Caribou, River, and Ocean"; Stewart, Keith, and Scottie, "Caribou Crossings and Cultural Meanings"; Keith, "Inuit Place Names and Land-Use History."

4 Harvaqtuurmiut Elders et al., *Harvaqtuuq*.

5 Ibid., 115.

6 Ibid., 113.

7 Stewart, Keith, and Scottie, "Caribou Crossings and Cultural Meanings."

8 Harvaqtuurmiut Elders et al., *Harvaqtuuq*, 102.

9 Parks Canada, *Fall Caribou Crossing National Historic Site*, Research Report No. 1995-028, 1995.

10 Sandlos, *Hunters at the Margins*.

11 Pelly, *Thelon: A River Sanctuary*.

12 Ibid.

13 Mannik, ed., *Inuit Nunamiut / Inland Inuit*.

14 Baker Lake Hunters and Trappers Organization, *Hanningajuq Project*, prepared by David Pelly, 2004.

15 A junior mining company is an exploration company in search of new deposits of gold, silver, uranium, or other precious metals. These companies are highly speculative, and almost never bring a mine into production on their own. Rather, they seek to develop interest in a deposit, in the hopes that a larger company will buy them out. They are often viewed as being aggressive in their business practices, and focused less on building long-term relationships with nearby communities than on making quick profits for their investors.

16 Government of Nunavut, Comments on NIRB Screening of Uravan's Garry Lakes Project, NIRB File No. 08EN037, 23 April 2008.

17 Beverly and Qamanirjuaq Caribou Management Board, Comments on NIRB Screening of Uravan's Garry Lakes Project, NIRB File No. 08EN037, 23 April 2008.

18 Lutsel K'e Dene First Nation, Comments on NIRB Screening of Uravan's Garry Lakes Project, NIRB File No. 08EN037, 9 June 2008.

19 Athabasca Denesuline Negotiating Team, Comments on NIRB Screening of Uravan's Garry Lakes Project, NIRB File No. 08EN037, 9 June 2008.

20 Nunavut Impact Review Board, Screening Decision Report for Uravan's Garry Lakes Project, NIRB File No. 08EN037, 27 June 2008.

21 Kivalliq Inuit Association and Nunavut Tunngavik Inc., Comments on the Draft Scope for Uravan's Garry Lakes Project, NIRB File No. 08EN037, 28 October 2008.

22 Kivalliq Inuit Association and Nunavut Tunngavik Inc., Additional Comments on the Draft Scope for Uravan's Garry Lakes Project, NIRB File No. 08EN037, 31 October 2008.

23 Indian and Northern Affairs Canada, Inspector's Direction, NWB File No. 2BE-GAR0710, 15 December 2009.

24 Uravan, Response to Inspector's Direction, NWB File No. 2BE-GAR0710, 31 December 2009.

25 Aboriginal Affairs and Northern Development Canada, Water Use Inspection Report, NWB File No. 2BE-GAR0710, 30 June 2012.

26 Uravan, Compliance Plan, NWB File No. 2BE-GAR0710, 17 October 2012.

27 "Email chain between Christine Wilson (a federal Resource Management Officer) and Larry Lahusen (CEO of Uravan)," NWB File No. 2BE-GAR0710, [2012–2013?].

28 Indigenous Affairs and Northern Development Canada, Final Inspection Report, NWB File No. 2BE-GAR0710, 24 August 2017.

29 +/- 106,600.

30 The results of these surveys are summarized in Campbell et al., "Calving Ground Abundance Estimates."

31 Ibid.

32 Adamczewski et al., "What Happened to the Beverly Caribou Herd after 1994?"

33 Campbell et al., "Calving Ground Abundance Estimates"; Adamczewski et al., "What Happened to the Beverly Caribou Herd after 1994?"

34 Nunavut Impact Review Board, Screening Decision Report for Anconia's Marce Lake Project, NIRB File No. 11EN046, 5 March 2012.

35 Baker Lake Hunters and Trappers Organization, Comments on Anconia's Marce Lake Project, 21 June 2012.

36 Aqigiq Hunters and Trappers Organization, Comments on Anconia's Marce Lake Project, 13 February 2013.

37 Issatik Hunters and Trappers Organization, Comments on Anconia's Marce Lake Project, 28 February 2013.

38 Kangiqliniq Hunters and Trappers Organization, Comments on Anconia's Marce Lake Project, 20 March 2013.

39 Aboriginal Affairs and Northern Development Canada, Letter to Anconia Resources Re: Compliance, NWB File No. 2BE-MRC1217, 16 September 2013.

40 Anconia Resources, Letter to AANDC Re: Expiry of Permit, NIRB File No. 11EN046, 14 January 2016.

41 Aboriginal Affairs and Northern Development Canada, Land Use Permit Inspection Form, NWB File No. 2BE-MRC1217, 26 July 2016.

42 Rodon, "Land-Use Co-Management in Canada"; Dyck, *Community Politics, Governance, and Land Use Planning*.

43 Kivalliq Wildlife Board Motion #KWB-2013-005.

44 Baker Lake Hunters and Trappers Organization, Comments on Draft Nunavut Land Use Plan, 10 October 2013.

45 Arviq Hunters and Trappers Organization, Comments on the Draft Nunavut Land Use Plan, 10 February 2014.

46 Aqigiq Hunters and Trappers Organization, Comments on the Draft Nunavut Land Use Plan, 18 September 2015.

47 Issatik Hunters and Trappers Organization, Comments on the Draft Nunavut Land Use Plan, 30 September 2015.

48 Arviat Hunters and Trappers Organization, Comments on the Draft Nunavut Land Use Plan, 24 September 2015.

49 Nunavut Wildlife Management Board, Comments on the Draft Nunavut Land Use Plan, 21 May 2014.

50 Lutsel K'e Dene First Nation, Comments on the Draft Nunavut Land Use Plan, 31 January 2014.

51 Northwest Territories Métis Council, Comments on the Draft Nunavut Land Use Plan, 21 February 2014.

52 Fort Smith Métis Council, Comments on the Draft Nunavut Land Use Plan, 4 February 2014.

53 Athabasca Denesuline Negotiating Team, Comments on the Draft Nunavut Land Use Plan, 20 October 2014.

54 Northlands Dene First Nation, Comments on the Draft Nunavut Land Use Plan, 27 May 2014.

55 Sayisi Dene First Nation, Comments on the Draft Nunavut Land Use Plan, 15 May 2014.

56 Beverly and Qamanirjuaq Caribou Management Board, Comments on the Draft Nunavut Land Use Plan, 14 February 2014.

57 Government of Nunavut, Comments on the Draft Nunavut Land Use Plan, 28 May 2014.

58 The "core" calving grounds were defined by GN Department of Environment biologists, using information gathered from radio tracking collars.

59 Nunavut Planning Commission, Transcript of Fourth Technical Meeting, 23–26 March 2016.

60 Kivalliq Inuit Association, Comments on the Draft Nunavut Land Use Plan, 13 October 2013.

61 Kivalliq Inuit Association, Written Submission for the NPC Fourth Technical Meeting, 21 February 2016.

62 Kivalliq Inuit Association, Comments on the Draft Nunavut Land Use Plan, 18 January 2017.

63 NWT and Nunavut Chamber of Mines, "Statistics Project Exploration Down in NWT and Really Down in Nunavut," press release, 13 March 2018.

64 Nunavut Tunngavik Incorporated, NTI and RIAs Joint Submission on DNLUP, 28 November 2018.

65 Ferguson Lake Natives, Comments on Starfield Resources Proposed Airstrip and Right of Way, NIRB File No. 07EN001, 31 January 2007.

66 Starfield Resources Inc., Response on Comments for the Application of an Airstrip for the Ferguson Lake Project, NIRB File No. 07EN001, 9 February 2007.

67 Nunavut Impact Review Board, Screening Decision Report for Starfield Resources' Ferguson Lake Camp Airstrip, NIRB File No. 07EN001, 2007.

68 Starfield Resources Inc., *Preliminary Economic Assessment of the Ferguson Lake Project, Nunavut, Canada*, prepared by Roscoe Postle Associates Inc., 30 November 2011.

69 Starfield Resources Inc., "Starfield Resources Inc. Makes an Assignment in Bankruptcy under the Bankruptcy and Insolvency Act (Canada)," news release, 2 July 2013.

70 Campbell, "Finding Canada's Centre."

Conclusion

1 Indigenous legal scholar John Borrows has also argued that Inuit traditional rules about the environment could form the basis for land use planning in Nunavut (Borrows, "Canada's Indigenous Constitution").

2 Coulthard, *Red Skin, White Masks*; Kulchyski, "Trail to Tears"; Alfred, *Wasáse*.

3 Berger, *Village Journey*.

Acknowledgements

1 Bernauer, "The Limits to Extraction."

2 Bernauer, "Land Claims and Caribou Habitat."

3 Kulchyski and Bernauer, "Modern Treaties."

4 Bernauer, "Land Claims and Resource Conflicts."

Glossary of Selected Inuktitut Terms

Aglirniq. Traditional prohibitions / Taboos

Angatquq. Shaman (pl. Angatquit)

Iglu. Snow house (pl. igluit)

Ilirahungniq. An Inuktitut emotional concept that has no direct equivalent in English. "Intimidation" is the English term that comes closest to capturing the meaning of Ilirahungniq in English.

Nipku. Dried caribou meat

Qablunaaq. A non-Inuk of European descent. (pl. *qablunaat*)

Qamutiik. Sled (pl. qamutiit)

Qarmat. Skin roof

Qayaq. Kayak (pl. qayait)

Qimmiit. Sled dogs

Pitqussiit. Inuit rules, customs, and social norms

Bibliography

Abele, Frances. "Canadian Contradictions: Forty Years of Northern Political Development." *Arctic* 40, no. 4 (1987): 310–20.

Aboriginal Affairs and Northern Development Canada. "Land Use Permit Inspection Form." NWB File No. 2BE-MRC1217. 26 July 2016.

———. "Letter to Anconia Resources Re: Compliance." NWB File No. 2BE-MRC1217. 16 September 2013.

———. "Water Use Inspection Report." NWB File No. 2BE-GAR0710." 30 June 2012.

Adamczewski, Jan, Anne Gunn, Kim G. Poole, Alex Hall, John Nishi, and John Boulanger. "What Happened to the Beverly Caribou Herd after 1994?" *Arctic* 68, no. 4 (2015): 407–21.

Aglu Consulting. "Agnico Kivalliq Projects 2019 Socio-Economic Monitoring Report." NIRB File No. 03MN107. March 2020.

Aglukark, Susan. "A Culture of Inertia." *Susan Aglukark* (blog). 13 April 2017. https://www.susanaglukark.com/culture-of-inertia/.

———. "Ilirasungniq." *Susan Aglukark* (blog). 2 June 2014. https://www.susanaglukark.com/ilirasungniq/.

Agnico Eagle. "Terrestrial Advisory Group Terms of Reference." NIRB File No. 16MN056. 24 October 2018.

———. "Terrestrial Ecosystem Management Plan for the Whale Tail Mine." Version 7. NIRB File No. 16MN056. 2019.

———. "Terrestrial Ecosystem Management Plan for the Whale Tail Mine." Version 8. NIRB File No. 16MN056. 2020.

———. "Terrestrial Ecosystem Management Plan Responses." NIRB File No. 16MN056. 13 July 2020.

Alfred, Taiaiake. *Wasáse: Indigenous Pathways of Action and Freedom*. Toronto: University of Toronto Press, 2005.

Anconia. "Letter to AANDC Re: Expiry of Permit." NIRB File No. 11EN046. 14 January 2016.

Aqigiq Hunters and Trappers Organization. "Comments on Anconia's Marce Lake Project." 13 February 2013.

———. "Comments on the Draft Nunavut Land Use Plan." 18 September 2015.

AREVA Resources. "Final Environmental Impact Statement for the Kiggavik Project." NIRB File No. 09MN003. 2014.

————. "The Kiggavik Project." NIRB File No. 09MN003. 2008.

Arima, Eugene Y. *A Contextual Study of the Caribou Eskimo Kayak*. Canadian Ethnology Service, Paper No. 25. Ottawa: National Museums of Canada, 1975.

Arragutainaq, Lucassie, Harry Flaherty, and Thomas Kabloona. Letter to NPC Chairperson Ron Roach, 6 May 2008.

Arviat Hunters and Trappers Organization. "Comments on the Draft Nunavut Land Use Plan." 24 September 2015.

Arviq Hunters and Trappers Organization. "Comments on the Draft Nunavut Land Use Plan." 10 February 2014.

Athabasca Denesuline Negotiating Team. "Comments on the Draft Nunavut Land Use Plan." 20 October 2014.

————. "Comments on NIRB Screening of Uravan's Garry Lakes Project." NIRB File No. 08EN037. 9 June 2008.

Baker Lake Hamlet Council. Special Meeting Minutes. 7 April 1978.

Baker Lake Hunters and Trappers Organization. "Changes to Agnico Eagle's Terrestrial Ecosystem Management Plan." NIRB File No. 16MN056. 30 April 2020.

————. "Comments on Anconia's Marce Lake Project." 21 June 2012.

————. "Comments on the Draft Guidelines for AREVA Resources' Proposed Kiggavik Project." NIRB File No. 08MN003. 27 February 2011.

————. "Comments on the Draft Nunavut Land Use Plan." 10 October 2013.

————. "Comments on the Revised Draft Guidelines for AREVA's Kiggavik Project." NIRB File No. 09MN003. 27 February 2011.

————. "Comments on Proposed Amaruq All-Season Road." NIRB File No. 11EN010. 2015.

————. *Hanningajuq Project*. Prepared by David Pelly. 2004.

————. "Re: The March 26th Letter from Agnico Eagle." NIRB File No. 16MN056. 10 April 2020.

————. "Technical Review Comments for the Whale Tail Expansion Project." NIRB File No. 16MN056. April 2019.

————. "Technical Review Comments on AREVA Resources Inc.'s Proposed Kiggavik Mine." NIRB File No. 09MN003. 14 January 2015.

Beach, Hugh. "Perceptions of risk, dilemmas of policy: Nuclear fallout in Swedish Lapland," *Social Science and Medicine* 30, no. 6 (1990): 729–38.

Bell, Jim. "Baker HTO Worried about Caribou Grounds." *Nunatsiaq News*, 17 February 2006. https://nunatsiaq.com/stories/article/baker_hto_worried_about_caribou_grounds/.

————. "Nunavut Uranium Forum Reveals Stark Divisions." *Nunatsiaq News*, 18 March 2011. https://nunatsiaq.com/stories/article/98789_nunavut_uranium_forum_reveals_stark_divisions/.

Berger, Thomas R. *Northern Frontier, Northern Homeland: The Report of the Mackenzie Valley Pipeline Inquiry.* Ottawa: Minister of Supply and Services, 1977.

———. *Village Journey: The Report of the Alaska Native Review Commission.* New York: Hill and Wang, 1985.

Bernauer, Warren. "Land Rights and Resource Conflicts in Nunavut." *Polar Geography* 42, no. 4 (2019): 253–66.

———. "The Limits to Extraction: Mining and Colonialism in Nunavut." *Canadian Journal of Development Studies* 40, no. 3 (2019): 404–22.

———. *Mining and the Social Economy in Baker Lake, Nunavut.* Saskatoon: University of Saskatchewan, Centre for the Study of Co-operatives, 2010.

———. "The Nunavut Land Claims Agreement and Caribou Habitat Management." *Canadian Journal of Native Studies* 35, no. 1 (2015): 5–32.

———. "Producing Consent: How Environmental Assessment Enabled Oil and Gas Extraction in the Qikiqtani Region of Nunavut." *Canadian Geographer* 64, no. 3 (2020): 489–501.

———. "The Uranium Controversy in Baker Lake." *Canadian Dimension* 46, no. 1 (2012): 35–39.

Beverly and Qamanirjuaq Caribou Management Board. "Comments on the Draft Nunavut Land Use Plan." 14 February 2014.

———. "Comments on NIRB Screening of Uravan's Garry Lakes Project." NIRB File No. 08EN037. 23 April 2008.

———. *Protecting Calving Grounds, Post-Calving Areas and Other Important Habitats for Beverly and Qamanirjuaq Caribou.* Position paper, 2004.

———. "Scheduling the Technical Meeting and Pre-Hearing Conference for the Kiggavik Technical Review." NIRB File No. 09MN003. 25 February 2013.

Birket-Smith, Kaj. *The Caribou Eskimos: Material and Social Life and Their Cultural Position, 2. Analytical Part.* Vol. 5 of *Report of the Fifth Thule Expedition 1921–24.* Copenhagen: Gyldendalske Boghandel, Nordisk Forlag, 1929.

Blangy, Sylvie, and Anna Deffner. "Impacts of Mining Development on Humans and Caribou in Qamani'tuaq." *Études Inuit Studies* 38 no. 1–2 (2014): 239–65.

Bliss L. Tracy, Gary H. Kramer, Jan M. Zielinski, and H. Jiang. "Radiocesium Body Burdens in Residents of Northern Canada from 1963–1990." *Health Physics* 72, no. 3 (1997): 431–42.

Borrows, John. *Canada's Indigenous Constitution.* Toronto: University of Toronto Press, 2010.

Bowman, Laura. "Sealing the Deal: Environmental and Indigenous Justice and Mining in Nunavut." *Review of European Comparative and International Environmental Law (RECIEL)* 20, no. 1 (2011): 19–28.

Brody, Hugh. *The Other Side of Eden: Hunters, Farmers and the Shaping of the World.* Vancouver: Douglas and McIntyre, 2000.

————. *The People's Land: Eskimos and Whites in the Eastern Arctic*. Vancouver: Douglas and McIntyre, 1975.

Burch, Ernest. "The Caribou Inuit." In *Native Peoples: The Canadian Experience*, edited by R. Bruce Morrison and C. Roderick Wilson, 106–33. Toronto: McClelland and Stewart, 1986.

Cameron, Emilie. *Far Off Metal River: Inuit Lands, Settler Stories, and the Making of the Contemporary Arctic*. Vancouver: UBC Press, 2015.

Campbell, Meagan. "Finding Canada's Centre." *Maclean's*, 14 July 2016. https://www. macleans.ca/how-to-find-the-centre-of-canada/.

Campbell, Mitch, John Boulanger, David S. Lee, Mathieu Dumond, and Justin McPherson. *Calving Ground Abundance Estimates of the Beverly and Ahiak Subpopulations of Barren-Ground Caribou* (Rangifer tarandus groenlandicus). Iqaluit, NU: Government of Nunavut, 2011.

Cater, Tara, and Arn Keeling. "'That's Where Our Future Came From': Mining, Landscape, and Memory in Rankin Inlet, Nunavut." *Études Inuit Studies* 37, no. 2 (2013): 59–82.

CBC Radio. "Deline and the Bomb." 6 August 2008. https://www.cbc.ca/player/play/ 2673194059.

Clark, Brenda L. *The Development of Caribou Eskimo Culture*. Archaeological Survey of Canada, Paper No. 59. Ottawa: National Museums of Canada, 1977.

Côté-Mantha, O., G. Gosselin, D. Vaillancourt, and A. Blackburn. "The Amaruq Deposits— Building a Customized Toolset and Using a Flexible Geomodel: Optimization from Discovery to Mine Development." In *Proceedings of Exploration 17: Sixth Decennial International Conference of Mineral Exploration*, edited by V. Tschirhart and M. Thomas, 553–67. 2017.

Coulthard, Glen Sean. *Red Skin, White Masks: Rejecting the Colonial Politics of Recognition*. Minneapolis: University of Minnesota Press, 2014.

Coupe, J., C. Bardeen, A. Robock, and O. Toon. "Nuclear Winter Responses to Nuclear War Between the United States and Russia." *Journal of Geophysical Research: Atmospheres* 124, no. 15 (2019): 8522–43.

Curly, Tagak. Open letter to Dennis Patterson, government leader of the Northwest Territories, 22 November 1988. Nunavummiut Makitagunarningit (Makita). https:// makitanunavut.files.wordpress.com/2012/04/01.pdf.

Dacks, Gurston. *A Choice of Futures: Politics in Canada's North*. Toronto: Methuen, 1981.

Dokis, Carly A. *Where the Rivers Meet: Pipelines, Participatory Resource Management, and Aboriginal-State Relations in the Northwest Territories*. Vancouver: UBC Press, 2015.

Duffy, R. Quinn. *The Road to Nunavut: The Progress of the Eastern Arctic Inuit since the Second World War*. Montreal and Kingston: McGill-Queen's University Press, 1988.

Dyck, S. "Community Politics, Governance, and Land-Use Planning in Nunavut." Master's thesis, University of Alberta, 2019.

Edwards, Gordon. "Canada's Nuclear Industry and the Myth of the Peaceful Atom." In *Canada and the Nuclear Arms Race*, edited by Ernie Regehr and Simon Rosenblum, 132–36. Toronto: Lorimer, 1983.

Edwards, Gordon, et al. "Uranium: A Discussion Guide." Canadian Coalition for Nuclear Responsibility. http://www.ccnr.org/nfb_uranium_0.html.

Ekho, Naqi, and Upsuralik Ottokie. *Childrearing Practices.* Vol. 3 of *Interviewing Inuit Elders*, edited by Jean Briggs. Iqaluit, NU: Nunavut Arctic College, 2000.

"Email chain between Christine Wilson (a federal Resource Management Officer) and Larry Lahusen (CEO of Uravan)." NWB File No. 2BE-GAR0710. [2012–2013?].

Ferguson Lake Natives. "Comments on Starfield Resources Proposed Airstrip and Right of Way." NIRB File No. 07EN001. 31 January 2007.

Fort Smith Métis Council. "Comments on the Draft Nunavut Land Use Plan." 4 February 2014.

Forum Uranium Corp. "Forum Consolidates North Thelon Properties by Acquiring 100% of Agnico Eagle's Claims Adjoining AREVA's Kiggavik Uranium Deposit." News release. 6 February 2014.

———. "Forum to Explore Nutaaq Rare Earth Property in Nunavut." Media release. 23 June 2011.

Freeman, M., ed. *Inuit Land Use and Occupancy Study.* Ottawa: Department of Indian and Northern Affairs, 1976.

Froese, Sarah, Nadja Kunz, and M.V. Ramana. "Too Small to Be Viable? The Potential Market for Small Modular Reactors in Mining and Remote Communities in Canada." *Energy Policy* 144 (2020): 111587.

Government of the Northwest Territories. *Hansard* of the Legislative Assembly of the Northwest Territories. 9th Assembly, 4th Session, 1981.

———. *Hansard* of the Legislative Assembly of the Northwest Territories. 10th Assembly, 7th Session, 19 June 1986.

Government of Nunavut. "Comments on the Draft Nunavut Land Use Plan." 28 May 2014.

———. "Comments on NIRB Screening of Uravan's Garry Lakes Project." NIRB File No. 08EN037. 23 April 2008.

———. "Changes to the Whale Tail Project's TEMP." NIRB File No. 16MN056. 22 May 2020.

———. *Hansard* of the Legislative Assembly of Nunavut. 2nd Assembly, 4th Session, 4 July 2007.

———. *Inuit Qaujimajatuqangit of Climate Change in Nunavut: A Sample of Inuit Experiences of Climate Change in Nunavut, Baker Lake and Arviat.* Iqaluit, NU: Department of Environment, 2005.

Göcke, Katja. "Uranium Mining in Nunavut." *The Yearbook of Polar Law Online* 5, no. 1 (2013): 119–42.

Green, Heather. "'There Is No Memory of It Here': Closure and Memory of the Polaris Mine in Resolute Bay, 1973–2012." In *Mining and Communities in Northern Canada*, edited by Arn Keeling and John Sandlos, 315–39. Calgary, AB: University of Calgary Press, 2015.

Green, Jim. "Nuclear Power's Economic Crisis and its Implications for Australia." Friends of the Earth Australia. December 2021. https://nuclear.foe.org.au/wp-content/uploads/Nuclear-power-economic-crisis-2021-FoE-Australia.pdf.

Gunn, Anne. *A Review of Research of the Effects of Human Activities on Barren-Ground Caribou of the Beverly and Kaminuriak Herds, Northwest Territories.* NWT Wildlife Service, File Report No. 43, 1984.

Hall, Rebecca Jane. *Refracted Economies: Diamond Mining and Social Reproduction in the North.* Toronto: University of Toronto Press, 2022.

Hamlet of Baker Lake. Untitled media release. 15 February 1990.

The Hamlet of Baker Lake v. The Min. of Ind. Aff. and North. Dev., [1979] 1 FC 487.

The Hamlet of Baker Lake v. The Min. of Ind. Aff. and North. Dev., [1980] 1 FC 518.

Harding, Jim. *Canada's Deadly Secret: Saskatchewan Uranium and the Global Nuclear System.* Halifax, NS: Fernwood Publishing, 2007.

Harper, Kenn. "The Answer the White Man Expects." *Nunatsiaq News,* 5 May 2010.

———. *In Those Days: Arctic Crime and Punishment.* Iqaluit, NU: Inhabit Media, 2015.

Harvaqtuurmiut Elders, Darren Keith, Joan Scottie, and Ruby Mautara'inaaq. *Harvaqtuuq: Place Names of the Lower Kazan River.* Ottawa: Canadian Heritage, 1996.

Hicks, Jack. "The Other Side of Kiggavik." *Nunatsiaq News,* 26 May 1995.

———. "On the Application of Theories of 'Internal Colonialism' to Inuit Societies." Paper presented at the 76th Annual Conference of the Canadian Political Science Association. Winnipeg, MB, 5 June 2004.

Hicks, Jack, and Graham White. *Made in Nunavut: An Experiment in Decentralized Government.* Vancouver: UBC Press, 2015.

———. "Nunavut: Inuit Self-Determination Through a Land Claim and Public Government?" In *Nunavut: Inuit Regain Control of Their Lands and Their Lives,* edited by Jens Dahl, Jack Hicks, and Peter Jull, 30–117. Copenhagen: International Work Group for Indigenous Affairs, 2000.

Hughson, Paula Kigjugalik. "Our Homeland for the Past, Present, and Future: Akulliqpaaq Qamaniq (Aberdeen Lake) and Qamaniq Tugliqpaaq (Schultz Lake) Landscapes Described by Elder John Killulark." Master's thesis, University of Manitoba, 2010.

"ICC Resolutions." *Inuit Today,* February 1984.

Indian [Indigenous] and Northern Affairs Canada. "Inspector's Direction." NWB File No. 2BE-GAR0710. 15 December 2009.

———. "Final Inspection Report." NWB File No. 2BE-GAR0710. 24 August 2017.

Indian and Northern Affairs Canada, Government of Nunavut, Canada-Nunavut Geoscience Office, and Nunavut Tunngavik Incorporated. *Nunavut Overview 2008: Mineral Exploration, Mining, and Geoscience.* Iqaluit, NU: Indian and Northern Affairs Canada, 2008.

Inter-Church Uranium Committee. "Atoms for War and Peace: The Saskatchewan Connection." Saskatoon, 1981.

Interdisciplinary Systems Ltd. *Effects of Exploration and Development in the Baker Lake Area.* Ottawa: Department of Indian Affairs and Northern Development, 1978.

"Inuit Circumpolar Conference." *Inuit Today*, September 1977.

"Inuit Protest War's Madness." *Inuit Today*, February 1984.

"Inuit Seek Court Protection for Baker Lake." *Inuit Today*, April/May 1978.

"Inuit Want Uranium Ban in North." *ITC News*, April 1980.

Issatik Hunters and Trappers Organization. "Comments on Anconia's Marce Lake Project." 28 February 2013.

———. "Comments on the Draft Nunavut Land Use Plan." 30 September 2015.

"ITC Calls for Land Freeze." *Inuit Today*, March/April 1977.

"ITC General Meeting." *Inuit Today*, April/May 1978.

Jaczko, Greg, Wolfgang Renneberg, Bernard Laponche, and Paul Dorfman. "Former Heads of US, German, French Nuclear Regulation and Secretary to UK Government Radiation Protection Committee: Nuclear Is Just not Part of any Feasible Strategy That Could Counter Climate Change." Nuclear Consulting Group. 6 January 2022. https://www.nuclearconsult.com/blog/former-heads-of-us-german-french-nuclear-regulation-and-secretary-to-uk-government-radiation-protection-committee-nuclear-is-just-not-part-of-any-feasible-strategy-that-could-counter-climate-chan/.

Johnson, Noor, Shari Gearheard, Jerry Natanine, and Shelly Elverum. "Community Actions to Address Seismic Testing in Nunavut, Canada: Building Capacity of Involvement." *Practicing Anthropology* 38, no. 3 (2016): 13–16.

Jones, Jen, and Ben Bradshaw. "Addressing Historical Impacts Through Impact and Benefit Agreements and Health Impact Assessment: Why it Matters for Indigenous Well-Being." *The Northern Review* 41 (2015): 81–109.

Kangiqliniq Hunters and Trappers Organization. "Comments on Anconia's Marce Lake Project." 20 March 2013.

Keeling, Arn. "'Born in an Atomic Test Tube': Landscapes of Cyclonic Development at Uranium City, Saskatchewan." *Canadian Geographer* 54, no. 2 (2010): 228–52.

Keewatin Inuit Association. Resolution #6-89 "Proposed Baker Lake Uranium Mine." Annual General Meeting, 1989.

Keith, Darren. "Caribou, River, and Ocean: Harvaqtuurmiut Landscape Organization and Orientation." *Études Inuit Studies* 28, no. 2 (2004): 39–56.

———. "Inuit Place Names and Land-Use History on the *Harvaqtuuq* [Kazan River], Nunavut Territory." Master's thesis, McGill University, 2000.

Kendrick, A. "Community Perceptions of the Beverly and Qamanirjuaq Caribou Management Board." *Canadian Journal of Native Studies* 20, no. 1 (2000): 1–33.

Kennedy Dalseg, Sheena. "Seeing Like a Community: Education, Citizenship, and Social Change in the Eastern Arctic." PhD. diss., Carleton University, 2018.

Keske, Catherine, Morgan Mills, Laura Tanguay, and Jason Dicker. "Waste Management in Labrador and Northern Communities." *The Northern Review* 47 (2018): 79–112.

"The Kiggavik Controversy." *Focus North*. CBC Television. 1990.

Kivalliq Inuit Association. "Comments on the Draft Nunavut Land Use Plan." 13 October 2013.

———. "Comments on the Draft Nunavut Land Use Plan." 18 January 2017.

———. "Review of KIA Involvement in the Development of TEMP Version 8." NIRB File No. 16MN056. 21 May 2020.

———. "Written Submission for the NPC Fourth Technical Meeting." 21 February 2016.

Kivalliq Inuit Association and Nunavut Tunngavik Inc. "Additional Comments on the Draft Scope for Uravan's Garry Lakes Project." NIRB File No. 08EN037. 31 October 2008.

Kivalliq Inuit Association and Nunavut Tunngavik Inc. "Comments on the Draft Scope for Uravan's Garry Lakes Project." NIRB File No. 08EN037. 28 October 2008.

Kivalliq Wildlife Board. "Motion #KWB-2013-005."

———. "Motion Regarding Proposed Kiggavik Mine. Final Hearing Exhibit No. 59." NIRB File No. 09MN003. 23 February 2015.

Kulchyski, Peter. "Trail to Tears: Concerning Modern Treaties in Northern Canada." *Canadian Journal of Native Studies* 35, no. 1 (2015): 69–81.

Kulchyski, Peter, and Warren Bernauer. "Modern Treaties, Extraction and Imperialism in Canada's Indigenous North: Two Case Studies." *Studies in Political Economy* 93, no. 1 (2014): 3–24.

Kulchyski, Peter, and Frank Tester. *Kiumajut (Talking Back): Game Management and Inuit Rights, 1900–70*. Vancouver: UBC Press, 2007.

Kuptana, Rosemarie. "Ilira, or Why it Was Unthinkable for Inuit to Challenge Qallunaat Authority." *Inuit Art Quarterly* 8, no. 3 (1993): 5–7.

Laugrand, Frédéric, and Jarich Oosten. *Hunters, Predators, and Prey: Inuit Perceptions of Animals*. New York: Berghahn Books, 2014.

Ljubicic, G., S. Okpakok, S. Robertson, and R. Mearns. "Inuit Approaches to Naming and Distinguishing Caribou: Considering Language, Place, and Homeland toward Improved Co-management." *Arctic* 71, no. 3 (2018): 309–33.

Loo, Tina. "Political Animals: Barren Ground Caribou and the Managers in a 'Post-Normal' Age." *Environmental History* 22, no. 3 (2017): 433–59.

Lutsel K'e Dene First Nation. "Comments on the Draft Nunavut Land Use Plan." 31 January 2014.

———. "Comments on NIRB Screening of Uravan's Garry Lakes Project." NIRB File No. 08EN037. 9 June 2008.

Lynge, Aqqaluk. *Inuit: The Story of the Inuit Circumpolar Conference*. Nuuk, Greenland: Atuakkiorfik, 1993.

———. *The Right to Return: Fifty Years of Struggle by Relocated Inughuit in Greenland*. Nuuk, Greenland: Forlaget Atuagkat, 2002.

"Makita Co-President Sandra Inutiq's Speech to the Government of Nunavut's Public Forum on Uranium Mining." Nunavummiut Makitagunarningit (Makita). https://makitanunavut.files.wordpress.com/2012/03/inutiq_gn_forums.pdf.

Maksimowski, Sophie. "Well-being and Mining in Baker Lake, Nunavut: Inuit Values, Practices and Strategies in the Transition to an Industrial Economy." Master's thesis, University of Guelph, 2014.

Mannik, Hattie, ed. *Inuit Nunamiut / Inland Inuit*. Altona, MB: Friesen, 1998.

Manuel, Arthur, and Ronald M. Derrickson. *Unsettling Canada: A National Wake-Up Call*. Toronto: Between the Lines Press, 2015.

Manuel, George, and Michael Posluns. *The Fourth World: An Indian Reality*. Toronto: Collier-Macmillan Canada, 1974.

Mawhiney, Anne-Marie, and Jane Pitblado, eds. *Boom Town Blues: Elliot Lake—Collapse and Revival in a Single-Industry Community*. Toronto: Dundurn Press, 1999.

McKay, Paul. "Snow Job: Doing the Uranium Hustle in the NWT." *This Magazine*, July/August 1989.

McPherson, Robert. *New Owners in Their Own Land: Minerals and Inuit Land Claims*. Calgary, AB: University of Calgary Press, 2003.

Merritt, John, Terry Fenge, Randy Ames, and Peter Jull. *Nunavut: Political Choices and Manifest Destiny*. Ottawa: Canadian Arctic Resources Committee, 1989.

Metuzals, Jessica, and Myra J. Hird. "'The Disease that Knowledge Must Cure'? Sites of Uncertainty in Arctic Development." *Arctic Yearbook* 57 (2018): 1–17.

Mitchell, Marybelle. *From Talking Chiefs to a Native Corporate Elite: The Birth of Class and Nationalism among Canadian Inuit*. Montreal and Kingston: McGill-Queen's University Press, 1996.

Muellner, Nikolaus, Nikolaus Arnold, Klaus Gufler, Wolfgang Kromp, Wolfgang Renneberg, and Wolfgang Liebert. "Nuclear Energy—The Solution to Climate Change?" *Energy Policy* 155 (2021): 112363. https://doi.org/10.1016/j.enpol.2021.112363.

Nadasdy, Paul. *Hunters and Bureaucrats: Power, Knowledge, and Aboriginal-State Relations in the Southwest Yukon*. Vancouver: UBC Press, 2003.

National Inquiry into Missing and Murdered Indigenous Women and Girls. *Reclaiming Power and Place: The Final Report of the National Inquiry into Missing and Murdered Indigenous Women and Girls*. Ottawa: National Inquiry into Missing and Murdered Indigenous Women and Girls, 2019.

Natural Resources Canada. "Canada's Small Modular Reactor Action Plan." Government of Canada, 2022. https://www.nrcan.gc.ca/our-natural-resources/energy-sources-distribution/nuclear-energy-uranium/canadas-small-nuclear-reactor-action-plan/21183.

Nightingale, Elana, Karina Czyzewski, Frank Tester, and Nadia Aaruaq. "The Effects of Resource Extraction on Inuit Women and Their Families: Evidence from Canada." *Gender and Development* 25, no. 3 (2017): 367–85.

North Slave Métis Alliance. "Re: Makita Letter to the NIRB Regarding Review Timelines." NIRB File No. 09MN003. 6 December 2012.

Northlands Dene First Nation. "Comments on the Draft Nunavut Land Use Plan." 27 May 2014.

Northwest Territories Legislative Assembly. Motion #05-90(1) "Opposition to Exploration and Mining of Uranium in the NWT." 27 February 1990.

Northwest Territories Métis Council. "Comments on the Draft Nunavut Land Use Plan." 21 February 2014.

NWT and Nunavut Chamber of Mines. "Statistics Project Exploration Down in NWT and Really Down in Nunavut." Press release. 13 March 2018. https://www.miningnorth.com/chamber-news/101522.

Nunavummiut Makitagunarningit. "Comments on the Draft Guidelines for AREVA Resources' Proposed Kiggavik Project." NIRB File No. 08MN003. 24 January 2011.

———. "Comments on the Revised Draft Guidelines for AREVA Resources' Proposed Kiggavik Project." NIRB File No. 08MN003. 2 March 2011.

———. "In Defense of Emotionalism, Makita Responds." *Nunatsiaq News*, 31 March 2011. https://nunatsiaq.com/stories/article/31446_in_defense_of_emotionalism_makita_responds/.

———. "Makita Says the NIRB's Failure to Translate Draft EIS Guidelines Shows Flagrant Disregard for Inuit Rights." Media release. 18 November 2010. https://makitanunavut.files.wordpress.com/2012/03/media-release-nirb-translation.pdf.

———. "NIRB Timelines for Kiggavik Project Review." NIRB File No. 09MN003. 3 December 2012.

———. "Nunavut Voters Should Decide Uranium Policy in Public Vote." *Nunatsiaq News*, 17 March 2011. https://nunatsiaq.com/stories/article/98789_nunavut_voters_should_decide_uranium_policy_in_public_vote/.

———. "Why Nunavut Needs a Public Inquiry into Uranium Mining." *Nunatsiaq News*, 29 June 2010. https://nunatsiaq.com/stories/article/why_nunavut_needs_a_public_inquiry_into_uranium_mining/.

Nunavut Impact Review Board. "Final EIS Guidelines for the Kiggavik Project." NIRB File No. 09MN003. 3 May 2011.

———. "Final Hearing Report for Agnico Eagle's Whale Tail Pit Project." NIRB File No. 16MN056. November 2017.

———. "Final Hearing Report for AREVA's Kiggavik Proposal." NIRB File No. 09MN003. 2015.

———. "Final Hearing Report for the Meadowbank Gold Project." NIRB File No. 03MN107. August 2006.

———. "Final Hearing Transcript for AREVA's Kiggavik Proposal." NIRB File No. 09MN003. 2015.

———. "Final Hearing Transcript for the Kiggavik Project." NIRB File No. 09MN003. March 2015.

———. "Final Hearing Transcript for the Meadowbank Gold Project." NIRB File No. 03MN107. 2006.

———. "Final Hearing Transcript for the Meliadine Gold Project." NIRB File No. 11MN034. August 2014.

———. "Final Hearing Transcript for the Whale Tail Proposal." NIRB File No. 16MN056. 2017.

———. "Final Hearing Transcript for the Whale Tail Expansion Project." NIRB File No. 16MN056. 2019.

———. "Preliminary Hearing Conference Decision Concerning the Kiggavik Proposal." NIRB File No. 09MN003. 2013.

———. "Project Certificate for the Whale Tail Mine." NIRB File No. 16MN056. 15 March 2018.

———. "Public Information Sessions Summary Report." NIRB File No. 09MN003. June 2012.

———. "Public Scoping Meetings Summary Report." NIRB File No. 09MN003. June 2010.

———. "Reconsideration Report and Recommendations for the Whale Tail Pit Expansion Project." NIRB File No. 16MN056. October 2019.

———. "Screening Decision Report for the Amaruq Advanced Exploration and Bulk Sample Project." NIRB File No. 11EN010. 5 October 2016.

———. "Screening Decision Report for the Amaruq Exploration Access Road." NIRB File No. 11EN010. 4 November 2015.

———. "Screening Decision Report for the Amaruq Winter Access Road." NIRB File No. 11EN010. 10 February 2015.

———. "Screening Decision Report for the Amaruq, Meadowbank, and White Hills Exploration Project." NIRB File No. 15EN050. 15 January 2016.

———. "Screening Decision Report for Anconia's Marce Lake Project." NIRB File No. 11EN046. 5 March 2012.

———. "Screening Decision Report for Starfield Resources' Ferguson Lake Camp Airstrip." NIRB File No. 07EN001. 2007.

———. "Screening Decision Report for Uravan's Garry Lakes Project." NIRB File No. 08EN037. 27 June 2008.

———. "SDR for AREVA's Kiggavik Proposal." NIRB File No. 09MN003. 2009.

———. "2013–2014 Annual Monitoring Report for the Meadowbank Gold Project." NIRB File No. 03MN107. 2014.

———. "2015–2016 Annual Monitoring Report for the Meadowbank Gold Project." NIRB File No. 03MN107. 2016.

———. "2017–2018 Annual Monitoring Report for the Meadowbank and Whale Tail Projects." NIRB File No. 16MN056. 2018.

————. "2018–2019 Annual Monitoring Report for the Meadowbank and Whale Tail Projects." NIRB File No. 16MN056. 2019.

Nunavut Planning Commission. "NPC Uranium Workshop Transcript." 5–7 June 2007.

————. "Report on Public Consultation on the Draft Nunavut Land Use Plan in Chesterfield Inlet." November 2014.

————. "Transcript of Fourth Technical Meeting." 23–26 March 2016.

Nunavut Tunngavik Incorporated. "Clarification on Agnico Eagle TEMP Version 8." NIRB File No. 16MN056. 13 May 2020.

————. "NTI and Forum Uranium Corp. Sign MOU." News release. 8 December 2008. https://makitanunavut.files.wordpress.com/2012/07/nr-08-44-mou-eng-nti-and-forum-sign-mou.pdf.

————. "NTI and RIAs Joint Submission on DNLUP." 28 November 2018.

Nunavut Wildlife Management Board. "Comments on the Draft Nunavut Land Use Plan." 20 May 2014.

O'Neill, Dan. *The Firecracker Boys: H-Bombs, Inupiat Eskimos, and the Roots of the Environmental Movement.* New York: Basic Books, 1995.

Oosten, Jarich, Frederic Laugrand, and Willem Rasing, eds. *Inuit Laws: Tirigusuusiit, Piqujait, and Maligait.* Iqaluit: Nunavut Arctic College Media, 2017.

Parks Canada. *Fall Caribou Crossing National Historic Site.* Research Report No. 1995-028. 1995.

Pauktuutit. *The Impact of Resource Extraction on Inuit Women and Families in Qamani'tuaq, Nunavut: A Qualitative Assessment.* Pauktuutit Inuit Women of Canada and the University of British Columbia School of Social Work, 2016.

Pelly, David F. *The Ancestors Are Happy: True Tales of the Arctic.* St. Marys, ON: Crossfield Publishing, 2021.

————. *Thelon: A River Sanctuary.* Toronto: Dundurn Press, 1996.

Peterson, Kelsey. "Community Experiences of Mining in Baker Lake, Nunavut." Master's thesis, University of Guelph, 2012.

Physicians for Social Responsibility. "The Myth of the European Nuclear Renaissance." 20 May 2009. https://web.archive.org/web/20130728115821/http://www.psr.org/safe-energy/the-myth-of-the-european.html.

Proctor, Andrea. "Uranium, Inuit Rights, and Emergent Neoliberalism in Labrador: 1956–2012." In *Mining and Communities in Northern Canada: History, Politics, and Memory,* edited by Arn Keeling and John Sandlos, 233–58. Calgary, AB: University of Calgary Press, 2015.

"Prospecting Deferred in Keewatin." *Inuit Today,* June/July 1977.

Qikiqtani Truth Commission. *Illinniarniq: Schooling in Qikiqtaaluk.* Iqaluit, NU: Qikiqtani Inuit Association, 2013.

————. *Nuutauniq: Moves in Inuit Life.* Iqaluit, NU: Qikiqtani Inuit Association, 2013.

————. *Paliisikkut: Policing in Qikiqtaaluk.* Iqaluit, NU: Qikiqtani Inuit Association, 2013.

————. *QTC Final Report: Achieving Saimaqatigiingniq*. Iqaluit, NU: Qikiqtani Inuit Association, 2013.

Ramana, M.V. "Small Modular and Advanced Nuclear Reactors: A Reality Check." *IEEE Access* 9 (2021): 42090–99.

Rand, Lisa Ruth. "Falling Cosmos: Nuclear Reentry and the Environmental History of Earth Orbit." *Environmental History* 24, no. 1 (2019): 78–103.

Rasmussen, Knud. *Observations on the Intellectual Culture of the Caribou Eskimos*. Vol. 7, no. 2 of *Report of the Fifth Thule Expedition*. Copenhagen: Gyldendalske Boghandel, Nordisk Forlag, 1930.

Ray, Arthur. *The Canadian Fur Trade in the Industrial Age*. Toronto: University of Toronto Press, 1990.

Riewe, Rick, ed. *Nunavut Atlas*. Edmonton, AB: Canadian Circumpolar Institute and Tunngavik Federation of Nunavut, 1992.

Rixen, Annabel, and Sylvie Blangy. "Life after Meadowbank: Exploring Gold Mine Closure Scenarios with the Residents of Qamini'tuaq (Baker Lake), Nunavut." *Extractive Industries and Society* 3, no. 2 (2016): 297–312.

Robertson, Sean, Simon Okpakok, and Gita Ljubicic. "Territorializing Piquhiit in Uqsuqtuuq (Gjoa Haven, Nunavut, Canada): Negotiating Homeland through an Inuit Normative System." *Territory, Politics, Governance* (2020): 1–20.

Robock, A. "Nuclear Winter." *WIREs Climate Change* 1, no. 3 (2010): 418–28.

Rodgers, Kathleen, and Darcy Ingram. "Decolonizing Environmentalism in the Arctic? Greenpeace, Complicity and Negotiating the Contradictions of Solidarity in the Inuit Nunangat." *Interface* 11, no. 2 (2019): 11–34.

Rodon, Thierry. "Institutional Development and Resource Development: The Case of Canada's Indigenous Peoples." *Canadian Journal of Development Studies* 39, no. 1 (2018): 119–36.

————. "Land-Use Co-Management in Canada." In: *Finnmark Act 15 Years After*. Copenhagen: Glydendal, 2021.

Ross, W. Gillies. "Whaling, Inuit and the Arctic Islands." In *Interpreting Canada's North: Selected Readings*, edited by Kenneth S. Coates and William R. Morrison, 235–51. Toronto: Copp Clark Pitman, 1989.

Royal Canadian Mounted Police. *Camp Conditions—General—Baker Lake Detachment Area*. 25 February 1960.

————. *Conditions Amongst Eskimos Generally, Annual Report—Period Ending December 31, 1959 Baker Lake District NWT*. Division File TA 1491-2-1-2 (59). 11 January 1960.

Royal Commission on Aboriginal Peoples. *Report of the Royal Commission on Aboriginal Peoples*. Vol. 1, *Looking Forward, Looking Back*. Ottawa: Canada Communication Group Publishing, 1996.

Sayisi Dene First Nation. "Comments on the Draft Nunavut Land Use Plan." 15 May 2014.

Scobie, Willow, and Kathleen Rodgers. "Contestations of Resource Extraction Projects via Digital Media in Two Nunavut Communities." *Études Inuit Studies* 37, no. 2 (2013): 83–101.

Scottie, Joan. "Is NTI Irresponsibly Endorsing Uranium Mining?" *Nunatsiaq News*, 2 June 2006. https://nunatsiaq.com/stories/article/is_nti_irresponsibly_ endorsing_uranium_mines/.

———. "NTI, Inuit Associations Do Not Serve Inuit." *Nunatsiaq News*, 21 November 2008.

Shuttleworth, Judy. "Baker Lake Wants Kiggavik Abandoned." *News/North*, 23 April 1990.

Simon, Mary May. *Inuit: One Future—One Arctic*. Peterborough, ON: Cider Press, 1996.

———. "Militarization and the Aboriginal Peoples." In *Arctic Alternatives: Civility or Militarism in the Circumpolar North*, edited by Franklyn Griffiths, 55–67." Toronto: Dundurn, 1992.

Smellie, Janet. "Motion Opposing Kiggavik Stalled by Legislative Assembly." *Nunatsiaq News*, 9 March 1990.

Smith, Garry. Open letter to M. Stuart, executive vice-president of Urangesellschaft Canada, 3 April 1990. Nunavummiut Makitagunarningit (Makita). https://makitanunavut.files. wordpress.com/2012/04/15.pdf.

Sovacool, Benjamin K. "Critically Weighing the Costs and Benefits of a Nuclear Renaissance." *Journal of Integrative Environmental Sciences* 7, no. 2 (2010): 105–23.

Starfield Resources Inc. *Preliminary Economic Assessment of the Ferguson Lake Project, Nunavut, Canada*. Prepared by Roscoe Postle Associates Inc. 30 November 2011.

———. "Response on Comments for the Application of an Airstrip for the Ferguson Lake Project." NIRB File No. 07EN001. 9 February 2007.

———. "Starfield Resources Inc. Makes an Assignment in Bankruptcy under the Bankruptcy and Insolvency Act (Canada)." Media release. 2 July 2013. https://www.newswire.ca/ news-releases/starfield-resources-inc-makes-an-assignment-in-bankruptcy-under-the-bankruptcy-and-insolvency-act-canada-512675391.html.

Steenhoven, Geert van den. *Leadership and Law Among the Eskimos of the Keewatin District, Northwest Territories*. Rijswijk, Netherlands: Uitgeverij Excelsior, 1962.

Stewart, Andrew M., Darren Keith, and Joan Scottie. "Caribou Crossings and Cultural Meanings: Placing Traditional Knowledge and Archaeology in Context in an Inuit Landscape." *Journal of Archaeological Method and Theory* 11, no. 2 (2004): 183–211.

Stratos Inc. "Meadowbank Gold Mine 2015 Socio-Economic Monitoring Report." NIRB File No. 03MN107. December 2016.

"Survival of the Inuit Culture vs Mining." *ITC News*, September 1979.

"Tea and Biscuits." *Inuit Monthly*, May/June 1974.

Tester, Frank. *Socio-economic and Environmental Impacts of the Polar Gas Pipeline—Keewatin District*. Ottawa: Department of Indian Affairs and Northern Development, 1978.

Tester, Frank, and Peter Kulchyski. *Tammarniit (Mistakes): Inuit Relocation in the Eastern Arctic, 1939–63*. Vancouver: UBC Press, 1994.

Tester, Frank James, Drummond E.J. Lambert, and Tee Wern Lim. "Wistful Thinking: Making Inuit Labour and the Nanisivik Mine near Ikpiarjuk (Arctic Bay), Northern Baffin Island." *Études Inuit Studies* 37, no. 2 (2013): 15–36.

Trott, Christopher. "Mission and Opposition in North Baffin Island." *Journal of the Canadian Church Historical Society* 40, no. 1 (1998): 31–55.

Truth and Reconciliation Commission of Canada. *Final Report of the Truth and Reconciliation Commission of Canada*. Vol. 2, *Canada's Residential Schools: The Inuit and Northern Experience*. Ottawa: Truth and Reconciliation Commission of Canada, 2015.

Tunngavik Federation of Nunavut.

United Nations General Assembly. *10th Special Session, 6th Plenary Meeting – Official Records*. 26 May 1978, p. 95.

Urangesellschaft Canada. Untitled press release. 5 July 1990.

Uravan. "Compliance Plan." NWB File No. 2BE-GAR0710. 17 October 2012.

———. "Response to Inspector's Direction." NWB File No. 2BE-GAR0710. 31 December 2009.

Usher, Peter. "The Class System, Metropolitan Dominance and Northern Development in Canada." *Antipode* 8, no. 3 (1976): 28–32.

———. "The North: One Land, Two Ways of Life." In *Heartland and Hinterland: A Regional Geography of Canada*, 3rd edition, edited by Larry McCann and Angus Gunn, 357–94. Toronto: Prentice Hall, 1998.

Vallee, Frank G. *Kabloona and Eskimo in the Central Keewatin*. Ottawa: Canadian Research Centre for Anthropology, 1968.

Wachowich, Nancy. *Saqiyuq: Stories from the Lives of Three Inuit Women*. Montreal: McGill-Queen's University Press, 2001.

Watt-Cloutier, Sheila. *The Right to Be Cold: One Woman's Story of Protecting Her Culture, the Arctic and the Whole Planet*. Toronto: Penguin Canada, 2015.

Webster, Deborah Kigjugalik. *Harvaqtuurmiut Heritage: The Heritage of the Inuit of the Lower Kazan River*. Yellowknife, NT: Artisan Press, 2001.

Welland, Tony. "Inuit Land Use in Keewatin District and Southampton Island." In *Inuit Land Use and Occupancy Project: Volume 1*, edited by Milton M.R. Freeman, 83–122. Ottawa: Department of Indian and Northern Affairs, 1976.

White, Graham. "Cultures in Collision: Traditional Knowledge and Euro-Canadian Governance Processes in Northern Land-Claim Boards." *Arctic* 59, no. 4 (2006): 401–14.

Wilt, James. "'The Ice Can Be Conquered': Scientific Knowledge and Mobilizing Arctic Gas." Master's thesis, University of Manitoba, 2020.

Index

A

Aariak, Eva, 145

aglirniq (taboos), 26, 63, 73

Aglukark, Susan, 43–44

Agnico Eagle: Amaruq deposit, 118–19; dust suppression, 115–16, 119; *ilirahungniq* (intimated), 124; projects, 5; protection measures affect profitability, 120, 121; revenues from Meadowbank gold mine, 114, 123; Terrestrial Advisory Group, 120–21; threat of layoffs, 120, 123; Whale Tail mine, 5, 106, 116, 117–18, 119–21. *see also* Meadowbank gold mine

Ahiak caribou herd, 182–83

Ahiarmiut, 13

Akilinirmiut, 13, 14

akiumilitat (placing pad), 21, 30

Aksawnee, Richard, 162, 166

Alerk, Michael, 17

Allmand, Warren, 61–62

Amarook, Michael, 61–62, 67

amauti (carrying coat), 17, 21

anaiyautit (wipers), 29, 30

Anawak, Jack, 88

Anconia Resources, Marce Lake project, 183–84, 185

angatquq/angatquit (shamans), 26–27, 45

Anglican Church, 26, 46, 49, 50

anthropologists, 13, 26, 44, 67, 212n19–12n20

anti-nuclear movement, 8, 89–90

aqnakuluugavit (you are cursed), 37–38

Arbuckle, Les, 18, 20

archaeology, 67, 175, 212n20

AREVA Resources' Kiggavik mine proposal: acquisition of Urangesellschaft's project, 125; Carolyn Bennett letter, 168; community engagement meetings, 142; in compliance with Keewatin Region Land Use Plan, 141; Environmental Impact Statement (EIS), 150, 155–56, 159–60; final hearings, 161–66; gaining community support, 131–32; Golder Associates, 145, 155–56; misleading statements, 158–59; NIRB environmental assessment, 7, 154–55; NIRB public meetings, 156–59; no clear timelines given, 159, 160, 161, 162, 163, 167, 195; promise of benefits to Inuit, 136; rejected, 150–51; summary, 149; Warren Bernauer, 8

Arnatsiaq-Murphy, Siobhan, 142

Arngna'naaq, Silas, 163, 166

Arviat Hunters and Trappers Organization (HTO), 183–84, 186

Asmara Minerals, 112. *see also* gold mining

Atangat, Mary, 17, creating insulting songs, 28; on gender roles, 21; Hitkati's spouse, 15–17; and Lucy Qaunnaq, 32; move to Baker Lake, 54;

Athabasca Denesuline, 163

Athabasca Denesuline Negotiating Team, 179–80, 187

atigi (woman's coat), 32

Atomic Energy of Canada Limited (AECL), 90

At Work in the Fields of the Bomb (Del Tredici), 92

aul'laqutit (flags), 24, 182

Aupaluktuq, Moses, 145

Australia, 60

autonomy, 2, 41, 170

Avaala, John, 67

B

Baffin region. *see* Qikiqtani region (Baffin region)

Baker Lake: business owners on mining, 85, 88, 114, 158, 194; healthcare as reason to relocate, 48–49; Inuit housing/ accommodations, 49, 53–54, 55; Operation Morning Light, 81; trading post, 23, 26–27. *see also* AREVA Resources' Kiggavik mine proposal; Baker Lake Hamlet Council; the Hamlet of Baker Lake; Urangesellschaft Kiggavik mine proposal

Baker Lake Concerned Citizens Committee (BLCCC): Barnabas Piryuaq, 75, 97; challenge of translation, 77; disbanded, 142; Fred Ford, 75; gives voice to regular people, 197; Martin Kreelak, 75; and Northern Anti-Uranium Coalition (NAUC), 75–76, 84, 87, 88, 92–96; Nunavut Planning Commission uranium workshop, 139–40; opposition to uranium mining, 152–53; request of support

J

James, Canon, 46, 47

Jorah, Samson, 75

Julie (at tuberculosis sanatorium), 32

K

Keewatin Inuit Association (KIA): Louis Pilakapsi, 98; member of Northern Anti-Uranium Coalition (NAUC), 84; motion to opposed Kiggavik mine, 83; "Opposition to Exploration and Mining of Uranium in the NWT" motion, 100; Scottie, Joan (Paningaya'naaq), 8. *see also* Kivalliq Inuit Association (KIA)

Keewatin Regional Council (KRC), 8, 83

Keewatin Regional Health Board (KRHB), 84–85

Keewatin Regional Land Use Plan: gold mining, 112; Nunavut Planning Commission (NPC), 126–27; prohibition of uranium mining, 125; Term 3.5, 139, 140; Term 3.6, 140–41, 153–54. *see also* Nunavut Land Use Plan

Keewatin Wildlife Federation (KWF), 82–83, 84, 86–87, 100. *see also* Kivalliq Wildlife Board (KWB)

Keith, Darren, 39, 127, 176–77

Kiggavik mine proposals. *see* AREVA Resources' Kiggavik mine proposal; Urangesellschaft's Kiggavik mine proposal

Kigjugalik Hughson, Paula, 163, 164

Kitts Michelini mine, 79

Kivalliq Energy, 137, 164

Kivalliq Inuit Association (KIA): area covered, 108; AREVA Resources' Kiggavik mine proposal, 141, 162; conditional support for uranium mining, 154; Ferguson Lake project, 191; on Garry Lakes proposal, 180; Inuit Owned Lands (IOL), 114, 191, 192; Marce Lake project, 183, 184; on protected calving grounds, 188–89; revenues from Meadowbank gold mine, 114–15; Terrestrial Ecosystem Management Plan, 121. *see also* Keewatin Inuit Association

Kivalliq region: Inuit groups, 13–14; map, 14; uranium mining industry, 6

Kivalliq Wildlife Board (KWB), 108, 161–62, 186

Kneen, Jamie, 197

Kreelak, Martin, 75

Kudloo, Rebecca, 164

Kudloo, Thomas, 87

Kuptana, Rosemarie, 44

L

land claims, 102, 196. *see also* Nunavut Land Claims Agreement (Nunavut Agreement)

Langenham, Mikle, 91

language: challenge of translation, 77, 158; forced use of English, 117; interpretation, 58–59, 81, 91, 139; lack of translation, 89, 151, 155, 161, 168; unilingual Elders, 155, 161, 173;

Lutsel K'e Dene First Nation, 135, 163, 166, 179–80, 187

Lynge, Aqqaluk, 82

M

Maclean's, 190

MacQuarrie, Bob, 87

Makita. *see* Nunavummiut Makitagunarningit (Makita)

Makkovik, Nunatsiavut, 79

Manitoba, 79, 187

Mannik, Hattie, 178

Manuel, George, 9

Marce Lake project, 183–84, 185

marine mammals, 5, 113, 116

Mautari'naaq, Suzanne Paalak, 96

McCallum, Barry, 131–32, 159

McKay, Paul, 89

McPherson, Robert, 10–11

Meadowbank gold mine, 75; Baker Lake, 5; benefits and profits, 114–15, 123, 133; environmental effects, 115–16; example of needing to hold companies accountable, 186; impact, 115–118; Inuit employment, 114, 117, 118; proposal, 112–14; and Whale Tail gold mine, 106, 119–20

methodology. *see* book methodology

military bases, 42, 80

mineral rights, 10, 107, 133

mining in Nunavut, 2, 108–10; Aboriginal title not honoured, 105; Baffinland Iron Mines, 5; Baker Lake court case, 66–68; Baker Lake study, 62–64; camp radio used by Hitkati, 46; camp supplied materials for Hitkati's cabin, 21–22; clean up, 1; cobalt, 190; copper, 189, 190; cultural importance of land to Inuit, 68–69; decisions made by non-Inuit, 5, 6, 106, 107; diamonds, 5; exploration activity and caribou, 6, 57, 64, 68, 189–90; exploration at Ferguson Lake, 3, 18, 57, 189–91; Inuit knowledge study, 155–56; MiningWatch Canada, 146; Nanisivik, 4–5; nickel, 3, 189, 190; NWT and Nunavut Chamber of Mines, 84, 185–186, 188–189; offshore seismic exploration, 3, 5; oil and gas, 3, 5, 54, 194,